THOSE THEY CALLED

IDIOTS

The idea of the disabled mind
from 1700 to the present day

SIMON JARRETT

REAKTION BOOKS

For Dianne and, of course, for Hana

Published by
REAKTION BOOKS LTD
Unit 32, Waterside
44–48 Wharf Road
London N1 7UX, UK
www.reaktionbooks.co.uk

First published 2020
Copyright © Simon Jarrett 2020

Printed and bound in Great Britain
by TJ Books Ltd, Padstow, Cornwall

A catalogue record for this book is available from the British
Library

ISBN 978 1 78914 301 0

CONTENTS

Introduction

As a young nursing assistant in the 1980s, I began work at a small, all-male 'mental handicap hospital' in southern England. Many of its elderly male patients had been admitted as children, in the 1920s and '30s. At the end of my first shift, I read through the file of G, an elderly patient who, dressed in the remnants of a battered suit, helped around the ward during the day. The file contained the notes of his admission in 1924, aged six, which began: 'G is a bat-eared cretin.' I recoiled at the harsh and degrading language used to describe such a young child. I would later learn that he was, in fact, being described in the correct, clinical language of his time. This language had made a journey, perhaps not a lengthy one, from authoritative medical terminology to street-level abuse during G's sixty-year sojourn on these wards. Other things had changed in that time also. There had been the General Strike, the Great Depression, the rise of Fascism, the Second World War, the Holocaust, the birth of the NHS, the end of the British Empire, the Cold War, the Swinging Sixties, the Civil Rights Movement, the Vietnam War and Thatcherism. Yet in all that time, as G grew from a boy into a man and now approached the end of his life, things for him had changed very little. Along with the other men (or 'boys' as they were known in the town), his hair had perhaps got longer, his girth thicker, his jumpers brighter and the wards a little less spartan. Yet as the world had changed outside he had followed the same routines, eaten the same three stodgy meals a day, gone to bed at 7.30 each night, got up at 6.30 each morning, and passed the time each day. He would die at some point having lived a strange Peter Pan sort of existence, never allowed to grow, hope or see beyond the immediacy of this unending daily routine. He came into the world 'a bat-eared cretin', and was never allowed to be anything else. Why?

There were many more questions as I worked over the ensuing decades with people whom I first knew as people with mental handicaps, then people with learning disabilities/difficulties, then as the intellectually disabled, and who, at other times, had been known as mentally subnormal, defectives, morons, cretins, feeble-minded, mentally retarded, idiots and many other terms. Why did the name keep changing? Who were these people? Who decided that they were these people? Why, if not ill, were they managed and treated by doctors? Had they always lived in asylums, or had there been another time, when they had lived in another way, or perhaps not been 'them' at all?

Almost as intriguing as their history was the lack of historical curiosity shown by most of the army of professionals employed in the modern state to work with them. For many, these people did not really have a history. They were an unchanging, universal phenomenon over time. 'Treatment' methods and public policy constantly changed, but this was because the past was always wrong; the present was always putting it right.

Inside or outside the asylum, this group seemed to live in a strange parallel world. The general rules of Western modernity – freedom to live as you choose, earn money, enjoy rights – seemed not to apply to them. They were of this world, but not in it. I came to know many people labelled intellectually disabled as individuals, as hopeful, striving human beings, often with the same preoccupations and aspirations as me. Unlike me, however, they were only seen as human in certain ways, and somehow not accorded full human status. Their preoccupations and aspirations would go, largely, unheard. Who were they? Where did they come from? What was their story?

Such questions and enquiries led to this book. I wanted to understand what happened in the past to those people we today call people with intellectual disabilities. What sort of lives did they lead? How were they seen by others? How did they see themselves? There were other questions too. Why have the words we have used to describe them changed so often, and what did these changes signify? Is it the same sorts of people we talk about when we use these different terms, or does society's view of what, and who, merits exclusion on the grounds of mental capacity change over time? I hoped that these enquiries would lead to a better understanding of the status of intellectually disabled people in society today.

I found that most historical enquiry focused either on the immediate past of 'care in the community' or on the asylum period from the mid-nineteenth century, implying that people with intellectual disabilities had achieved historical focus only when they became objects of the institution. But how did they live before there were asylums? Were they an accepted part of their communities, or were they ostracized? They must surely have been there, known, talked about, with their families, in their communities, living their daily lives in some way. Something must then have changed for them to come to be seen no longer as people who could live their lives in those communities and families, but as people who should live separately, 'cared for' by professionals behind the high walls of the asylum. There had clearly been a transformation through the eighteenth century and into the nineteenth, much of it in people's minds, from communities that had among them those they called idiots, to the opening of the world's first specialist idiot asylum at Earlswood, Surrey, in 1855, managed by the famous Dr John Langdon Down (the 'discoverer' of what he called 'Mongolian imbecility', which today is known as Down syndrome). What was this road, this journey of a mentality, that led to Dr Down's idiot asylum? And then there was another journey, another social transformation, when after 140 years of incarceration people came back out of the idiot and imbecile asylums, mental deficiency colonies and mental handicap hospitals (as they eventually become known), and back into society, in the latter part of the twentieth century. It is that three-hundred-year return journey, from the communities of the eighteenth century, into the asylums of the nineteenth and eventually back to the communities of the twentieth century, that this book describes.

I argue that there was a time, before the asylum era, when the class of people described as idiots and imbeciles lived as integrated members of the communities of eighteenth- and early nineteenth-century England. They were members of families, of neighbourly and employment networks, and were loved, protected and accepted by those who knew them. They were sometimes seen as strange, often seen as amusing, and their mental shortcomings were noticed and commented upon. Nevertheless they were accepted, they belonged, and were seen as naturally belonging, their differences absorbed into the everyday lives of communities. In the absence of state infrastructure and institutions to isolate those seen as not fitting in, these communities were by necessity flexible and accommodating. In the eighteenth century, to be born into a community was qualification enough to be part of that community, whatever a person's deviation from any sort of social norm. Communities adapted to people rather than people having to adapt to them. You did not have to pass some sort of mental test to gain a certificate of human belonging. To be sure, there were times when so-called idiots and imbeciles were bullied, abused, despised, loathed or held in contempt – but always there was a countervailing response of protection, love and acceptance.

I believe this holds important lessons for the status of those we call people with intellectual disabilities in our society today. First, we should understand that the period we can call 'the great incarceration', from the mid-nineteenth century to the 1980s, which involved the move of tens of thousands of people into institutions on the grounds that they lacked the mental capacity to belong to mainstream society, was an anomaly, not the norm. For the thousand years of recorded history in England before then, those deemed to have been born lacking mental faculty lived in their communities, not in institutions. 'Idiots', people with intellectual disabilities, are not natural creatures of the asylum – they were simply perceived and categorized as such during the 140 years or so of the great incarceration. Many factors contributed to this, and most of them had their roots in Enlightenment thought – the mania for classification and diagnosis, the construction of a set of mental attributes that constituted 'human' – and the rise of a centralizing and bureaucratic state that took the 'different' into its 'care' and out of society. There were also new notions of citizenship that required certain reciprocal duties, responsibilities and mental abilities from each individual before a badge of social belonging could be conferred. As these core Enlightenment ideas, nourished and polished in the eighteenth century, seeped into public thought and policy-making from the early nineteenth century, driven by a newly emboldened and empowered medical profession, so the idiot and the imbecile lost their toehold in society and slipped quietly into institutional oblivion.

Since the 'great release' that began in the 1980s, as the old institutions were closed down and the move to 'care in the community' began, we have congratulated ourselves on our enlightened modernity. Certainly there have been considerable gains and progress in the last few decades. However, it would be wrong to believe that we are the first to have pioneered a world in which people with intellectual disabilities live in the same communities as the rest of us. We should also note that what we offer is 'access' to communities, often through a series of bureaucratized assessments, risk profiles, funding decisions and personalized plans, rather than unconditional acceptance. We grant a form of conditional social tenure, a precarious semi-acceptance in which people can belong so long as they recognize a set of limitations and restrictions that we place around them, an invisible asylum wall constructed from the bricks of bureaucracy and social policy. Our society often does not change or soften itself to adapt to those who cannot conform to the prevailing norm – we allow instead the level of belonging people are deemed to be capable of. The long shadow of the nineteenth-century asylum still falls across our assumptions and perceptions.

The eighteenth century can teach us much about how society needs to reshape itself to accommodate all its members, to take them for who they are, to allow them to be who they want to be. We often ask ourselves the question: what does it mean to be human? We give many answers – to know that we know things, to be rational, empathetic, logical, have a sense of futurity, be able to form relationships, be duplicitous or have a sense of humour. All such answers can be used (usually unjustifiably) to exclude the idiotic, the imbecilic, the stupid, the dull, the moron, the cretin, the intellectually disabled person. We rarely, or possibly never, say that to be human is simply to be born to human parents – the one answer that would not exclude our group. This book argues that this is how people with intellectual disabilities should be understood: simply as humans, without having to jump through a series of meritocratic hoops before society is prepared to accept them as such. Once this is understood, it becomes clear why those labelled as belonging to this group should hold full human rights, and why they should not have to plead for their personhood before psychiatrists, psychologists, social workers and judges. There are areas in which people with intellectual disabilities lack, to varying levels, certain types of capacity. A good society is one that sees this as a cause for flexibility, adaptation and acceptance, not a cause for exclusion based on either pity or hostility.

AT THIS POINT the difference between intellectual disability and mental illness, 'idiocy' and 'lunacy', needs to be made clear. In general when we talk about a person having an intellectual disability (and all the terms that have been used to describe the condition before it), we mean that they have been born with some lack of mental faculty which can make it difficult for them to understand what most other people can understand, to learn in the educational sense, and to have the skills necessary to live an independent life. It is a lifelong condition and does not change or get 'cured', although this does not mean that the person cannot develop over their lifetime and, in many cases, achieve a high level of independence. The severity of the condition can vary considerably, from the profoundly disabled person who lacks verbal communication and may have physical disabilities, epilepsy and other conditions on top of their intellectual disability, to the more mildly disabled person whose disability is much less visible, but who has a low intellectual capacity as defined by IQ. Those with 'mild' disabilities have been described as 'morons' and 'imbeciles' in the relatively recent past, and often live their lives on the borderland of social belonging. Quite who belongs in this group has been contested over time, and the definition is often closely linked to social beliefs and assumptions.

Mental illness (or insanity, lunacy or madness, as it was known in the past) is a different matter. In most cases (and I generalize here) a mental illness is acquired during a person's lifetime rather than being something they are born with. People who acquire a mental illness will often have been born within the normal range of intelligence as it is defined by IQ, or even display a very high level of intelligence. The range of conditions that fall within mental illness today is extensive, from depression and anxiety through to schizophrenia and psychosis, and levels of severity within each of these conditions can vary extensively. Unlike intellectual disability there is often the potential for a person to recover from a mental illness or, as it would more likely have been termed in the past, be 'cured'. Importantly, this means that they might be able to recover the capacity their illness caused them to lose, and so the law might restore any rights that they have been deprived of – something that does not happen in the case of the lifelong intellectually disabled person.

Despite the extensive differences between intellectual disability and mental illness, they are often confused, because they are both seen as mental afflictions of some sort. It is intellectual disability that is the subject of this book, not mental illness. The life experiences of a person with an intellectual disability, the social context within which they live and the assumptions made about them are very different to those that occur in the lives of people with mental illness. It is also the case that by definition people with intellectual disabilities leave little written record of themselves, given that a high level of literacy eludes them, unlike the numerous accounts of mental illness left by those who have endured or encountered it. This contributes to the dearth of historical accounts of 'idiocy' in contrast to the plethora of accounts of mental illness. Do the two overlap in any way? It is certainly the case that a person with an intellectual disability, like anyone else, can also acquire a mental illness, but this does not mean they will inevitably do so. Terms like imbecility have changed over time, used in the seventeenth and early eighteenth centuries to describe anyone whose mind was perceived as feeble in some way, such as some elderly or physically ill people, but gradually narrowing in definition to mean those born with a lack of intellectual capacity who were not fully 'idiotic' but not of 'normal' capacity either. Conditions such as dementia, and brain injuries acquired during a person's life through accident or illness, can have effects similar to an intellectual disability, but differ in that they have not been lifetime conditions and represent a change in a person's mental faculties rather than the mental faculties they have always lived with. However, despite all the differences between them, the insane and the idiotic have often been lumped together, in asylums, in diagnoses, in legislation, in historical writing and in public perception.

The people we describe today as having intellectual disabilities are most often seen as marginal or unworthy of attention by historians. As one historian has noted, 'historically, the social marginality of people with learning disabilities has been mirrored by their academic marginality.'[1] It is perhaps inevitable that many of those academics who live their lives powered by the finest intellects that nature can supply should find the idea of an intellectual disability, or some sort of absence of intellect, hard to contemplate or accept. It is also the case that lunacy history, the history of madness or mental illness, has overshadowed the history of idiocy. As one great historian observed, 'madness continues to exercise its mystique, but mindlessness holds no mystique.'[2] The normal or even genius mind afflicted by derangement has been of more interest than a mind that has been 'dull' from birth.

It is perhaps no surprise that the first histories of 'idiocy' were written by medical clinicians and social scientists, who saw and claimed the idiot as a (passive) player in their own historical accounts. These were really books about the history of the medical profession and its heroic role in rescuing idiots from the cruel outside world, or protecting society from them through the asylum system, and these ideas persist today in some accounts.[3] They portray the idiot population before the welcome arrival of the asylum as beleaguered and abused, living in a state of appalling misery where they were 'chained, beaten and half-starved . . . lived in cellars and garrets, in prisons and workhouses'. They were saved only by 'a new spirit of humanity, a rising class of important asylum doctors'.[4]

Starting in the 1990s this medical account of history began to be challenged, and an important series of revisionist accounts placed the intellectually disabled at the heart of the story as people in their own right, worthy of respectful historical investigation, rather than as objects of medical investigation. They also analysed developments such as eugenic science and institutionalization as ideological movements with significant impact on the lives of individuals, and extended the historical study of idiocy to the medieval and early modern periods. For the first time, a presentation of the pre-asylum era was not predicated on themes of marginalization, abuse and persecution, but showed the idiot recognized and sustained within communities without recourse to institutionalization as a punitive or rescuing solution.[5]

Since then the field has widened and developed, with extensive work on inclusive history, including oral histories of twentieth-century institutionalization and the move to care in the community. There have also been detailed accounts of the eugenics and mental deficiency period of the late nineteenth and early twentieth centuries, and of the Victorian asylum era.[6]

The most recent wave of intellectual disability history, to which this book owes much, has argued that the term 'intellectual disability' is not a stable historical concept itself. We cannot simply seek out and identify current notions of intellectual disability in earlier periods to underpin a narrative of progress, or suggest that there has always been an easily identifiable, universally recognizable outgroup of the intellectually unfortunate whose nomenclature just happens to have changed with alarming regularity over the last several centuries. Psychology and medicine do not produce indisputable scientific knowledge about what constitutes idiocy, but rather each age and each society constructs a version of idiocy (and a new name for it) that reflects their own anxieties and concerns, to form an ultimate outsider group from whom the rest of us draw our feeling of inclusion. This is why exploring notions of intellectual disability (or the lack of them) prior to the nineteenth century is of particular importance. We have to understand that the medicalized notion of idiocy that formed in the nineteenth century and lingers with us today is just one formulation of many that have been made over time about those deemed to be lacking in certain types of intellectual faculty. Intellectual disability is an *idea*, one which changes over time and which has an overweening impact on those whose lives are lived within the definitional walls it places around them.[7]

This book takes the early eighteenth century as its starting point, but rather than assuming the existence of some form of cruel marginalization and exclusion it seeks out the 'idiot' as part of everyday society. I have looked therefore in the sources for everyday life of the eighteenth century: in reports from the civil and criminal courts, in the jokes people told and the slang they used, in novels, poetry, caricature and art, in popular fiction and plays, in accounts by travellers. Sure enough, the idiot is there, a feature of everyday life and a member of communities, seen as somewhat strange, sometimes amusing or even an object of ridicule, but very much there, in the world, in society. From these sources we find people named as idiots who are loved by their families, defended by their communities, kindly treated by juries, often in work, sometimes married, always visible, and all of this usually in an unobtrusive, quiet, unremarkable way.

The story this book goes on to tell is how and why this changed; how people who had been accepted as members of their community in the eighteenth century became creatures of the asylum by the end of the nineteenth, deemed unfit to be part of the communities to which they had once belonged. The book traces the changes in thought, humour, morality, ideology, public opinion, manners and concepts of citizenship that brought about this shift in mentality. It also describes the bizarre entanglement of ideas of idiocy and imbecility with ideas of race and intelligence, a process that began with global exploration in the eighteenth century and ended in the scientific racism of the mid-nineteenth century, and the highly racialized eugenic science of degeneration after Darwin. Idiocy moved from being something harmless, if a little odd, to a much darker idea of existential racial threat and danger. A universal indictment developed both against those deemed to have low intellectual faculty and against the non-white races of the world. The idea of intellectual disability was key to all of this. The book then tells the latest episode of the story: how after a dark century of incarceration, exile, indictment, neglect and abuse, which included the horrors of the Nazi mass killings of the mentally unfit from 1939 to 1945, a new chapter opened, with the closure of the institutions in the late twentieth century and the return to some form of community life. The book examines how and why this occurred and explores the successes and failures of the 'great return'.

This story roams across Europe and North America at times, and indeed across Britain's growing empire in the eighteenth and nineteenth centuries, but it is very much a story of idiocy in England and how Enlightenment thinking impacted on English perceptions and assumptions about idiocy, intelligence and the importance of mind, both at home and in the expanding empire.

Thinking elsewhere, particularly in France and the United States from the early nineteenth century, was often influential on English thought and attitudes, and there were many close parallels between developments in England and the u.s. throughout the nineteenth and twentieth centuries. Yet important differences remained, particularly in the English privileging (certainly in their own country) of individual liberty over state protection and intervention. The lead-up to and implementation of the mass killing of disabled people in Nazi Germany is examined here for its impact on pre- and post-war thinking about intellectual disability in England (and the wider United Kingdom by this time), where, while eugenic thinking thrived, libertarians, religious campaigners and a pervasive suspicion of state authority conspired to ensure that similar murderous excesses did not occur.[8]

Ever-changing terminology is something that anyone working in this field of history has to grapple with. It is in itself a revealing aspect of the history of intellectual disability and presents a challenge to historians. The possible meanings and roots of these rapid changes are discussed at various points in the book. The term 'intellectual disability' is used as the current accepted academic term to describe what practitioners in Britain call 'learning disability' and in the United States 'mental retardation'. To avoid ahistoricism, and to capture important truths about periods in history, the terminology in use at the various time periods described is used; this includes idiocy, imbecility, mental deficiency, moron, mental handicap and so on. None of these of course is acceptable terminology outside their historical context in public discourse today, all having become terms of abuse or anachronistic. It is worth reflecting on why there has been such a rapid turnover in terminology. Does each new term reflect a power claim by a professional group – doctors, psychologists, educationalists, advocates or even historians – asserting the right to identify, treat and control the group they are naming? Do the terms reflect the hidden fears of those who apply them? What would be more disturbing to a late nineteenth-century doctor seeking to cure all disease than something defective? Likewise, do psychologists most fear a cognitive disability, do members of a meritocracy most fear a learning disability, academics an intellectual disability? Or does language just change because it has to, as clinical terms slip rapidly into terms of abuse, a vivid illustration of excluded status? There is probably something of all three in the never-ending terminological procession.

The title of this book, *Those They Called Idiots: The Idea of the Disabled Mind from 1700 to the Present Day,* seeks to highlight the archaeology beneath these never-ending changes in terminology. There was in the beginning one all-embracing term – 'idiot' – that described a group seen as lacking something mentally, in a way that differentiated them from others. This term has long since become nothing more than a gratuitous insult. However, there has always been such a group. The idiot group has been regularly renamed, over the past 250 years, and the criteria for membership has fluctuated with equal regularity. Their level of acceptance and belonging in wider society has also changed with, for example, high levels of belonging in the eighteenth century and almost total exclusion for much of the nineteenth. But there has always been the 'idiot', repackaged and re-presented by varieties of professionals over time, and the book's title seeks to reflect this underlying reality.

The following pages portray a mentality and how it was formed and reformed in England over three centuries. It is clearly no linear story of progress and improvement, and I conclude by highlighting the new uncertainties and anxieties we face today. Shared social assumptions determine who belongs inside society and who should be outside it. For those people who have been characterized as idiotic or imbecile, or whatever else they have been called, shifts in communal mentality, what happens in other people's minds, have always had profound implications. Specific ideas about idiocy are inextricably linked to wider ideas about humanity, mind, identity, race and rights. The idiot population moved from a group seen as odd, different, vulnerable but ultimately belonging to their communities, to people who needed to be shut away, kept separate, and who did not belong. Then, eventually, they were 'allowed' to return to society, under certain conditions of acceptance. It was a journey from the centre to the margins, and back again. Its effects remain with us today as the newly constituted class of the intellectually disabled struggle to gain readmission to the communities which were once their own. Much of this struggle is because of the past – which is why the stories of the past must matter to us.

PART ONE

Idiocy and Imbecility in the Eighteenth Century, *c.* 1700–1812

1

Poor Foolish Lads
and Weak Easy Girls:
Legal Ideas of Idiocy

The idea of an idiotic person has been part of law since antiquity. In early Greek society *idiota* signified a private person, living in solitude and divorced from public and social life. For the Romans, such a person was *illiteratus*. This concept of the solitary person, isolated from the social and public connections and networks that most people enjoy, underpinned early English legal understandings of idiocy. It was the 'naturalness' of the condition, the fact that it was there from birth, that exercised legal minds. Did such a person, born this way, count as a full person or not under the law? The British legal writer John Cowell explained in 1607 that those whom the Greeks called *idiota*, and whom the Romans called *illiteratus*, are 'taken . . . in our Law for *non-compos mentis* or a natural fool'.[1] The idiot was a person alien from human society from birth, illiterate, uncommunicating and locked into a private mental world. An immediate question that arose from this was whether such a way of living made that person dangerously alien and unpredictable, or simply a harmless person living in a state of benign innocence. The precise status and location of the idiot between these two poles, benign or malign, has been debated for centuries.

A feature of Roman and Byzantine law was to make those deemed idiotic through lack of judgement and comprehension wards of either their families or their lords. In England such wardship became the responsibility of the monarch from the late thirteenth century (under Edward I) as part of the Prerogativa Regis, a medieval document asserting the rights of the Crown over those considered to lack mental capacity.[2] Idiots were perceived as, in a childlike way, lacking capacity to contribute to the affairs of the nation, and also represented a threat to healthy bloodlines. This incurred obligations from the monarch of both protection and control, and gave the crown rights over their land and assets.[3] The Prerogativa gave the sovereign custody of the lands of 'natural fools', with an obligation to maintain the person during their life-time. It also sought to distinguish between the natural fool, whose condition would never change, and the lunatic or mad person, whose loss of mind might be temporary and who might recover or have lucid intervals. Lunatics therefore enjoyed greater rights.[4]

Idiots, from the medieval period onwards, were identified through inquisitions ordered by the monarch and carried out by lay (never medical) officials.[5] These centred on numeracy, knowledge of others and knowledge of self.[6] By the seventeenth century more sophisticated knowledge was required, including weights and measures and days of the week.[7] Idiocy was seen as a legal problem with implications for wealth and property, which meant that for the landless labouring poor it was not an issue. Bloodline and the protection of family wealth and inher-itance were all-important. As far as the small educated elite were concerned, the great masses of the poor, for whom illiteracy was the norm and inheritance irrelevant, were all idiotic.

In 1540, under Henry VIII, the Tudor administration estab-lished a powerful Court of Wards.[8] This brought a sharper definition of and focus on what constituted legal incapacity after the loose and sporadically used medieval guidance.[9] This court consolidated and shaped the conventions and practices of the legal treatment of those deemed incapacitated through idiocy into a form that persisted through the eighteenth and nineteenth centuries.[10] Despite the abolition of the Court of Wards in 1661, after the Civil War and the restoration of the Stuart monarchy, its functions simply passed over to the Court of Chancery (they survive today in the Court of Protection).[11]

As the state strengthened, and increasingly profited from, the law on capacity, it faced growing challenges from families to eliminate the use of 'idiocy grants': permanent confiscation by the state, in the name of the monarch, of the land and assets of people deemed idiots under law, which was seen as unfair and punitive. The pressure rose as the early Stuart kings in England, James I and Charles I, milked the court for all they could gain from it. Gradually, in response to this pressure, terms and conditions for idiots moved into line with those for lunatics, meaning that their estates were not permanently confiscated, there was proper accounting for profits, and maintenance of both idiots and their families had to be in line with their degree and estate in life.[12]

The still quite vague legal definition of what constituted idiocy was shaken up by the jurist Lord Coke in 1628. He defined four categories of 'non compos mentis', or those of unsound mind, the first of which was the 'idiot': 'Idiota . . . from his nativitie, by a perpetuall infirmitie'. The other categories were those who had accidentally lost their understanding though sickness or accident; lunatics who slipped in and out of understanding; and people who lost understanding through their own fault, such as drunks. However, Coke then added something of a catch-all fifth category of incapacity, which he defined as 'all other persons, who from *natural imbecility*, disease, old age or any such causes, are incapable of managing their own affairs'.[13] These 'natural imbeciles' were a new legal concept. They were not idiots, but they had an impaired mind from birth and a question mark over their capacity. On which side of the capacity border did they lie? This was the point at which the idea of the imbecile as a type of idiot – a person mentally feeble from birth but not quite idiotic – was born. The meaning of the word 'imbecile' began to pass from a general concept of mental and physical weakness to a more specific notion of a person born with a dull intellect. The effect was to widen the segment of the population whose mental capacity from birth to be full members of society came under question.

This, then, was the legal understanding of the idiot with which the eighteenth century began. Idiots were solitary beings, unable to understand money, numbers or social relationships and lacking self-awareness and memory. In an increasingly dynamic and commercial society in which growing numbers were escaping from the poorest class, it was becoming harder for the idiot to blend in unseen as part of the illiterate masses. Unchanging idiots were joined by the scanty outline of a new imbecile class, the simpleton group also challenged by the demands of the rapidly changing world around them. Through 'mere weakness of understanding',[14] their right to social status was being questioned. The idiot in law was coming into sharper social focus, becoming a complex and noteworthy matter, with families increasingly in conflict with the state and its over-mighty laws of appropriation of the lands and wealth of idiots.

At this juncture in 1700 the lawyer John Brydall produced a book called *Non Compos Mentis; or, The Law Relating to Natural Fools, Mad-Folks and Lunatick Persons*, which gives us an excellent summary of both the law and common understandings of idiocy at the beginning of the eighteenth century.[15] He described the system of 'begging an idiot', which referred to the process of demanding an inquiry by the Court of Chancery to determine whether a person was legally idiotic or not. From this derives our modern saying 'Do you take me for an idiot?' According to Brydall, the king's right to identify idiots and take possession of their lands remained intact at this point. He also stated that idiots could be easily discerned by appearance, could not make a promise or a contract, marry, make a will or give voluntary consent. They were distinguished from lunatics and others of unsound mind in that they were 'wholly destitute of reason . . . by a perpetual infirmity, as . . . *Fools Natural*'.[16]

He then tackled what was evidently a tricky legal question. This was an apparent paradox whereby idiots could sometimes appear perfectly reasonable by making a rational remark and 'it may appear, then such a one is no idiot naturally.' If they were capable of such rational glimmers of light, did this not mean that

The 18th-century view: 'John Donaldson, A Poor Idiot who usually walked before Funeral Processions at Edinburgh', etching published by Henry Sawyer.

JOHN DONALDSON,
A Poor Idiot who usually walked before Funeral Processions at Edinburgh.
Published by Henry Sawyer, Dean S.t Soho.

they were in fact capable of having sufficient reason to make a lawful contract? Yet how could they be both an irrational idiot and say rational things at the same time? Brydall's answer to this paradox was that such moments were a divine act, 'because Almighty God doth sometimes so illuminate the Minds of the foolish they are not much inferior to the wise'. These random rational remarks were the appearance of reason, but not its substance.[17]

How could the law distinguish between the two? Brydall raised the stakes for qualification as a fully rational human. This would now include the ability to understand abstractions, ideas and meanings rather than simple facts. Therefore, an apparently reasonable testament made by an idiot was insufficient in law, because it would not display true understanding. Even if what they said was reasonable, the idiot would not have intended it.

Saying the right words, in the right order, even if these words were given by God, was not enough. The words of idiots had no meaning because they lacked understanding or intention and meant no more than 'a Parrot speaking to the Passengers [passers-by]'. Brydall left a small amount of room for conjecture, suggesting that if further proof of reason and understanding could be provided then an idiot's testimony might be allowed to stand. However, his argument was clear – even those idiots who could speak did not understand language, they merely parroted it, however wise their words might seem at times.[18]

Brydall also had words to say about the imbecile. There was, he argued, a human type 'that only is of mean capacity or understanding, or one who is, as it were betwixt a man of Ordinary Capacity and a Fool' and who, it appeared, could make a testament. However, this should only be with the proviso 'that he understands the nature of a Testament – if not, [he] is not fit to make a Will'. The mental shortcomings of the person of 'dull capacity . . . lacking virtue moral and theological, or to be of a quick understanding' did not in themselves justify depriving them of their legal rights. Yet nor did it mean they were automatically entitled to them. Although seen ambivalently as somewhere on the cusp between having capacity and lacking it, the idea of the lifelong born imbecile class, a cut above the idiot but below the rest of humankind, began to take legal shape. The law must in future consider how to respond to their complexity.[19]

How was legal knowledge about idiocy being formed and transmitted? It was not simply a top-down formation from sharp legal minds. The idiot not only had a legal identity by the beginning of the eighteenth century but occupied a space in the minds of people, defined in popular terms and talked about in jokes, slang and everyday conversation. As well as using case law and earlier legal theory, Brydall drew on this popular cultural wisdom, this 'common sense' and cultural understanding about what constituted idiocy. He acknowledged the interplay between common understanding and formal, legalistic definitions: 'Idiot signifies commonly an unlearned or illiterate person, but among the English Jurists is a term of law, and taken for one that is wholly deprived of his Reason and Understanding from his birth and . . . in our common speech is called a *fool natural*.'[20] To explain the idea of the 'glimmer of reason' that could occur with idiots, he described at length a 'merry accident' that occurred in Paris when an idiot was asked to judge a dispute between a diner and a cook.[21] This apparent real-life account had in fact appeared, much more concisely, in a jestbook thirty years earlier:

> A fellow in a Cook's shop in France filled his belly only with standing by whilst the meal was dished up, and the Cook would be paid for a meal. So it was left to the decision of the next Passenger [passer-by], which happened to be an Idiot, who said that the man's money should be put between two dishes, ringing it for a time, and the Cook should be content with the jingling of the money as the man was satisfied with the smelling of the meat.[22]

The (rather excruciatingly laboured) joke was that a person was satisfying his hunger simply by smelling, rather than eating, the cook's food, and refusing to pay for the privilege: the idiot had wisely, yet also naively, solved the dispute by judging that if the customer was only smelling the food, the cook should only hear the money. Brydall presented this as a 'case', demonstrating the ability of the irrational idiot to appear to have a rational thought. He acknowledged that it had been recounted by 'divers credible writers'.[23] The use of a joke as an illustration in a book of legal theory is one of many examples of knowledge passing both ways between popular knowledge and legal theory. The popular idea of the idiot having a lucky, random lucid thought would endure: 'Well Mr Random, a lucky thought may come into a fool's head sometimes,' Tobias Smollett's eponymous hero was told half a century later.[24]

It was a commonly shared public belief that an idiot could be easily discerned by appearance alone. Ordinary Londoners echoed Brydall's depictions of 'dunces' and 'dull pates' with a rich vernacular. In criminal cases at the Old Bailey, witnesses confidently described the idiotic when giving testimony in criminal cases: 'he was a soft-pated fellow,' 'He was of such a slow and dull apprehension.'[25] It surfaced in everyday street language, where the 'dullard', 'dull swift', 'dulpickle', 'addle-pate', 'leaden pate' and all the other 'windy fellows' (those without sense or reason) were identified, targeted and teased by Londoners of all classes.[26] The concepts of idiocy and capacity lived in the minds of people as well as in legal theory and ideas passed upwards from the streets into lawyerly discourse as well as down from the legal caste. Notably, no flow of knowledge came from medical men – idiocy was a matter for the lawyers, and the public, to determine. This unchanging, untreatable, God-given condition was of no interest to doctors at all.

In both legal theory and popular wisdom, therefore, the early eighteenth-century idiot was conceived as irrational,

Thomas Rowlandson, 'Wonderfully mended; should't have known you again!,' 1807, watercolour print depicting the consulting room of a quack; 18th-century doctors had no interest in 'incurable idiots'.

vulnerable, easily duped, lacking understanding of everyday social commerce and, in theory at least, owned by the monarch. As the Prussian officer, historian and traveller Johann Wilhelm von Archenholz succinctly put it later in the century, the king 'is the guardian of all the fools in the kingdome, and he inherits the estates of all those who die without heirs.'[27] Yet this same idiot could have glimmers of reason and, however apart in mind, was very much physically embedded among England's families and communities. Next to the idiot stood a perplexing type who was becoming known as the imbecile: dull, slow, soft and weak from birth, and somewhere between the sound and the unsound.

In the Courtroom: Civil Courts

How did these understandings of idiocy and imbecility manifest themselves in the daily exchanges of the eighteenth-century courtroom? There were two arenas in which idiots and imbeciles appeared before the courts to be talked about, described, characterized and judged. They appeared before ecclesiastical or civil courts to establish whether they had capacity in order to determine the legitimacy of marriages, or to do the same for wills. And they appeared before the criminal courts, such as London's Old Bailey, to face charges of felony. There was a distinct class chasm between those who featured in civil cases and those who featured in criminal cases. Those appearing before the civil and ecclesiastical courts were from families with property or other assets, and therefore almost entirely from the upper or middling classes. In these cases, important issues of inheritance and bloodline were at stake. In criminal cases, those appearing in the dock at the Old Bailey were almost entirely from the poorer classes. Drawn from the teeming streets of plebeian London and accused of what appear to modern eyes to be minor thefts, such as pickpocketing or shoplifting, their own lives were at stake as they stood trial under what was known as the 'Bloody Code' of English eighteenth-century law.

Civil cases illuminate the variety of understandings of idiocy among the higher orders that pertained in the eighteenth-century courtroom, and also illustrate the extraordinary lives that those labelled idiotic might experience. Particularly striking was the strange life and last testament of Sir John Leigh, a wealthy Surrey property owner, who came under the legal gaze in the ecclesi-astical courts from 1739. He was alleged by his solicitor to have lacked sufficient judgement, capacity and understanding since birth, and to be no more capable than a child of seven years.[28] He had married and had a son but, once Sir John was widowed, his son managed his estate for him, being 'aware of the weakness of his father's capacity and understanding'.[29] Sir John spoke strangely and monosyllabically, saying *'yes yes yes by Chris [Christ] no no no by Chris'*, and was seated separately from the family when dining. On hearing in 1731 that his only son had died young, Sir John showed no reaction; yet this was to be a turning point. As a 58-year-old weak-minded man with 'very unsound and imperfect judgement', without a known heir and with a considerable estate, he was an obvious target for predators. A group of family friends attempted to protect and oversee him, but this stable grouping of support was quickly displaced by a band of local gentlemen who moved in to take over the house and estate. They called themselves, without legal sanction, Sir John's commissioners, and spent their time in 'rioting, drinking and other excesses'.[30]

An apothecary called William Vade moved in when Sir John developed pain in his foot in 1732, and appeared to exert growing power and control over him. The scheming Vade, sensing Sir John's gullibility, assured him after his toe was amputated that it would grow again. In fact his whole foot was then amputated, much to Sir John's fury, although this was vented on others rather than William Vade. Vade continued to dominate him, allowing no visitors without his permission, including two pre-viously unknown cousins, now next of kin, tracked down by Sir John's solicitor, whom Vade persistently obstructed. In 1733, despite Sir John having recently exclaimed, 'Chris God! I to be married? I know nothing of going to be married!'[31] Vade took him to London by stagecoach for just that purpose. A marriage ceremony was performed between sixty-year-old Sir John, made drunk to the point where he fell over, and his new sixteen-year-old bride. The new Lady Elizabeth was none other than Elizabeth Vade, William Vade's daughter.[32] On hearing of this marriage Sir John's cousins took out a commission to prove incapacity and force annulment of the marriage. However, because he could answer some questions 'tolerably' and now had a wife to help manage his affairs, he was found of sound mind.[33] From this point William Vade took total control of Sir John's life. In 1736, Lady Elizabeth, aged just eighteen, died suddenly. Vade's hold on Sir John's estate for himself and his family was again threatened. Three days later he called Sir John to a part of the house where he had grouped an attorney and several witnesses. Servants heard shouting, and by the end of the day there was a new will, leaving all to William Vade. When John Leigh died the next year, Vade inherited.[34]

At the final appeal of the lengthy case against the will brought by Sir John's cousins, Lord Hardwicke pronounced it 'the greatest instance of weakness he had ever met with'. He accepted the finding of a Commission of Lunacy in 1733 that Sir John was not idiotic, but stated that the boundary was so narrow between a person non compos mentis, and one as weak as Sir John, that he upheld the complaint.[35] While this was good news for Sir John's cousins, who were now able to inherit his fortune despite never having known him during his lifetime, in legal terms it represented a dramatic expansion of the territory of incapacity and imbecility, because it drew those just beyond the current boundaries of unsoundness of mind into the orbit of those whom the law must protect. The judgment suggested that those described in Brydall's book of law as 'neither of the wisest sort, nor of the foolish'st but ... betwixt a wise man and a fool',[36] those weak-minded imbeciles, should be brought into the realm of incapacity because of their vulnerability to exploitation, as so dramatically illustrated in Sir John's life.

The instinctive inclination towards Sir John, despite his clear vulnerability, had been to value individual liberty over statutory interference. His gentleman acquaintances had sought to create an informal network of protection, and the Commission of Lunacy jury opted for non-intervention. The locus of care for those who could not support themselves was still perceived to rest in the informal realm of family and acquaintances, not with the state or institutions. However, in his case these informal networks failed or became, in the person of his bride, an instrument of the exploitative forces ranged against him. Seeing this, Lord Hardwicke's verdict effectively asserted the right of the state legal apparatus to intervene in an expanding territory of imbecility. The state's right to protect assets and bloodlines was asserted over the claims of neighbourhood and family protectors. As Arthur Onslow, Speaker of the House of Commons, who knew Sir John's family, tried to tell him, his duty was 'to ensure that what had descended *to* him descended correctly *from* him'.[37] It was Sir John's inability to preserve bloodline and family entitlement that led to Hardwicke's judgment.

William Hogarth, *The Polling*, plate III from 'Four Prints of an Election', 1758, engraving showing a mentally disabled man brought to vote.

The complex association of the idiot with value in relation to heritable assets dominated civil legal proceedings. Idiots could represent value in that they could be seen as commodities, associated with inherited wealth. They also represented a threat to value, in that they were thought not to understand or appreciate their assets, and thus through profligacy, simplicity or vulnerability could squander estates and end bloodlines unless the law intervened. Finally, they also represented valuelessness, in the sense that the common human comforts, luxuries and opportunities that money could bring were perceived not to have any meaning for them. Their inability to understand, or value, money was key in this perception. For a certain human type not to value what was valued by common human assumption was unnerving and raised questions about human status.

These themes loomed large in the case of Henry Roberts, who, according to an anonymous polemical broadside published after his death, 'by unparalleled cruelty was deprived of his estate under the pretence of idiocy'.[38] Roberts inherited from his parents a very large fortune, including Barbados slave estates. After the death of his sister and heir in 1742 a commission was brought on the grounds of his 'weak mind'. The anonymous author described farcical proceedings as Roberts was bullied and heckled in an Exeter courtroom, taken to a tavern forcibly by a mob, manhandled to the balcony and displayed to a baying crowd, his wig removed. At an equally colourful appeal, witnesses testified that Roberts lacked 'common humanity' and that any correct answers he gave resulted from a system of nods and winks from his supporters in the courtroom. Childlike behaviour was the main evidence given of his idiocy: shooting with a bow and arrow, blowing feathers, tossing up his hat and catching it, kicking pebble stones and needing help to sign his name. Roberts complained bitterly that he had been confused by the jurors:

> They came round me and asked their Questions together, without giving me Time to answer. They asked me what

a *Lamb*, and what a *Calf* was called at one, two and three years old. They gave me a Sum of Money to tell, which I miscounted, and then I heard them say, he is not capable of managing his affairs, we will return him incapable.

This combination of childlike behaviour, simplicity and eccentricity was sufficient for an 'unsound' finding.[39]

In 1743 Roberts, now worth £400 a year, passed into the hands of his appointed guardian, Dr John Lynch, Dean of Canterbury, a notoriously 'acquisitive accumulator of preferments'.[40] Lynch swiftly moved to add the estate of Roberts's sister and the Barbados plantations to his existing wealth.[41] The certificate confirming that Roberts was of unsound mind was signed by the Archbishop.[42] Roberts, now an imbecile caught in a classic web of eighteenth-century corruption, was lodged at the top (the poorest part) of an 'ordinary house' in Canterbury, with one servant. Falling ill in 1746, he deteriorated rapidly and died aged 28. His estate, now worth £3,000 a year, descended to Dr Lynch.[43]

Anonymous, 'An Ass loaded with Church Preferments', 1737, cartoon satirizing William Wake, Archbishop of Canterbury (holding whip), for bestowing on his son-in-law the notoriously acquisitive Dr Lynch (ass) lucrative ecclesiastical appointments and neglecting the advancement of other clergymen.

Roberts's journey from a life of wealth and ease when his family was alive to legalized imbecility, poverty and a lonely death, was not unique. In an acquisitive and corrupt economic culture where many sought preferment and easy wealth, a vulnerable, unprotected idiot with a large, or even modest, estate was an obvious target. The wealth, status and well-being of newly parentless idiots could be drained, the idiot seen as a commodity to be plundered despite a system ostensibly designed to protect them and continue the support previously given by their family. In mid-century, Andrew Birkbeck, an idiot, lived with his stepmother for a year after the death of his wealthy father. The stepmother then put him out to lodgings with a 'keeper' where he would receive 'meat, drink, washing and lodging and . . . necessary care' for five shillings a week. Soon he was moved elsewhere at three shillings and sixpence per week, and within a year to yet another keeper at two shillings and sixpence per week. By this time it was necessary for 'the Parish over and above [to] find him cloaths' through Poor Law funds.[44] The value, both physical and moral, of the idiot declined as his assets were stripped and the right to physical comfort and luxury denied. It was seen as natural that the Poor Law, designed to give minimum ease to the most destitute, should release funds to sustain a delegitimized idiot inheritor like Andrew Birkbeck, despite ostensible personal wealth.

Exploitative designs came in many forms, both from within and outside the family. There was, however, always a counterbalancing group, seeking to protect idiots and maintain their human and fiscal status. In the cases of Sir John Leigh and Henry Roberts, this involved informal friendship groupings battling predatory outsiders. In the extraordinary case of Fanny Fust it was her family who led the battle, in a complex case highlighting the disputed demarcation lines between choice and protection, freedom and vulnerability.[45]

In 1786 Fust, aged 22, was heiress to several substantial family fortunes. Living near Bath with servants, carriages and a well-connected family, she was also, according to her mother, an idiot, 'in a state of total . . . imbecility of mind and is in every respect of as weak a state of mind as she was when only three years of age'. Evidence of her idiocy was her inability 'of counting twenty, of knowing her right hand from her left, one kind of animal or vegetable food from another, the Sun from the Moon, the value and difference of the most common English coins, of knowing the days of the week and the difference of times and seasons'. Once, when out walking in a storm and seeing lightning, 'she called out in a very childish manner "do it again" meaning that the people with her should make the lightening happen again.' As well as lacking basic knowledge and understanding, she was perceived to exhibit dangerously transgressive behaviour that threatened both class and sexual propriety; she had 'in the presence of men servants pulled up her petticoats with an intention of making water'. She needed constant attendance to help with dressing, eating and protection from danger, such as falling into the garden pond. After seven years of schooling she could do no more than write her name, with help.[46]

Henry Bowerman, an army lieutenant who scarcely knew Fust, was accused of hatching an elaborate plot with co-conspirators to kidnap and marry her in order to obtain her fortune. The plot involved enticing her to tea at the house of a former school companion. Five conspirators waiting there took her, on the pretence of going to eat strawberries and cream, to a nearby village. There, a post-chaise with two horses was waiting. Fust was separated from the trustworthy companion her mother had insisted should accompany her and taken to the Bath–London road, where Bowerman was waiting with three further conspirators and a coach and horses. The entire group, with Fust, then drove through the night to Dover and sailed to France, where Bowerman made repeated attempts in Calais, Lille and Tournay to find a priest to perform a marriage. None agreed to do so, because Fust's idiocy (and therefore incapacity to consent) was apparently evident to them through her appearance and behaviour. Bowerman eventually found a troubled

Church of England priest called Robert Popkin in Lille, who at first refused to conduct a ceremony but was plied with alcohol and persuaded to perform it. He was carried home intoxicated and then fetched from his bed at dawn to conduct the nuptials.[47]

Meanwhile, Fust's well-resourced mother discovered she was in France and dispatched four investigators, one armed with a request from the Secretary of State for Foreign Affairs to Louis XVI in Paris, to make an order for her return. The order was granted, and Fust was tracked down to a private house in Lille rented by Bowerman and returned to Calais accompanied by three French Cavaliers and the investigators, and thence to Bath. When asked in a French court why she had come to France, Fust replied that she 'came to eat strawberries and cream'. A long hearing in the ecclesiastical Court of Delegates eventually resulted in the annulment of the marriage. Bowerman appealed, claiming Fust had only appeared idiotic because her mother gave her strong alcoholic drinks. In 1787 Fust's mother reluctantly took out a commission of lunacy for guardianship. Having avoided this previously because it would be too distressing for her 'on account of her maternal affection and extreme tenderness for her daughter', she was now 'by experience convinced how ready and desirous the wicked part of mankind were to take advantage of such the imbecility of her daughter'. The commission declared Fust of unsound mind, as she was unable to give sensible answers about whom in the courtroom she would like to marry and whether her property was worth more than five guineas.[48] Deemed unable to understand money or marriage, her marriage was annulled and Fanny Bowerman became Fanny Fust again, now officially an adult idiot in the custody of her mother. The case formally ended in 1790.[49]

The Fust case sheds interesting light on late eighteenth-century ideas of idiocy. In over a thousand pages of testimony no reference is made to medical evidence of her imbecility. Instead, appeals are made throughout to 'common sense' and to the circular notion that Miss Fust must be an idiot because she appears to be an idiot and behaves like an idiot, lacking what the witness testimony refers to as 'common capacity'. She was observed by all, claimed the deposition, to be 'short, fat, deformed, squinting and weak in her understanding'. The judges in France determined the case on 'the appearance of Fanny Fust' as well as her 'strange behaviour and irrational answers'. The public could easily determine her idiocy. The crew on the Channel steamer were 'convinced by Fanny's gestures, manners and appearance that she was insane or an ideot'. French passers-by spontaneously exclaimed what a fool she was, 'not merely from the bodily infirmities . . . but from the mental defects which very visibly appeared in her manner and deportment'.[50]

There was therefore common sense about idiocy: the legal profession simply confirmed what the public already discerned. If a woman was prepared to sell her property for less than five guineas, urinate in front of menservants and did not understand the science of lightning, she could not understand the complex abstractions of wealth, propriety and science that underpinned polite and commercial society. However, this visible idiocy was discernible not only to those who sought to support and protect Fust, but to those who wished to exploit her, 'the wicked part of mankind' as her mother called them. Those operating informal social or family networks of support came under siege from rapacious predators hunting assets. Fust's mother had to resort to law to fight the pervasive, sophisticated corruption ensnaring the asset that was her daughter. The informal system, widely accepted as the proper means of idiot support, was threatened, and resort to the law was the best option for those families able to afford it. A new acceptance of legal rather than informal processes to manage idiocy was evident. Courts had been loath to provide protection to Sir John Leigh and Henry Roberts, either through a reluctance to interfere in individual liberty (Leigh) or through a corrupt bias in favour of those mining an idiot's wealth (Roberts). In the case of Fanny Fust the family fought back and bent the legal process to their own will.

In the Courtroom: Criminal Courts

In trials at the Old Bailey, despite the vast differences in wealth, social class and status between those who appeared in the criminal dock and their more affluent counterparts in civil cases, a similar pattern is discernible of people living within their communities rather than in institutions, supported by informal networks of friends, neighbours and family who sought to protect them not only against those who might exploit them but against the harshness of the criminal justice system. Sentencing decisions generally reflected an assumption that people defined as idiots were members of their communities. Even if guilty of a crime, dispatch to any sort of an institution was never a consideration, even while their intellectual limitations were understood to make them not fully responsible for their own actions. So

William Hogarth, 'The Bench', 1758–64, engraving. Judges showed surprising leniency towards idiots in 18th-century courtrooms.

long as networks of support were perceived to be in place, or if the idiot defendant was perceived to be harmless, acquittals were common, even if it was evident that they had committed the crime they had been apprehended for, as the trial of Mary Bradshaw in 1710 demonstrates:

> Mary Bradshaw, alias Seymour, of St Giles without Cripplegate was indicted for feloniously stealing 2 stuff gowns, value 20s, a Stuff Petticoat 3s with other things, the Goods of Elizabeth Morgan. A cloth petticoat 5s[,] a Stuff Petticoat 3s, 3 Dowlace Smocks 15s, the Goods of Anne Downing. The Fact was plainly prov'd upon the Prisoner, but sufficient Proof being given in Court that she was an Idiot, the Jury acquitted her.[51]

Given that anyone on trial for a felony at the Old Bailey in this period was on trial for their lives, such acquittals were a way of withholding punishment on the grounds of the person's incapacity or harmlessness, or confidence in the ability of their community and family network to keep them out of trouble in the future. Even if death sentences were commuted, as they frequently were, 'lesser' sentences were harsh, and included transportation (to America in the earlier part of the century, later to Australia) or physical punishments such as whipping or branding. Acquittals of people who, like Mary Bradshaw, were deemed to have committed a crime but were shown leniency on the grounds of their idiocy or simplicity, and associated lack of responsibility, endured throughout the century. In 1719, when Mary Tame was accused of killing her two-year-old sister by drowning, the jury heard the 'evidence that the Prisoner was an Ideot' and 'considering the Matter acquitted her'.[52] Robert Left, on trial for stealing a brass weight in 1748, was acquitted by the jury, who 'said they thought he was an idiot'.[53] As late as 1804, 'Charles Viton was indicted for feloniously stealing, on the 23rd of October, one pair of breeches, value 12s, the property of Moses Levi, and Mary Jones. It appearing to the Court that the prisoner was an ideot, or lunatic, and subject to fits, he was acquitted.'[54] Two other men were acquitted in the same year on the grounds that 'it (appeared) to the court that the prisoner was an ideot, and subject to fits.'[55]

Idiots who faced trial in the Old Bailey were, for most of the eighteenth century, subject to the process of law in the same way as their fellow citizens. An idiot accused of committing a crime had to face justice; under English law at the time there could be no exceptions in the case of felonies. Pre-trial determinations by magistrates and grand juries[56] concentrated only on whether a crime was a felony or misdemeanour, with no consideration of a defendant's fitness to stand trial. Most thefts were considered felonies, and therefore capital offences,[57] and so idiots, reflecting the experience of the wider population, appeared on trial for their lives before the highest criminal court for the most minor of thefts – stealing a brass weight, a coat, some ribbon, a pair of breeches, a saw or a frock[58] – alongside those accused of murder, manslaughter or violent assault.

Once inside the courtroom, however, the possibility of exceptionality came into play. Being an idiot considerably raised the defendant's likelihood of being acquitted for anything seen as a relatively minor crime, or of escaping a death sentence through a reduced charge, even if the crime clearly had been committed. It was common for juries in cases involving idiot defendants to deliver 'partial verdicts' finding defendants guilty of a 'lesser offence', a non-capital charge that would avoid incurring the death penalty.[59] For example, in 1723 Thomas Allen, a 'soft-pated' fellow, was charged with stealing goods worth fourteen shillings but was found guilty of stealing goods worth less than one shilling, allowing him to escape the gallows.[60]

Driving these decisions were the testimonies of neighbours, friends, families, employers and workmates, whose assurances of good character and future support within strong community networks were an important factor in jury and judge decisions to show mercy. Representation by members of these social and work networks, appearing as witnesses on behalf of idiot defendants, followed a largely consistent pattern. Their intent was usually to demonstrate both the limiting impact of the person's idiocy and the positive character attributes of the idiot in the dock. To achieve this and demonstrate credibility to the court, they would adopt formal, respectable language in their rhetorical appeals for mercy. Eighteenth-century London was rich in slang terms denoting gullibility and low intelligence. Slang dictionaries had over 160 terms to denote the vulnerable idiot, most of them derisory, such as beetle head, blockstock, bottle-head, cake, clodpate, dog booby, empty-skulled, looby, nickum-poop, shallow-pate and wooly-crown.[61] However, such terms were not used in court, where witnesses adopted milder, more respectable and more morally neutral terms such as silly, foolish, ignorant, soft and weak, to which the slang terms formed a linguistic subset. Thus witnesses would present in respectable language a character who was intellectually weak but morally strong and respectable: 'a very honest, but a very silly ignorant fellow', 'I never heard anything amiss of him, but took him to be a little soft (or foolish)' and 'I always was of opinion that he was soft, but with respect to his honesty, I never heard a bad character of him in my life' were typical examples.[62]

Close relatives adopted a more emotive tone, emphasizing the vulnerability and harmlessness of the defendants. 'He is a harmless, half-witted, foolish lad,'[63] pleaded the mother of John Longmore at his trial for assault in 1732. Sometimes they explained the origins and extent of their relative's idiocy. 'His head was torn to pieces by a dog when he was 2 or 3 years of age' was the explanation of one brother, while a father said of his son that 'when he was between 6 and 7 years he was taken with a putrid fever, when he got better he was deprived of his speech.'[64] They would also seek compassion and urge sympathy, emphasizing the strong, loving family bonds that would ensure the defendant would stay out of trouble in future if spared. The father of 'foolish' epileptic Elizabeth Camell appealed directly to judge and jury that 'she is all the children I have out of fifteen, God bless you use her as well as you can. If she is released I'll

Thomas Rowlandson,
'A Cake in Danger',
1806, hand-coloured
etching. Dull-
wittedness made
rural vistors to
London easy prey.

take care to send her far enough from London, if she has got into ill Company.'[65] There was an urgency and desperation to the appeals of family members urging juries (usually successfully) to accept the harmlessness, naivety and incapacity of the defendant, and the respectability and devotion of the family, as factors deserving a merciful determination. The sincerity of their love for the idiot family member was clearly apparent.

There were sometimes extraordinary levels of commitment and devotion shown to idiot defendants by friends and workmates, revealing genuine friendships between idiots and non-idiots. In the 1732 trial of a gang accused of highway robbery, one of the accused made a dramatic intervention on behalf of a fellow gang member, half-witted, foolish John Longmore (whose mother's pleas for him we have already encountered): 'I own I am guilty of the fact, and desire to dye for it, but Longmore is innocent.'[66] Deep emotional and social ties were also evident. When seven witnesses, all workmates, lined up to defend Peter Cunniford, who was accused of theft, one of them revealed that he had 'lodged with the prisoner about 4 or 5 years and worked with him as long'. Another added, 'I have known him for several years and have worked with him in several places. I never heard the least stain on his character in the world. I never knew him but an honest fellow. I take him to be very foolish.'[67]

In 1780, a casually employed young skin-gatherer from the meat markets of London called Thomas Baggott went on trial accused of participation in the anti-Catholic Gordon Riots that convulsed London that year.[68] One hundred properties were destroyed, 285 rioters killed, 450 arrested, 160 tried and 25 hanged.[69] The government, shocked at the insurrectionary nature of the violence, urged retributive, exemplary justice. Baggott was described in court as 'almost an idiot . . . very weak . . . a poor foolish lad'. A succession of witnesses, six in total, provided alibis for him for the two-hour time period when it was claimed he had been seen 'stupefied with liquor' and helping to destroy a Catholic woman's house. Witnesses included male and female workmates, his employer, his sister and his mother. A further three people provided character witness statements. An examination of the statements makes it clear that perjury was being committed, at great personal risk, by at least some, if not all, of these witnesses, as their accounts contradicted each other, although they were consistent in exculpating Baggott. The judge noted this and at one point warned, 'I caution you, to be careful what you say,' to which a witness replied, 'I am very careful, and very sure he was employed in the yard until dinner-time.' A witness was cross-examined on his motive for appearing on Baggott's behalf and replied, 'my Master said I was to prove the time he was with me to serve a friend, not to forswear myself.' The witnesses acknowledged Baggott's idiocy and his faults, pointing out that 'he will work sometimes, but when he has got a few halfpence in his pocket he will not work' and acknowledging that 'when he had drank a little liquor, did not know what he did'. The lone prosecution witness, exasperated, pointed out the contradictory testimonies the court was hearing. Yet even he knew Baggott well, commenting, 'I have seen the boys after him in Newgate-market making game of him; he is almost an idiot . . . He used to gather skins in the market,' and testifying that when he spotted Baggott among the rioters he addressed him not as an idiot, but by his occupation: 'I said you skin gathering rascal, get away.' Baggot was acquitted: the jury colluded with this display of solidarity, perhaps assured that the existence of this supportive network would deter him from serious crime, perhaps believing him not responsible for his own actions. There were hints that others marginalized and exploited him: 'I have seen the boys . . . making game of him.' Yet when crisis came, Thomas Baggott was an idiot whose life meant something to others, whose membership of his community was validated by those who went to court prepared to take risks to save him.

Witnesses worked hard to present to the court an image of the defendant distinct from their alleged crime; embedded in ordinary life within family, work and neighbourhood; and imbued with moral integrity and valuable personal characteristics such as honesty and diligence. In doing this they revealed a world in which the idiot was understood as far more than an idiot, where bonds of love, friendship, kinship and economic relations placed them strongly within the circles of community that formed eighteenth-century London. Central to this was a belief, shared by witnesses, judges and jurors, that those on trial were not intrinsically dangerous as a consequence of their idiocy, and that they were well known and unlikely to commit serious crimes in future. Despite its harshness, the eighteenth-century justice system offered a discretionary space that allowed for mercy, acquittal or leniency, and those perceived as idiots occupied a favourable position within it. Most were deemed troublesome but unthreatening and therefore worthy of mercy. Very occasionally, we hear an idiot defendant making a rhetorical plea for their own life. Ann Wildman, a 'very weak, easy, foolish girl, next a kin to an idiot', indicted for shoplifting ribbon, denied her crime and pleaded:

'I hope your lordship and the jury will take it into consideration not to hurt me.'[70] She was acquitted.

However, where idiots had committed more serious crimes such as those involving killing or violent assault, and particularly if they were regarded as serial offenders, mercy was far less likely to be shown. In such cases those few deemed dangerous or likely to commit serious crime were judged by the same standards as non-idiots, their idiocy not seen as a contributory factor to their dangerousness. In 1716 Richard Price, who like Thomas Baggott was accused of involvement in demolishing a house during a religious street riot, was found guilty and hanged. An apprentice described by his master as 'a very silly ignorant fellow', Price, unlike Baggott, was a recent arrival in London and had no community or family roots, there thus being no guarantee that he would not simply drift back into dangerous behaviour if acquitted.[71] Mary Radford, 'a very silly creature and a half natural', was hanged for infanticide in 1723.[72] Multiple offences also attracted death sentences, recidivism seen as dangerous whatever the capacity and level of responsibility of the offender. Half-witted, foolish John Longmore, despite the pleas we have seen from his mother and his comrade in crime, was acquitted of his first two offences – violent theft and assault – but hanged in 1732 for his third, a highway robbery. Two years later James Belford, 'of weak understanding and a very silly weak man', suffered a similar fate for his second offence of highway robbery.[73]

At the heart of the criminal justice system, as in the civil courts, was the question of a defendant's character and the capacity of the judge and jury to observe and determine it. If a person was to be recognized as an idiot, that recognition would take place in the courtroom, by those whose duty was to judge them. Rapid character judgements by juries and judges based on appearance and behaviour were the norm. Once recognized, idiocy did not guarantee acquittal, but largely it attracted lenient treatment. The trial itself was 'essentially a direct confrontation between the victim and the prisoner, moderated by the judge, in which each party was responsible for

Isaac Cruikshank, 'The Deaf Judge; or, Mutual Misunderstanding', 1796,
satirical print of a scene at the Old Bailey.

providing whatever witnesses and evidence they could muster
in their support'.[74] Lawyers did not begin to appear in Old
Bailey cases, and then only sporadically, until the last quarter of
the century. The courtroom, until the introduction of counsel,
was not seen as the domain of the professional, apart from the
judge,[75] who examined victims, prosecutors and witnesses and
moderated procedure.[76] Guilt or innocence were perceived as
discernible in the defendant's 'immediate and unrehearsed
responses' to the evidence.[77] In the absence of forensic evidence
and with the victim (also the prosecutor) often the sole witness,
a defendant's character was central to the determination of the
truth. The focus was therefore on the quality of character witness testimony and the accused's response to the charges laid.[78]
As John H. Langbein has written, 'the logic of the early modern

trial was to pressure the accused to speak, either to clear himself, or hang himself.'[79]

For someone perceived as an idiot the need to conduct their own evidence presented both a problem and an advantage. If unable to communicate clearly, think quickly or understand the process, they risked self-incrimination. Sixteen-year-old 'Foolish Johnny Leck' contradicted himself as he both admitted and denied his theft. 'I will never do so any more; I should not have done it now, but another boy did it first,' he admitted. Yet minutes later he denied the crime: 'I did not do it, another boy began at first, and then he ran away, I will never touch anything again.' However, such defendants were likely also to benefit from what the legal scholar William Hawkins has described as the jury's duty to detect 'simplicity and . . . artless and ingenuous behaviour', where 'the very speech, gesture and countenance . . . may often help to disclose the truth.'[80] Criminality was located in the appearance, attitude and conduct of the defendant, and juries made their own amateur assessments of the potential risks and harm that the offender represented.[81] A 'simple' person who had committed an offence unwittingly or through their perceived stupidity stood a strong chance of being deemed low-risk and acquitted.

BY THE END of the eighteenth century, therefore, the early modern legal idea of idiocy was still intact, and discernible in the arena of both the civil and criminal courts. Idiocy was something you could see marked on the face and body of the person who carried it; idiots themselves were generally harmless, if strange, and the natural place for them to function was within their families and communities, under the informal protection of family members, friendship groups and neighbourly networks. The law, in its role as representative of the state, needed to do little to intervene in their lives. Criminal courts on the whole acquitted or showed leniency, while civil courts preferred informal solutions to state intervention. However, towards the end of the century the stability and borders of this definition were threatened by exploitative corruption and crumbling informal networks, which led to a perceived need for greater legal intervention and protection in civil cases. The early 1800s would show a similar trend in criminal trials, although some leniency persisted. On the whole, judges and juries would become less tolerant and forgiving and began to impose harsher and more punitive judgments and sentences on idiot defendants. They would increasingly question a person's right to remain within their community.

The trends discernible in trials were reflected in two early nineteenth-century works: the legal writer Anthony Highmore's *A Treatise on the Law of Idiocy and Lunacy* in 1807,[82] and the barrister George Dale Collinson's *Treatise on the Law concerning Idiots, Lunatics, and Other Persons Non Compotes Mentis* in 1812.[83] There had been greater focus as the eighteenth century developed on the levels of knowledge and understanding necessary to constitute full human understanding and permission to participate in the 'offices of life'. These had moved far from the ability to count to twenty and recognize one's mother and father. Legal theorists began to take greater interest in idiocy and, more broadly, imbecility, with a growing canon of case law and law reports on which to build. The borderlands of idiocy became more fluid as the contested new class of lifelong imbecile was consistently reinvented. Collinson was clear that things had moved on since Lord Hardwicke's pronouncement on Sir John Leigh's case, which situated him just the other side of the border of unsound-mindedness. Now, 'non compos mentis comprehends, not only idiots and lunatics, but all other persons who from *natural imbecility* . . . are incapable of managing their own affairs.'[84] The courts were extending to 'persons incapable of managing their own affairs through mere weakness of understanding . . . the same relief as to lunatics'. Lord Chancellor Eldon had pronounced that he was not prepared to correct any judgment that had classified a person naturally weak of mind but non-idiotic, as non-compos mentis, thus giving legal status to the lifelong imbecile.[85]

Alongside this extension of the boundaries of definition, however, state intervention in idiocy became less revenue-driven and arose more from family concerns about exploitation or inheritance. Collinson noted that 'the king's interest in the property of idiots has long been considered a hardship' but added that in fact 'few instances can be given of the oppressive exertion of it.'[86] It became increasingly rare for the Crown to claim its confiscation entitlement. There was a wider political reluctance to interfere with and thereby to undermine individual and private decision-making, individual liberty of conscience and action. Collinson urged 'to take care not to extend the prerogative of the Crown so as to restrain the liberty of the subject, and his power over his person and property, further than the law allowed'. He argued that 'there cannot be an act of greater oppression than to interfere with the economy of domestic life.'[87] Informal family and friendship networks were, however, coming under siege from perceived acquisitive exploiters, while families, as in the Fanny Fust case, began to see legal intervention and state protection as a new, more formal and effective option.

However significant these changes, Highmore's and Collinson's concept of the idiot remained broadly recognizable: as instantly discernible by the layman, with idiocy evident in appearance as much as action or thought (or lack of it) – unlike lunacy, which could be concealed. The idiot was easily exploited and cut off by their mental incapacity from the norms and assumptions of daily society. The idea of idiocy was constructed as much by popular perception as legal theorization. Collinson even recycled the now very ancient joke about the idiot in the Paris cookshop to illustrate that although the idiot could sound reasonable, 'to do a sensible act, is no certain proof of a sound mind.'[88] Institutionalization was never mentioned; expert medical opinion never sought. There was no intimation, as reflected in both the civil and criminal courts, that idiots as a class were dangerous. As Highmore put it, 'Ideots are afflicted with no turbulent passions; they are innocent and harmless, and often excite pity, but never occasion fear.' They could, however, be a danger to themselves, and face danger from others. The purpose of the law, in the eyes of the legal theorist, was 'securing them against injury from their own hands and from the self-interest of others'. Families provided for them and friends rushed to defend them. The law saw one of its primary aims as ensuring that the 'interests of their families are preserved'.[89] The idiot remained at the heart of communities; challenged, vulnerable, perceived as different and lacking capacity but with sufficient personal capital in the eyes of others to be worth defending.

2

Billy-noodles and Bird-wits:
Cultural Ideas of Idiocy

During the eighteenth century it was very rare for anyone labelled an idiot or imbecile to be confined to an institution. The locus of care and support, if needed, was the community. While the occasional person might find themselves almost accidentally consigned to one of the small emerging places of institutional confinement for those with disordered minds – Guy's, St Luke's or Bethlem hospitals, for example – the institution was not seen as the natural place for the idiot. Indeed, some actively sought to exclude idiots on the grounds that they would block up the system for more needy 'lunacy' cases.[1] Idiocy was not seen as a medical matter. Medical men – and they were all men – were in the business of payment by results, recompense for curing whatever was wrong with a person. Idiots and imbeciles were not ill, and therefore could not be cured, which made them a matter of supreme indifference to the medical profession. The asylum movement's argument that idiocy was a matter for medical incarceration and supervision would not gather true momentum until well into the nineteenth century.

If we seek to discover the eighteenth-century experience of those who lived their lives perceived as idiots, imbeciles or just dull-witted, and to understand the social assumptions that were made about them, we must therefore look elsewhere, outside the institution. They lived their lives in communities, as part of general society, and so we find them where we find everybody else. They are to be discovered in jokes, in the rich slang of the eighteenth-century street, in novels, cheap fiction and poetry, in art and caricature and in religious sermons preached by evangelicals to huge crowds. We hear about them, as we have already seen, in criminal trials and civil legal proceedings, sometimes even catching, very faintly, their own voices. It is through a reconstruction of these glimpses that we can begin to build a picture of how the idiot and the imbecile were perceived, talked about, laughed about and understood in the societies they lived in. We can also develop an idea of how they lived their lives, their experience of family, community and society in the eighteenth century.

As the Prussian visitor to England Archenholz remarked in 1789, 'There [in England], as everywhere else, they laugh at a ridiculous person, but they treat him with a great deal of indulgence; and they do not esteem a gentleman less on account of his oddity, provided he hurts no one.'[2] Humour was a highly prized part of eighteenth-century British culture, reflected in fiction, art, caricature and not least in the pervasive popularity of jokes and slang language. Those called idiots and imbeciles, stupid or simple, lived their lives under the amused gaze of their fellow citizens: this could be either malicious or sympathetic. In the cultural imagination idiots loomed large. They were a stock feature of jokes, in many guises. They were also a pervasive and significant presence in street slang.

Jokes, Slang and Stories

The everyday humour of the eighteenth century has survived predominantly in the jestbooks and chapbooks that were produced in their tens of thousands throughout the century, and in dictionaries of slang terms from the London streets. There were hundreds of different jestbook titles, and while it is difficult to ascertain precisely the extent of readership, they were clearly popular and widely read, as each season mainstream publishers issued reprints of old favourites and up to twenty new titles.[3]

They would not, it can be assumed, have done this had demand not existed. Such works came in a range of genres, including bound books, retailing at around a shilling and targeted at those with disposable income. These encompassed titles such as *Coffee-House Jests, Being a Merry Companion* (1760), *The Macaroni Jester and Pantheon of Wit* (1773) and *The Sailor's Jester; or, Merry Lad's Companion* (1790). There were also penny chapbooks or single quarto sheets (with titles such as *The Penny Budget of Wit*), sold for as little as a farthing by chapmen door to door or on the streets. These were affordable even for the barely literate poor. The humour cut across classes, with the same jokes appearing in the more expensive books and the cheaper pamphlets, and some fashionable jestbooks were abridged as chapbooks or sold in weekly parts to poorer consumers.[4] Listening to, reading and laughing about jokes were therefore activities that could appeal to the disparate populations and classes of eighteenth-century Britain. Some books were read aloud by literate members of communities; others were specifically designed to be carried around in the pocket to provide a supply of ready wit to impress friends and acquaintances.[5]

Slang, like jokes, built group identity in communities, with its origins in the so-called canting language of criminals, from which the modern term 'cant', now meaning hypocritical and sanctimonious talk, is derived. It was devised to deceive, defraud and conceal as well as create a distinctive alternative subculture.[6] The ability of slang to hide meanings from the unsuspecting meant that it was ideally applied against outsiders, highlighting their oddity, their vulnerability and their unfamiliarity with the shared cultural codes and practices of those among whom they found themselves.[7] We owe our knowledge of eighteenth-century slang to antiquarian gentlemen such as 'B. E.' (his full identity has never been discovered), who published a dictionary of *The Terms Ancient and Modern of the Canting Crew* in 1699, and, most famously, Francis Grose, whose *Classical Dictionary of the Vulgar Tongue* of 1784 remains the most comprehensive repository of the street language of the time. Grose, it was claimed, toured the back slums and drinking dens of St Giles, the notorious poverty-stricken and crime-ridden area around present-day Tottenham Court Road in London, with his serving man, Batch. He was simultaneously repelled and fascinated by the sharp argot of London's poor – the hawkers, labourers, prostitutes and criminals – and from 'these nocturnal sallies, and the *slang* expressions which continually assaulted his ears',[8] he compiled his dictionary, laying before the world the secret codes of the London poor.

Street slang showed that the population had a sharp eye for those they regarded as mentally dull-witted. Slang, like fashion, is used 'to define in-groups and out-groups'.[9] The ability of slang to hide meanings from the unsuspecting meant that its main concerns were always matters that speakers wished to disguise, such as sexual relations or criminal activity. A principal aim was to identify the vulnerable:[10] easy prey, the empty-headed victim or the easily manipulated accomplice. Slang is therefore a rich source for popular opinions about the looks and behaviour

Nathaniel Dance, portrait of Francis Grose, frontispiece to *Supplement to The Antiquities of England and Wales* (1777).

of the idiotic, dull-witted and exploitable. They were 'culls' and 'bubbles', 'silly easy fellows' who could be easily 'buttoned' or drawn in. There were 'billy-noodles' and 'bird-wits', 'empty fellows' and 'goose-caps', 'nizies' and 'nockys', each of them a way of describing the idiotic, the dim and the dull.

A particular target of slang and jokes were the rustic idiots, the unintelligent country simpletons who flocked to London and were ripe for the picking on its streets, dull, slow and stupid. At the beginning of the century, this notion of the rural idiot represented an entire idiot class without distinction of rank or wealth. The 'rich bumpkin' and the county squire were just as stupid, to the smart city-dweller, as the ditch digger or plough-man. In jestbooks, countrymen see large ships in the London docks and on being told they are a year old, wonder how large they will be by the time they are adults;[11] they observe the new St Paul's Cathedral being built and marvel that it must have cost even more than they spent on their new barn;[12] they are called 'loggerheads' by smart city boy apprentices.[13] 'Ignorant

A Natural Crop; – alias – A Norfolk Dumpling

James Gillray, 'A Natural Crop; – alias – A Norfolk Dumpling', 1791, hand-coloured etching. 'Norfolk Dumpling' was a slang term for a rural idiot.

clowns' think they can read, but misread signs with comical effects and fall on their backsides on London's streets, crying, 'London can kiss my arse!'[14] The same jokes were plagiarized and recycled throughout the century.[15]

An enormous array of slang terms and nicknames described the idiot countryman: 'booby', 'chaw-bacon', 'clodpate', 'hick jop', 'bumpkin', 'clouted shoon', 'hobinail', 'milestone', 'country put' and 'clown' all captured his dull slowness of wit.[16] The rustic idiot was barely distinguishable from the animals and birds among which he dwelt. He was a bull calf, a donkey, a pea goose and a sheep's head. Popular rural names became nouns to denote stupidity: an idiot figure was a Ben, Dick, Roger, Sam, Jack Adams, Johnny Raw, Simkin, Simon or Donkey Dick. The rural idiot was characterized by a thick, impenetrable skull and did not feel pain in the same way as others. Thus he was a puzzle (or puzzel) pate or hulver-head, hulver being Norfolk dialect for a hard, solid wood, and Norfolk being the epicentre of rural stupidity, epitomized by the Norfolk Dumpling, a particularly egregious form of rural idiot.[17] In cheap popular drama aimed at mass audiences, characters called Hob and Dick became engaged in cudgel fights with their neighbours Puzzel Pate and Roger, with a prize for the first to break the skull of another. No matter how hard their skulls were hit, they came back, still alive, for more. As Puzzel Pate put it, 'I have had enough on' en already, for he broke my Head but last week.'[18] There was clearly little brain to be damaged.

Writers and caricaturists drew on the slang and jokes and added their own versions of the idiot, which in turn fed back into the ideas swirling in the minds of the public, high and low. In Fanny Burney's *Camilla* (1796), the intellectually challenged Sir Hugh, with his 'poor capacity' and 'poor weak head',[19] is referred to by his exploitative nephews as 'blockhead', 'old gull', 'ninny' and 'numps',[20] all terms lifted directly from the slang dictionaries to denote an idiot, vulnerable simpleton. Caricaturists drew the jokes they had read in the jestbooks, bringing visual form to their idiot characters; bamboozled idiot countrymen found themselves paying to walk in London sedan chairs which had had their floors removed, and rustic simpletons misunderstood and were baffled by the questions of their intelligent visitors from London.[21] Idiot characters stared, eyes half-shut, from caricatures, displaying the low 'beetle-brows' and sloping 'bullet-heads' that Grose had gleaned from his vicarious fascination with London's low-life talk. The idiotic 'lowbrow' even became a term to define low culture. The idiot, and ideas about the idiot, unobtrusively permeated culture at all levels. Patrick McDonagh has written about how nineteenth-century cultural works 'express culturally charged beliefs about the subtexts or connotations' of notions of idiocy.[22] So it was in the eighteenth century: the casual humour betrayed deeply held cultural assumptions.

The country idiot was not simply a witty conceit but occupied a meaningful space in the consciousness of the eighteenth-century city-dweller. Amused Old Bailey juries would acquit an accused felon on the grounds that 'he was a poor silly country fellow and might be easily drawn in'.[23] Ideas of intellectual deficit since the medieval period were intimately tied up with ideas of class and poverty.[24] Members of the labouring classes were, to the elite, simply and irrevocably idiotic because they were born lower class and poor. However, over the eighteenth century there developed an increasing recognition that idiocy was more nuanced than this.[25] The countryman might appear idiotic due to lack of experience and education, but most had the capacity to learn and could demonstrate wit and intelligence, to the surprise of the urban sophisticate. A mid-century jest has Beau Nash, the famed dandy and leader of fashion, encountering an apparently gormless country porter, whom he abuses and tells mockingly to find 'a greater fool than yourself'. The porter goes off and promptly returns with the mayor of the town. Nash, surprised, appreciates the witty point the poor and uneducated porter has made, and asks him, 'Being a poor Man, what Business have you with Wit?' He and his newly respected countryman friend agree that too much wit only brings misfortune to rich and poor, while both rich and poor fools prosper. Nash gives him a guinea and advises him to 'go Home, and study Stupidity'.[26] The empathy between Nash and the porter is based on shared intelligence rather than class, which enables idiocy to be seen as a changeable and rectifiable phenomenon rather than a fixed function of social class. A clear distinction was beginning to develop between the 'real' idiot and those labelled as idiotic because of their foolish and exasperating behaviour. As the author of the short popular 'ramble' novel *The History of Tom Fool*, three years before the Nash anecdote, put it:

> By Ideots I don't mean those unhappy objects, whose defective Organs make them May-games to the sounder-formed part of the World. I mean . . . that Society of men, who are nicknamed Ideots by their Wives, their Brothers, their Friends, their Partners, Masters and kept Mistresses.[27]

A divide was appearing between the incorrigible born idiot, a perpetual target of amusement for the community, and the uneducated but improvable fool, country or otherwise, amusing but able to change.

This linked to a further strongly held notion of a certain type of idiot as a human unable to learn. The idiot's problem, it was believed, lay in their thick, inflexible, impenetrable, unproductive, empty head, skull or brain. As a typically scatological piece of graffiti from 1731 pronounced, 'Like Claret-Drinkers Stools, a Blockhead's Brain; / Hardly conceives what it brings forth in Pain.'[28] As well as thick-skulled idiots there were also their counterpart, the thin-skulled 'vapourish' type.[29] They were corky brain'd fellows, crakt-brains, jingle-brains or had their brains in their ballocks. Their skulls were soft, meaning that they were empty and unproductive. Thus they were paper skuls, num-skuls, sapsculls, empty skull'd, sap-pates and shallow-pates. A silly fellow is like a feather bed, explained a riddle, 'because he is soft'.[30] Their heads, though, as a rule were generally hard, signalling that nothing, including a cudgel, could penetrate the blockhead, fat-head, hulver-head, loggerhead or thick-head.

In this rigidity and inflexibility, the inability to read situations or learn from them, lay the humour of idiocy. It was believed that idiots persisted in doing the wrong thing because, as the law suggested, they were unable to abstract or apply knowledge flexibly, and the comic consequences of this incapacity permeated the jestbooks. An idiot on his death bed, assured by his friends that he will be carried to the graveyard, replies that he would prefer to make his own way there.[31] In more sinister vein, a fool, teased by a carpenter, gains his revenge by cutting off his head with an axe when he is asleep and hiding it. Asked later why he is laughing he replies, 'Oh, the bravest funn that ever you heard of . . . I laugh to think, when the carpenter wakes, how like a fool he'll look without a head, and lose his Afternoon's work, to find out where I have hid it.'[32] Idiots were the ultimate comic bystander, obstinately failing to learn, non-participants in the common human themes of life and death, startling in the sheer level of their ignorance. As Fanny Burney's Sir Hugh laments, however much he tries all this 'jingle jangle' (learning), 'I find myself turning out as sheer a blockhead as ever.'[33]

The Simple Simon character (a man, not a child) and other dull-witted anti-heroes endured throughout the century and became a motif for all forms of stupidity. British adults and children were assailed throughout their lives with folk tale accounts of variable, and often limited, intellectual faculty, the deeds of the stupid and the dull, the travails of the idiotic and imbecilic. As Robert Darnton has pointed out, in contrast to the cruelties, terrors and tortures of French peasant tales, British folk stories were awash with 'Jacks and Jocks, brave but lazy, good-natured but thick-headed'.[34] Grose in his slang dictionary captured Simon's multiple stupidities in his definition of the street-slang term: 'Simon: a sixpence. Simple Simon: a natural, a silly fellow. Simon Suck-egg, sold his wife for an addle duck egg.'[35] The significance of the sixpence was that it was a coin easily 'bent and distorted'.[36] The Simon Suck-egg folk rhyme alludes

simple simon

scathingly to the easily trickable idiot unable to understand value, or indeed family relationships. The Simple Simon rhyme, circulating as a ballad since at least the sixteenth century and in print as a chapbook from 1764,[37] encapsulates the human who lacks the basic capacity to understand what is necessary for everyday survival and who is also incapable of learning. He asks a pieman for a pie, but when asked to produce the money necessary for the exchange – 'Show me first your penny' – can only reply, 'Sir, I have not any.'

There were other versions of Simple Simon, outside the well-known ballad, that were part of the collective memory. One of the consistent, distinguishing and enduringly hilarious features of a Simon for eighteenth-century readers was his lack of masculinity, which condemned him to live inappropriately under the guiding hand of a kind mother or facing the blows of a shrewish, hectoring, permanently exasperated wife. A chapbook song about 'Poor Simon', a hapless simpleton living with his violent, hard-drinking wife Margery, shows him subjected to unremitting violence.[38] Margery successively lugs his ears, rings his nose, 'beat him till tears ran down to his hose' and belabours him with a large cudgel. Each act of violence is in response to Simon's acts of hopeless incapacity while trying to perform simple tasks.[39] Unable to perform the tasks of a man, Simon's stupidity threatens the livelihood and survival of the family, and economic unit, to which he clings so precariously and ambivalently. However, two events ensure his survival and stabilize his position. Pitying neighbours take him in after his own (inept) suicide attempt and Margery's attack with the cudgel, and summon Margery to their home: 'They sent for his wife, who came without fail / Their peace was made o'er a jug of ale.' After this drunken negotiation (quantities of 'canary', or sack, have already been consumed):

> The neighbours in merriment got him to bed
> That night no doubt he pleased his wife,
> For now he leads a happy life.[40]

Marjorie's relentless physical thrashings, and the suicidal intent they bring about in Simon, have passed beyond humour. Community intervention is necessary. Neighbours impose themselves, but also bring about a reassertion, or perhaps a first assertion, of Simon's masculine sexual duty to satisfy his wife and claim his 'proper' place. Any threat to the social or gender order is thus averted and happiness, order, prosperity and stability are restored.

Simple Simon and the shrewish Margery were repeatedly portrayed as the man without brains and the woman without restraint, locked in a violent and uncomprehending embrace. The violence is extreme. Simple Simon, who looks 'like one who had neither sense nor reason', stands gormlessly and insensibly in the face of events 'like one half-affronted out of his wits'.[41] Margery hits him with a staff – 'such a clank on the noddle, as made the blood spin' – ties him up and hauls him in a basket over a fire, where he is smoked for the night. Later Margery 'let fly an earthen pot at his head, which caused the blood to run about his ears', and whips him with a dog whip.[42] And yet, always, when he can endure no more, Simon the emasculated simple male weeps, and at last the community intervenes to plead, successfully, for the violence to stop and for order to be restored:

> She . . . carries on beating him until neighbours came in, persuading Margery to be pacified . . . 'A rascal,' said she, 'I can set him about nothing, but thus he serves me.' Yet still they interceded for Simon, until she excused him.[43]

In these portrayals, the simple idiot is a fool (and a hapless, annoying, useless fool at that), and yet he is the responsibility of the community. He must stay within it and be accorded some sort of status; the cruelty must stop and he must be protected from himself and others. If not, the disorder around him, and the subversion of the sexual order, are too threatening. He is, for better or worse, a part of the ordered community, and the instability he has brought to it needs to be corrected. His haplessness will be tolerated, but controlled, as will the disturbing masculine violence and rage of Margery.

Other dim-witted but ultimately amiable characters populated the ballads and tales that people listened to and told. Their stupidity is not necessarily an impediment to success and is often offset by admirable characteristics. The numbskull Jack (of beanstalk fame) 'trades the family cow for a few beans and then climbs his way to riches'.[44] In another tale, the good humour of Joseph Jollyboy makes up for his deficiency in 'brightness of facts' and wit.[45] Dull-witted simplicity might be an object of ridicule, but, we are reminded by one anonymous writer, 'the family of the Simples is as ancient a family as any in England.'[46] The inevitably named Simon Simple 'would do everything he was bid, and believed everything that he was told'; however, the reader is enjoined to remember that 'simplicity is a virtue, not a folly.'[47] There was something almost stirringly and patriotically English about lacking intellectual faculties but having a good heart. The idiotic, the foolish, the simple could be both perplexing and exasperating, but they held a necessary place in the social order, recognized by rich and poor. They were not a group to be victimized or banished but one rather to be laughed at for their foolishness, protected for their vulnerability and admired for their innocent and honest virtues.

The emasculated cuckold, as we have seen with Simple Simon, was one recurring image of the male idiot throughout the century. In slang, a 'nickum-poop' was not just a silly, soft, foolish fellow but also one who 'never saw his wife's ****'.[48] Joke makers scorned the trusting, naive, gullible idiot husband, startled by his wife's pregnancy after eight childless years, who exclaims 'I protest I had no hand in it' and innocently invites his cousin, the real father, to be the child's godfather.[49] A satirical jestbook poem in 1745 had yet another hilariously dim Simple Simon begging his friend Thomas to kiss his beautiful wife Susan, utterly oblivious to the affair they are having.[50]

However, far from these impotent idiot authors of their own matrimonial misfortune was a sharply different breed of intellectually challenged man: the well-endowed, sexually prodigious idiot, weak in mind but amply compensated in body. In John Cleland's pornographic work *Fanny Hill* (1748–9) the eponymous heroine seduces a servant named Will, fresh from the country, who is not only a 'very handsome young lad' but also a 'modest, innocent . . . blushing simpleton . . . in a strain of perfect nature'.[51] When Fanny, certainly no stranger to the male body, unbuttons Will's breeches she is astonished to encounter 'not the plaything of a boy, not the weapon of a man, but a maypole of so enormous a standard that, had proportions been observed, it must have belonged to a young giant'.[52] Cleland emphasizes the association of sexual endowment with idiocy, referring to the popular saying 'a fool's bauble is a Lady's play fellow,'[53] with 'bauble', as Grose recorded in his dictionary, being a slang word for testicle. The reason for the belief in an idiot's exceptionally sized genitalia was the idea of the compensatory faculty, whereby a bodily or mental inadequacy of one sort was made up for by exceptional gifts in another area. As Cleland put it about the simpleton Will: 'nature . . . made him amends, in her best bodily gifts, for her denial of the sublime intellectual ones . . . in short had done so much for him in these parts that she perhaps held herself acquitted in doing so little for his head.'[54] The idea of the well-endowed idiot was encapsulated in the term 'lob cock', which meant both 'a heavy dull inanimate fellow' and 'a large relaxed penis'.[55] This was also the theme of *The History of Tom Fool* in 1760, where the proliferation of the Fool family is attributed to 'Nature making amends for the Deficiency of Head, by a Superabundancy in other parts'.[56] Like *Fanny Hill*'s Will, Tom Fool is intellectually simple but physically handsome and attractive. As a lady's maid comments after catching him 'unlaced' one day, 'he's such an ignoramus, and so bashful . . . he looked so simple, and so innocent, that if I had been to be ravished by him, I must have forgiven him.'[57]

Fanny later encounters a youth named Good-natured Dick. 'Good-natured' in this sense means easy and pliable but also, more importantly, naturally well endowed. He is a local ragged flower-seller, 'a perfect changeling or idiot' stammering out 'the sounds that his half-dozen animal ideas prompted him to utter'. Though ragged, he is 'well made, stout, clean limbed'.[58] Fanny and her friend seduce him and find him 'rich in personal treasures . . . of so tremendous a size that, prepared as we were to see something extraordinary, it still, out of measure, surpassed our expectation and astonished even me, who had not been used to trade in trifles'.[59] Dick's mental faculties are considerably more impaired than Will's, so his physical compensation is proportionately greater. The popular idea of the handsome, well-endowed and somewhat unrestrained idiot was evident when Peter the Wild Boy, a strange youth discovered living wild in a German forest, was brought to the Hanoverian court in 1726. Courtiers were reported to have been disappointed by his indifference to women, after holding high expectations of the idiot youth's 'wild virility'.[60] Along with the savage man, the idiot could hold irresistible sexual appeal.[61] Notably absent from this understanding of idiocy was any sense of dangerousness, disgust or loathing, and nor was the thought of sexual liaison with a certain type of idiot perceived as taboo.

More ambivalent was the imagining of the idiot as incontinent, in the broadest senses of the word: physically, emotionally, verbally and morally. These multiple incontinences derived from a lack of control and self-restraint. Slang reflected this. Stupidity and the inability to control language were conflated. Thus a 'blab' was a prating stupid fellow who tells all he knows. Foolish, nonsensical ramblers were spoonys, rattle-pates or blubbers. There was no connection between idiots' facial expressions and the inner emotions they were supposed to reveal: they would grin, but for no reason. In Grose's dictionary a 'grinagog' was a foolish grinning fellow 'who grins without reason', while 'flearing fools' were grinning, silly fellows. Idiots were slow, clumsy, barely able to move their own dull, blockish bodies; they were clumpish, lumps and slubbers – all meaning heavy, stupid fellows. A 'drumbelo' was a dull, stupid slug of a man.

This lack of control over the body and mind clashed with growing expectations of control of bodily functions and emotional restraint, as bodily control became an indicator of social standing.[62] In this disparity between public aspiration and individual behaviour, humour flourished. Conduct and rule books tried to instil new standards of publicly restrained and hygienic behaviour, a sense of shame, delicacy and mutual obligation. In 1729 Jean-Baptiste de La Salle, the French rule-setter on manners, advised, 'it is very impolite to emit wind from your body when in company, either from above or below, even if it is done without noise . . . it is shameful and indecent to do it in a way that can be heard by others.'[63] Thirty years later, oblivious idiot jestbook characters were doing precisely that, and subsequently bragging about it: 'A simple fellow, before some Women did let a Crack [fart] behind, and then he said that he had a very good Rapport behind his back.' The punchline underscores the connection between the uncontrolled body and the unrestrained mind, as an observer tells the simple man: 'thy Tail [arse] can talk much better; for that has more wisdom in telling a Tale than thy Tongue.'[64]

La Salle also enjoined that 'it is never proper to speak of . . . certain bodily necessities to which nature has subjected us, or even to mention them.'[65] The enjoinment not to talk about such natural functions mingled with requirements, which had been developing since the medieval period, to use the right hand for clean and the left hand for dirty tasks, to improve hygiene.[66] Thus the jest about a fool's use of the wrong hand for greeting, and his explanation of why he had done it, was doubly shocking:

A natural fool was commanded to give such a Lord his Hand, which he presently did, but gave him his left Hand, for which his master chid him, and told him he should have given his Lord his Right hand. O fye, Master, says the Fool, I think you are more Fool than I, for that's an unseemly Thing indeed, to give to a great Lord that Hand which I wipe my Breech withal every day.[67]

These humorous observations indicate the opening up of a gap between the expectations and criteria that society was setting down for acceptability and what the idiot could achieve. Their unawareness of this and the resultant constant social faux pas were laughable matters and signified a growing alienation from the mainstream for an increasingly clearly defined born-idiot group. Alongside this, however, there existed a certain relish in the idiot's stubborn refusal to 'modernize'. The imprecations of La Salle and others, the exhortations to politeness and manners, were just that: imprecations and exhortations. Eighteenth-century society was not becoming an oasis of good manners and excellent personal hygiene simply because writers were suggesting that it should. There was a gulf, often humorously observed, between precept and practice. Ideals and exhortations to politeness were expressed precisely because it was not being attained, in an impolite world that talked about politeness.[68] People strained desperately to make themselves polite, to regulate their passions.[69] In 1740, *An Essay on Polite Behaviour* demanded: 'A Man must be Master of Himself, and his Words, Gestures and his Passions, that nothing offensive may escape him.'[70] 'One must conform', wrote the diarist Anna Larpent, 'to the World . . . I will do everything with the intention of doing right . . . I must learn to dissimulate in this world.'[71] The jesting satire was not directed only against the uncontrolled bodies and unmannerly behaviour of their idiot protagonists: it was also against those offended and discomfited by them, who were trying so hard not to be like them.

The most extreme and enduring image of the idiot body and its incontinence was the gaping, drivelling mouth. Idiots were imagined with mouths permanently open, the drooping lower lip pulled down like a hinge by the protruding lower jaw. The open mouth signified not only poor control over one's facial features and expressions, but a dull puzzlement at what was going on. Idiots roamed the streets 'mouth half cockt', as the slang dictionaries put it, 'gaping and staring at everything they see'.[72] Their slack jaws earned them the epithet 'gab'.[73] In the jestbooks, bemused country idiots wandering London's streets would address each other 'mouth at half cock',[74] while idiot country lads being asked the catechism 'stood gaping' as if they 'had heard Dutch spoken'.[75]

The open, uncontrolled mouth resulted in drivel, the idiot's internal fluids leaking from their bodies through this unguarded point of exit. The head-lopping fool of the carpenter joke laughed uncontrollably at what he had done, 'till he drivel'd again'.[76] Robert Nixon, the probably apocryphal protagonist of the immensely popular 1715 almanac *Nixon's Cheshire Prophecy*, was a 'sort of an idiot' from the reign of Charles II, widely believed to have the mysterious power to foresee momentous political events like Nostradamus.[77] Nixon was able to deliver prophecy with 'gravity and solemnity . . . speaking plainly and sensibly', despite being a 'Drivler [who] could not speak common sense when he was uninspired'.[78] As a typical idiot, Nixon displayed greedy, uncontrolled appetites and was locked in a cupboard by the king's cooks because he 'grew so troublesome in licking and picking the meat' in the royal kitchens.[79] He lacked any form of control, either in consuming or in his bodily emissions. Idiots were signified in portrayals by unrestrained and meaningless verbosity, combined with uncontrolled physical drooling.

The drivelling idiot could even be deceptively framed within a handsome beauty. In Burney's *Camilla*, the father of Eugenia arranges for her to encounter 'accidentally' a young woman who is 'a beautiful creature . . . fair, of a tall and striking figure, with features delicately regular'.[80] Eugenia, devastated by what she perceives as her own ugliness and physical deformity, is then astonished to see the beautiful stranger break into nonsensical chatter. On being asked if she is well, she responds, 'Give me a shilling!' while 'the slaver dribbled unrestrained from her mouth, rendering utterly disgusting a chin that a statuary might have wished to model.'[81] Eugenia understands immediately the moral message her father has arranged: 'beauty, without mind, is more dreadful than any deformity.'[82] Idiocy could be deceptive, but it would always become apparent, breaking out from any bodily disguise, the body unable to hold back its fluids, the mind unable to control its chuntering thoughtlessness. This image appeared in a distinctly unmerry poem in the *Merry Fellow* jestbook in 1757, called 'The Handsome Idiot'. The poet's heart is taken the moment he casts his eye on the young woman 'so heavenly fair, with eyes so bright', but:

> . . . soon as e'er the beauteous idiot spoke,
> Forth from her coral lips such folly broke;
> Like balm the trickling nonsense heal'd my wound,
> And what her *eyes* enthralled, her *tongue* unbound[83]

In these portrayals, the thick, solid head and body of the idiot concealed and unsuccessfully tried to contain the airy lightness and liquidity of the idiot mind. Idiocy oozed, trickled and dribbled into the sunlight and there, displayed on the chin or evident in meaningless babble, turned to something disgusting. Saliva and spit, La Salle implored, must be concealed:

> you should take great care never to spit on your clothes, or those of others . . . if you notice saliva on the ground, you should immediately put your foot adroitly on it. If you notice any on someone's coat, it is not polite to make it known; you should instruct a servant to remove it . . . for good breeding consists in not bringing to anyone's attention anything that might offend or confuse them.[84]

While clearly not all, particularly those of the lower orders, were conforming to La Salle's precepts, most did have the capacity to conform to polite standards if they wished. However, people now perceived a certain type of idiot, with their involuntary slavering, who simply lacked the capacity to respond to this clarion call for acceptable, mannerly behaviour.

Art and Caricature

The drivelling idiot found visual expression in a guide to caricature at the end of the century. Along with 'stupidity' and 'simplicity', 'drivelling idiotism' was one of fifteen 'easily recognisable' character types demonstrated by Alexander Beugo in 1801. A shaggy-haired, half-grinning youth with arched, thick 'beetle brows', drooping nose, sagging, fleshy lower lip, slack jaw and curving chin gazes downwards through half-shut eyes, a small but unmistakable streak of drool trickling from the side of his mouth. Beugo was demonstrating here the 'science' of physiognomy, the enduring and, by the end of the eighteenth century, increasingly codified belief that character and character types were indicated through facial features.[85] There was an almost unconscious sharing of ideas and assumptions about the look of human types between artist and viewer.[86] These signals of physiognomy were immediately apparent to eighteenth-century audiences, who understood the construction of the face through them.[87] Systematized by Johann Kaspar Lavater's hugely popular *Essays on Physiognomy* (1774–8), which had gone through 55 editions by 1810,[88] popular physiognomic beliefs that moral values and character could be read in the faces of people were a fundamental underpinning of the visual image.[89] The caricaturist James Gillray summarized this in 1798: 'if you could know men's hearts, look in their faces.'[90] This was not evidence-based science, although it posed as such; it was popular belief about the meanings of differently shaped noses, eyes, jaws and foreheads, captured and displayed as knowledge, making value judgements via facial features.[91] Caricature, therefore, offers important insights into popular assumptions and notions about idiocy.

For Beugo, idiocy could adopt a number of forms. Alongside his 'drivelling idiot' was 'stupidity', who had the same drooping lips, slack jaw and half-shut eyes but also a bulbous, misshapen head, presented in side view to show the prominence of the posterior of the brain. This signalled that the stupid person had

Alexander Beugo, face of a 'drivelling idiot', detail from *Fifteen Easy Lessons in Caracature*, 1801, hand-coloured etching with stipple.

animal-like feelings, passions and propensities, believed to reside in the base of the head, as opposed to the perceptive faculties which resided in the front of the brain and would be indicated by a fine, large, straight forehead.[92] Thus was visualized the un-thinking, sluggish animal dullness of the stupid person, with the low brow and 'jolter head' expressed so vividly in street slang. 'Simplicity' was characterized by a gaping mouth and snub nose with snout-like nostrils. Small noses, it was thought, indicated low intellect, compounded by an animalistic appearance. If slightly upturned, as in the case of Beugo's 'simplicity', this so-called 'celestial' nose further indicated a capacity for mischief and cunning.[93]

The discernible difference between the full-blown drivelling idiot and the simpleton was that the simpleton, despite their intellectual deficits, had some capacity to engage with the world around them. This was, however, in the dangerously amoral, devious, mischievous way that was characteristic of the imbe-cile figure beginning to be characterized by the medical theorists working in the great Paris hospitals in the early nineteenth century.[94] Between the drivelling idiot and the mischievous simpleton stood lumbering 'stupidity', largely dull, harmless and unfeeling but with an animal-like brain, able to perform menial and burdensome tasks at the instigation of others. There were common characteristics in the caricatures of the idiotic, the stupid and the simple person. Each had the prognathous (unusually projecting) lower jaw (as opposed to the more desirable, firmly right-angled 'orthognathous' jaw), the sloping forehead and the fleshy, drooping lips that signalled inherent lowness and consigned them to the general realm of dull intellect.[95] However, more subtle signifiers indicated the important differences between them, and ranked them according to ability

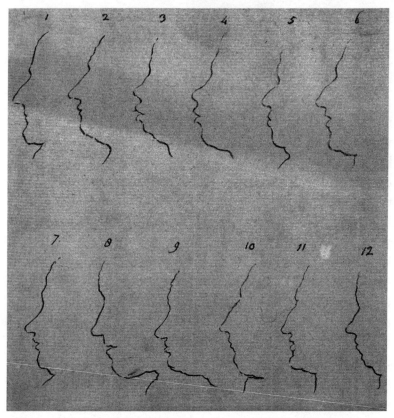

Outlines of twelve faces of mentally disabled people, drawing in John Caspar Lavater's *Essays on Physiognomy* (1789 edn). In the text, Lavater comments that 'an experienced observer will easily distinguish, in this series of faces, some idiots naturally such, and others who probably became so by the effects of disease or some accident.'

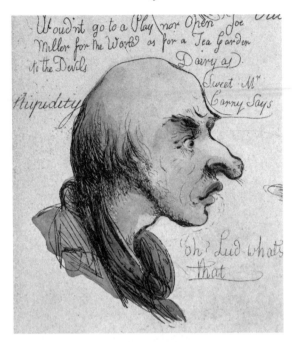

Alexander Beugo, face of 'stupidity', detail from *Fifteen Easy Lessons in Caracature*, 1801, hand-coloured etching with stipple.

and dangerousness. The idiot was the least able, the imbecile simpleton the most dangerous.

What, then, was the specific look of the idiot type? In Gillray's caricature 'Very Slippy-Weather' (1808), a gentleman slips on the ice having been too absorbed in checking the weather on his newfangled thermometer. Behind him a small crowd, their backs to Gillray, gazes at his prints in a print shop window. Apart and to the side of them, gazing though half-shut eyes not at the prints, the falling gentleman or anything else in particular, is a figure of indeterminate size, neither a child nor a man, a tiny snub nose barely protruding from his face. He is slope-backed and his knees are slightly flexed in a posture of inferiority. He has exaggeratedly fleshy, protruding, down-turned lips, a sloping forehead, a beetle brow, a slack, prognathous jaw and unkempt hair protruding from a scruffy hat. This was the idiot figure, a recurring type in late eighteenth- and early nineteenth-century caricature: always slightly removed from and unengaged with the action, unnaturally small, neither child nor adult, unkempt and uncared for and with all the physiognomic features of low intelligence. However,

Alexander Beugo, face of 'simplicity', detail from *Fifteen Easy Lessons in Caracature*, 1801, hand-coloured etching with stipple.

it is important to note that the joke is not on the affectionately drawn idiot character, but on the unworldly cleverness of the tumbling gentleman.

This characterization of the idiot was a consistent presence in caricatures, often seen in a servant role, legs flexed, mouth gaping, startled, bemused or detached from the world around him. The tiny idiot figure was the bemused servant boy, clothes patched, holding a container of cow-pock vaccine for Edward Jenner; the clumsy retainer spilling a basket of breads and precariously balancing a tray of drinks as he serves in the household of the nouveau riche Farmer Giles; and the gaping-mouthed, half-terrified footman not knowing whether he should serve drinks to his lady's unwelcome suitor. Beugo's stereotypes of idiotism, stupidity and simplicity played their parts in caricaturists' reflections of daily life. When medical men began to take an interest in the 'feeble-minded', it was on these popular notions that they drew to present what they passed as a form of medical knowledge about the idiot body and face. The

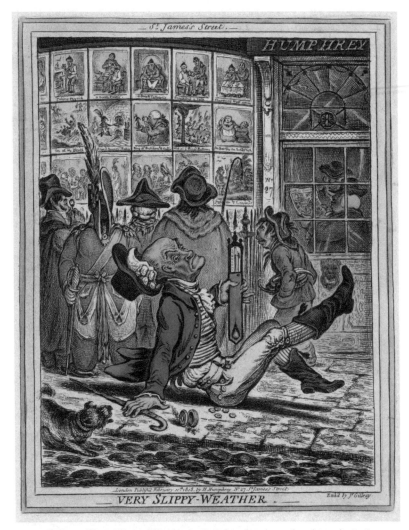

James Gillray, 'Very Slippy-Weather', 1808, hand-coloured etching depicting an elderly man slipping on the pavement outside a shop.

French medico-legal theorist Étienne-Jean Georget in 1820 saw an imbecile felon as having a 'low forehead, feeble constitution, under-developed for his age, he limps, his physiognomy expresses stupidity. It is known that most idiots have ill-formed heads, that they are small and suffer from rickets, that lack of intelligence is painted on their face.'[96] It was the great, popular eighteenth-century caricaturists who portrayed imbecilic low intelligence, and the public who immediately understood their

James Gillray, 'Very Slippy-Weather', 1808, detail of the idiot figure in the background.

Detail of the idiot servant (bottom left) in James Gillray, 'The Cow-Pock; or, the Wonderful Effects of the New Inoculation!', 1802, hand-coloured etching.

characterizations. Georget and his fellow medical theorists would later take this knowledge, repackage it and present it as medical authority.

These recurring images reflected popular wisdom about idiocy. Idiots were both present and liminal, hapless characters and a source of humour, but employable and generally amiable. They participated in the daily life of communities and families without having a great deal of influence, often there but forgotten, shabby figures relegated to the side. If they were noticed at all it was because they were about to spill drinks, misunderstand orders or commit the faux pas of serving an unwelcome guest. They were physically, socially and morally awkward, which of course meant they were also amusing and slightly unpredictable. They appeared as servants in caricatures because they worked as servants in real life. Eighteenth-century criminal

The idiot servant (far right) about to spill the drinks in James Gillray, 'Farmer Giles & his Wife, shewing off their daughter Betty to their Neighbours, on her return from School', 1809, colour etching.

trials revealed both fully embedded live-in servants such as Ann Wildman, 'next-akin to an idiot', whose mistress pledged to re-employ her if she was cleared of theft; and charwomen working for rich households, such as Mary Radford, a 'half-natural, very silly creature'.[97]

It was for this reason, knowing that his audience would recognize the type, that William Hogarth was able to portray an idiot servant in his *Marriage A-la-Mode* series, frozen and startled as he is about to be slapped by the enraged apothecary for having foolishly and unwittingly bought his lady the poison with which she has committed suicide. An eighteenth-century audience had no difficulty in recognizing and interpreting the idiot servant character. Georg Christoph Lichtenberg, the German commentator on Hogarth, saw immediately how the artist signalled his mental incompetence and lowly status: he wears the fine household livery that any servant would wear but it is clearly far too big for him, his coat 'buttoned up askew', and in typical idiot fashion his flexed legs showing 'the permanent curtsy of impotence which they are in the act of making'.[98] The final message to the audience lies in the blow that the apothecary is about to deliver to the idiot servant's face. While casual violence in the form of slaps, kicks and blows was a common, accepted feature of everyday life in the eighteenth century, blows to the face were taboo. 'Striking a man's face was completely unacceptable'[99] whatever the rank of the perpetrator, and reduced the person receiving the blow to the status of an animal. All of this was communicated between Hogarth and his audience in the minor character of his idiot servant: his tolerated but precarious status, his liminality, his personal incompetence, his bewilderment and almost comic incapacity to grasp the momentous personal tragedies unfolding around him.

Idiots and the simple-minded were, it is clear, often laughed at, or about. However, in eighteenth-century Britain this was not necessarily a sign of objectification or marginalization, as some historians have argued.[100] To be laughed at, to be seen as fair game for ridicule, was more complex than that. It meant that a person was noticed, accepted as part of the social fabric. Laughter and ridicule could of course be cruel and uncomfortable, and nobody escaped its barbs: as Simon Dickie has pointed

An idiot footman in a state of confusion in Isaac Cruikshank, 'Irish Fortune Hunter', *c.* 1800, pen and watercolour.

out, jestbooks featured 'blind men led into walls, dwarfs thrown out of windows, lame matrons tumbled into ditches'.[101] However, such laughter was not considered inherently objectifying by those who laughed. In Fanny Burney's *Camilla*, Mrs Arlebury defends herself and all other wits from the accusation of unfeeling cruelty:

> Never judge the heart of a wit by the tongue. We have often as good hearts, and as much good nature as the careful persons who utter nothing but what is right, or the heavy thinkers who have too little fancy to say anything that is wrong. But we have a pleasure in our rattle that cruelly runs away with our discretion.[102]

Beneath the 'rattle' lay good hearts and good nature. The idiot was accepted, indulged and sometimes even admired and desired by those good hearts and good natures, just as much as they

William Hogarth, 'Death of the Countess', *Marriage à la Mode*, Plate 6, 1745, engraving of the countess dying in a chair.

The idiot servant berated by the apothecary, detail from Hogarth, 'Death of the Countess'.

were laughed at and 'jeered'. In the age of ridicule and laughter, to be ignored, seen as beyond both, was the cruellest, most marginalizing fate. To be laughed at, however unpleasant it might be at times, was at least a sign of being present, noticed, and occupying a position in society, for those groups who in later times would come to be seen as fit only for exclusion to the institution.

Criminal Trials

This pervasive and accepted presence of idiots and imbeciles in communities is borne out by evidence and information given in Old Bailey trials, which illustrate how they were integral members of families, workplaces and neighbourhoods.

A high level of intellectual deficit was not necessarily an obstacle to marriage. John Thomas was described by his father-in-law as 'a simple lad, little better than an idiot'.[103] Sarah Holloway, whose husband accompanied her after her arrest, was 'silly . . . and when anybody has given her a farthing, she has stood laughing for half an hour; they used to call her foolish Nan.'[104] They were also people who worked. The women were predominantly employed in menial jobs, for instance as servants, charwomen or washerwomen. The 'half-natural, very silly creature' Mary Radford carried out charring tasks for richer households.[105] Some idiots operated within the marginal economy. Ann Terry, for example, 'a very silly foolish girl, not capable of taking care of herself', worked 'closing upper leathers for shoes'.[106] This meant that she was part of an organized group of pauper women in London known as 'translators' who took old shoes that had been begged and gave them new soles.[107] Robert Miller, 'much troubled with fits, and half an ideot', survived by running errands for gentlemen.[108]

Others were in more stable occupations. Peter Cunniford, an idiot since 'his head was torn to pieces by a dog when he was about two or three', had worked as a labourer in a building company for twelve years and was viewed by workmates as a hardworking, honest fellow.[109] Although most male idiots were employed as unskilled labourers or servants of some sort, a small number were in skilled occupations, such as bricklaying, carpentry and paper-hanging. Some were even involved in running small businesses, although usually with help. John Bullock kept a public house in Essex but as he was 'a silly innocent sort of a fellow . . . the management of the business lay altogether upon the wife'.[110] Idiots therefore were people who lived and worked in a variety of settings. Being an idiot did not in itself define a person. They could be seen as contributing workers with rounded personalities. Questions in court frequently concerned their 'living', rather than their idiocy.

The place in the community which such people occupied should not be over-romanticized, however. Trial evidence shows repeatedly that cruelty and ridicule were factors in their lives, with witnesses stating: 'I have seen 'em black his face, and carry him about in a basket, and then throw him out into a kennel [gutter]'; 'he is a poor silly fellow, laughed and jeered at by the rest'; 'people used to push him about and ill-use him.'[111] Those perceived as vulnerable or undesirable could easily be ostracized or attacked by sections of the community. However, in all the incidences of violence and bullying cited, there was a response from other community members who stood up in defence of the person concerned. Their place in the community was contested but over time retained its stability, even when under attack from those who saw them as an object of contempt or violence.

Sermons

A similar, broadly tolerant view of idiocy and simple-mindedness could also be discerned in the sermons preached by evangelicals on the streets of cities and towns during what became known as the Evangelical Revival or 'Great Awakening', led by the evangelical Methodists. Early eighteenth-century dissenting ministers such as Isaac Watts offered a passionate, evangelizing, emotional alternative to the stuffy, uninspiring Church of England. Methodists such as John and Charles Wesley, although remaining tenuously within the Anglican Church, likewise offered something entirely different to the traditional sermon – something more accessible and of far greater appeal to the mass of people.[112] From the 1730s, outdoor sermons were delivered to huge crowds across Britain.[113]

Many sermons preached to these crowds touched on matters of intelligence, stupidity, dullness, the feeble mind and the idiotic. The starting point was that all people were imperfect, and therefore any degree of deficit, deformity or incapacity was no sin in itself. Nor were learning and well-developed mental faculties in themselves virtues; what mattered was the use a person made of whatever faculties, of whatever quality, were bestowed upon them, and the intention or will with which they acted.[114] The well-educated, learned sinner was far worse than the ignorant dullard, as he had no excuse for any ignorance or indifference towards God. The misuse of the gift of intelligence would lead only to Hell.[115] The weak-minded, on the other hand, could find the grace of God, and salvation, provided they could apply their mind, however limited, to the works of God. As Isaac Watts preached: 'God beholds all men equally . . . the master and the servant, the prince and the subject, the learned and the ignorant, shall receive a recompense according to their works.'[116] The ignorant fool can indeed become a true believer, and one of the elect, if God wills it, and find favour above the reasoned intellect: 'He [God] takes pleasure to pour contempt in all the pride of human reason, by choosing a foolish man, and making him a humble believer. No man should despair of salvation.'[117] The intellectually dull formed part of God's will. To be deficient in reason, memory or intellectual faculty could not in any way be a sin, because such deficiencies had been bestowed by God. It was that person's will to faith, within their capacity, that mattered.

John Wesley shared Watts's suspicion of, and contempt for, the intellectually gifted and learned person who did not heed the word of God: 'the ignorance never so strongly glares, as in those who are termed, men of learning.'[118] The natural state of man, argued Wesley, is to be in a state of sleep until awakened to God, and therefore we are all in a state of supine stupidity and indolence: none is in a position to complain, therefore, about the stupidity of others.[119] Natural defect is God-given and cannot be helped, and therefore cannot be condemned. A person can only function within the level of capacity they have been given, within their allotted position.[120] Wesley listed the natural infirmities that are no person's fault, and for which no person can be condemned:

> The weakness or slowness of understanding, dullness or confusedness of apprehension, incoherence of thought . . . heaviness of imagination . . . the want of a ready or of a retentive memory . . . slowness of speech, impropriety of language, ungracefulness of pronunciation.[121]

Simplicity, dullness and intellectual limitation were not vices, and nor were they punishable. The job of each individual was simply to make the best of whatever gifts they had been given, however poor, and to achieve grace accordingly. The feebly endowed might need to be carried part of the way but they had as much chance as anyone else of crawling their way to salvation. This was the message given day after day, year after year, to the dissenting congregations and to the throngs who flocked to the great outdoor sermons.

THROUGH THE PRISM of jokes, slang, fiction, caricature, art, trials and sermons it is clear that idiots (and their imbecile and simple cousins) were an undeniable and pervasive presence in eighteenth-century society. They could often be peripheral, but were always present. A lack of intelligence, even to a substantial degree, was not necessarily seen as a barrier to belonging. The dim-witted could be seen as having other virtues – of reliability, steadfastness, honesty and loyalty. Physically, they could even be objects of desire, for their fabled compensatory bodily gifts. Spiritually, as the preachers constantly emphasized, simplicity of mind could be a positive advantage over the corrupt, dishonest, blasphemous minds of the highly educated and intellectually gifted elite.

They were everywhere and yet, as the same time, easy to miss; such a familiar yet unobtrusive presence that they could be both present and invisible. This is why, as will become evident, when later they began to slip from the public gaze and to be thought about in different ways, it was a quiet, barely perceptible and largely unnoticed process. But for now at least they remained a familiar feature of life, strange perhaps but accepted, included and woven strongly into the patterns of everyday existence in eighteenth-century society.

3

Idiots Abroad:
Racial Ideas of Idiocy

A strange thing happened as Europeans, and in particular Britons, intensified their exploration of the world during the eighteenth century, sailing to and trekking across lands they had never seen before, encountering peoples who were just as unfamiliar to them as these new landscapes. Being dutiful children of the Enlightenment, and bearers of the civilized virtues of rationality and science, they sought to explain and categorize the new types of human they came face to face with in Africa, the South Seas and Asia. Who were these people, recognizably human in physical form but culturally deeply alien to these European visitors? Many did not have systems of reading and writing. Their languages seemed impenetrable, their systems of justice brutal or non-existent, their morals alien or perverted, if discernible at all. They seemed to live without the luxuries and comforts which many Europeans had come to take for granted and, worse than that, to be entirely indifferent to them. In fact, in many ways they seemed not to have progressed or developed from the 'primitive man' of the deep past about whom Enlightenment philosophers speculated so much. Could it be, these explorers wondered, that these strange people represented whole races of mentally undeveloped humans? How else could they be explained, categorized? Perhaps the unclothed, hut-dwelling, indifferent, lethargic, barely communicative 'savages' that they perceived were like the indifferent, lethargic, barely communicative 'idiots' they had encountered at home. What about the more 'advanced' races, such as the peoples of India and China, who had clearly made some progress but still, our intrepid Europeans felt, fell short of European civilized norms? Perhaps these seemingly clever, duplicitous, mischievous and sometimes cruel 'barbarians' were like the clever, duplicitous, mischievous and sometimes cruel imbeciles who were starting to find their way into the medical and legal textbooks of Europe.

The remarkable story of the fallacious intertwining of ideas of race and intelligence began on the ships and in the expeditions of Enlightenment men who traversed the globe throughout the eighteenth century. The fatal and disastrous consequences of this spurious entanglement of ideas, misperception, misinterpretation and moral blindness have endured and wrought their calamitous effects for three centuries. They have been calamitous for whole races of people, and also for great swathes of humanity in all societies, deemed to lack sufficient intelligence to qualify for full human status.

A good point to begin to unravel this complex story is in the 1770s, when on one side of the world Captain James Cook's ship *Endeavour* sailed to the eastern shore of the land that would become known as Australia, while back in England an English clergyman and naturalist published a short book on the natural history of his small village in the county of Hampshire in England.

On 28 April 1770, the winds at last being favourable, the crew of the *Endeavour* gratefully guided their vessel into a calm, deep bay (now known as Jervis Bay[1]) on the eastern shore of the land then called New Holland.[2] On board, the naturalist Joseph Banks, one of the mixed cohort of men of science who had joined this momentous voyage of European discovery, noticed something strange. Just inside the bay were four small canoes from which indigenous inhabitants of this 'new' land were catching fish: 'these people seemed to be almost totally engag'd in what they were about: the ship passed within a quarter of a mile of them and yet they scarce lifted their eyes from their employment,' Banks wrote in his journal.[3] This first encounter between

William Hodges, *A View of Maitavie Bay*, [*in the Island of*] *Otaheite* [*Tahiti*], 1776, oil on canvas showing Captain Cook's ships at anchor in Tahiti.

Europeans and the eastern indigenous people of this land then became, for Banks, even stranger:

> At 1 we came to an anchor abreast of a small village consisting of about 6 or 8 houses. Soon after this an old woman followd by 3 children came out of the wood; she carried several peice [sic] of stick and the children also had their burthens . . . She often lookd at the ship but expressd neither surprize nor concern. Soon after this the . . . four canoes came in from fishing; the people landed, hauled up their boats and began to dress their dinner to all appearances totally unmov'd at us, tho' we were within a little more than ½ a mile of them . . . myself to the best of my judgement plainly discerned that the woman did not copy our mother Eve even in the fig leaf.[4]

For Banks and his shipmates, it was a puzzle. How could these naked, wild primitives, with virtually no marks of civilization, be so resolutely indifferent to the splendour of the *Endeavour*, its

THOSE THEY CALLED IDIOTS

equally splendid uniformed crew of white men, and its artfully constructed accoutrements? What sort of minds did they have, that they remained absorbed in their own world? Why was no impression made on these incurious people?

In the ostensibly less exotic surroundings of the small Hampshire village of Selborne, the naturalist Gilbert White was also puzzling over some strange behaviour he had observed. White recalled, shortly after the completion of Cook's first voyage, a strange boy who had lived in Selborne twenty years earlier: 'We had in this village . . . an idiot boy . . . who, from a child, shewed a strong propensity to bees; they were his food, his amusement his sole object . . . this lad exerted all his few faculties in this one pursuit.'[5] This idiot-boy, whom White named 'the bee-boy', when not showing extraordinary skill in plunging into and upending hives, extracting honey and drinking what he called 'bee-wine', did nothing and noticed nothing: 'In the winter he dozed away his time, within his father's house, by the fire side, in a kind of torpid state, seldom departing from the chimney corner . . . and, except in his favourite pursuit, in which he was wonderfully adroit, discovered no manner of understanding.'[6] The puzzle for White was how a member of the human species could be so absorbed, alert and adroit in one area of activity and yet so ignorant, incurious and, indeed, oblivious to all other aspects of the world around him. For White the answer lay in the idiot's lack of faculty: 'this lad exerted all his few faculties in this one pursuit.'[7] There was simply insufficient capacity left to inspire curiosity, learning or any sort of mental development.

What linked these two apparently highly disparate but contemporaneous observations from opposite ends of the earth? The two accounts, one about 'savagery', the other about 'idiocy', were in fact connected in important ways. White and Banks knew each other well. They had met in London in 1767, shortly before the *Endeavour* voyage had begun, and subsequently corresponded. White enthusiastically followed the progress of Banks's voyage.[8] They were both part of the elite late eighteenth-century network of gentleman natural scientists and natural philosophers who eagerly shared and exchanged observations, findings and classifications.[9] The work of these densely interconnected intellectual communities drove what has been described as 'the global accumulation of natural knowledge that marks the latter half of the eighteenth century'.[10] The interests of natural scientists in this pre-specialist era were eclectic: they included zoology, botany, geology, astronomy and, of course, the 'science of Man'. Just as White studied the people, including Gypsies and idiots, alongside the natural phenomena of his native Hampshire, so Cook and his team of scientists were deputed to study the native peoples of the lands they encountered, alongside the birds, animals and rocks. (They were also, of course, expected to chart the lands and claim them for the British state.) The admiralty's secret instructions for the *Endeavour*'s voyage included the following:

> You are likewise to observe the genius, temper, disposition and number of the natives, if there be any, endeavour by all proper means to cultivate a friendship and alliance with them, making them presents of such trifles as they may value, and showing them every kind of civility and regard: taking care however not to suffer yourself to be surprised by them, but to be always upon your guard against any accident.[11]

Clearly, expectations concerning native encounters were ambivalent. They were to be observed, mapped and described, just like the flora and fauna of the lands they occupied. There could be trade, but there was already an expectation that this would be unequal, with the natives valuing only cheap 'trifles'. They might be friendly, but an undercurrent of danger could also lurk. The job of the scientific team would be to encounter, observe, characterize and finally categorize the savage inhabitants of the new lands they would encounter, and some assumptions about them were already at work – their potential dangerousness and their susceptibility to flattery and cheap trifles.

This dynamic interchange of knowledge between daring global explorers like Banks and more sedentary gentleman naturalists like White was facilitated by the Linnaean system of classification. Carl Linnaeus' *Systema naturae* of 1758 had been the first major systematic attempt to categorize all natural phenomena, including the races and types of 'Man'. The power of this system lay in 'its capacity to effectively travel across space, to render knowledge of nature mobile and allow global comparison'.[12] White and Banks were thus two links in a 'community of knowledge [encompassing] rural informants, metropolitan correspondents and a fully European republic of letters'.[13] Of most interest to the processes of categorization in which these networks of individuals were involved were its anomalies: types which appeared to display new and previously unknown characteristics, or whose characteristics were so unusual that they challenged existing categories, dissolving borders and undermining assumed certainties. Two groups of humans in particular puzzled, worried and therefore attracted the interest of natural scientists. Each appeared to challenge neat systematization of what constituted humanity. First, there were the 'savages' of the newly discovered lands, whose customs, modes of living and ways of speaking were so far removed from the 'civilized' European's experience that,

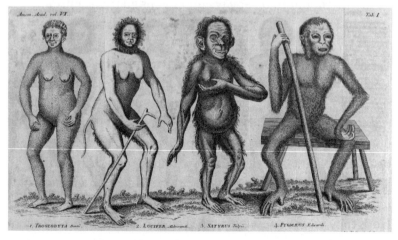

Illustrations of four figures becoming progressively less human-like and more ape-like, from Carl Linnaeus, *Amoenitates academicae* (1763).

when encountered, they continually caused astonishment and raised speculation. Second there was the idiot and imbecile population, who had human form but seemed to lack many of the prerequisites that defined, in the Enlightenment mind, a human being: reasoning power, the ability to abstract, language, ability to form social relations, emotional sensibility, capacity for intellectual development and curiosity about the world around them.

The anomalous nature of these two human categories inevitably invited comparison, and the more natural scientists gazed and compared, the more intersections and apparent similarities they believed they found. Indifference and a lack of curiosity coupled with absorption in trinkets and their own trivial or peculiar tasks were long-standing stereotypes in the characterization of the idiot. The social reformer Francis Place described an episode from the 1790s where a family carried out an elaborate deception to ensnare an orphan idiot woman, with an inheritance worth £1,000 per annum, into marriage with their eldest son, and thereby secured her inheritance. Once married, the son took a mistress with whom he slept in the family home, while his wife was given a separate room:

> The poor ideot wife never suspected, or never gave herself the trouble to enquire about the matter. Her husband gave himself no concern about her, and so long as she was dressed in fine cloaths and treated as a child she was contented.[14]

At the end of the eighteenth century the French medico-legal theorist François-Emmanuel Fodéré gave medical authority to the idea of the indifferent, indolent, incurious idiot when he analysed the characteristics of the 'cretins' of the Swiss Alps (a group later to be classified as suffering from congenital hypothyroidism). Where cretinism is prevalent, he argued:

> Here one no longer recognizes the man, amazed in his distinctive characters of thought and language . . . who

calculates the immensity of the heavens and who writes about heavenly movements . . . It is no longer that animated physiognomy, that superb eye, where the will is painted, it is a dumb face, similar to those old pieces of money, where usage has effaced the imprint.[15]

The next year, from his observations of idiots at the two great Paris asylums, the Bicêtre and the Salpêtrière, Phillippe Pinel concluded: 'Their face is expressionless, their senses dulled . . . and there may be a constant state of stupor. A kind of insuperable inertia makes up their character.'[16]

Travellers throughout the eighteenth century made remarkably similar observations about the non-European peoples they encountered. Stung by these people's refusal to react with wonder and amazement to the ships, technologies and cultivated appearances that the Europeans displayed before them, they attributed this to idiotic indolence and incuriosity. 'Nor did they seem to admire anything we had,' wrote the baffled sea captain and 'buccaneer' William Dampier in 1697. Indeed, 'they took no notice of the ship or anything on it.'[17] The priest-explorer Louis Hennepin concluded, from his lengthy treks across the North American interior, 'generally speaking, all the savages . . . I have seen in the Northern *America*, have an extream indifference for all things; they . . . set no great value upon the most precious things they have.'[18] As the century progressed, European travellers continued to marvel at the idiotic indifference they encountered everywhere they went. Among the common 'Mohamadens' of India, complained Jemima Kindersley in 1777, 'their minds . . . [are] no more informed than the beasts . . . whether punished by cold, or enervated by heat, indolence equally prevails, to such a degree as seems to absorb every faculty; even immediate self-preservation scarcely rouses them from it.'[19]

Watkin Tench, a British naval officer involved in the establishment of the new settlement of Sydney at the end of the century, concluded that no attachment was formed between the new colonizing settlers and the indigenous inhabitants because the native population, 'like all other savages, are either too indolent, too indifferent or too fearful, to form an attachment on easy terms, with those who differ in habits and manners so widely from themselves'.[20] This dull, apathetic stupor of the non-European mind appeared, to European observers, to be a global phenomenon, and the virulence with which travellers noted it increased as the century drew to a close. As well as in Native Americans, 'Mohamadens' and eastern Australians, it was discernible in Bengali Hindus: 'the apathy with which a Hindoo views all persons and interests unconnected with himself, is such as excites the indignation of Europeans.'[21] Banks himself noted it among the Khoekhoe, or Khoikhoi, people of southern Africa – then known as Hottentots – who he claimed 'have not the least idea of . . . what all other people deem to be necessaries of life'.[22] The anthropologist François Péron, part of Nicolas Baudin's expedition to explore Tasmania in 1803, saw it in a young Tasmanian man whom he attempted to embrace: 'Mr Frejanet having embraced him, I did the same, but from the air of indifference with which he welcomed this the evidence of our intent it was easy for us to recognise that it had no significance.'[23]

A correlation thus began to emerge in traveller accounts between the behaviour and look of those they encountered in their extra-European adventures and the defining accounts of idiocy they knew from their homelands. Indifference and indolence were not the only markers of idiocy they believed they were seeing. There was the innocent simplicity of the savage, prone to irrational outbursts of laughter, strongly reminiscent of the recurring idiot character in eighteenth-century jokes. The indigenous Americans of Carolina were 'an easy credulous people',[24] while the uncultivated minds of the people of Guiana rendered them susceptible to 'puerile mirth, dancing or immoderate laughter'.[25] Descriptions of savage appearance recalled the idiots of eighteenth-century caricature: they 'stood gaping around',[26] gazing through half-closed eyelids,[27] their uncouth flat faces, small black eyes, low foreheads and flat noses[28] complementing their distended bellies and weak, slender, over-extended arms and legs,[29] according to the gaze of the European.

Idiots, their senses perceived to be dulled and with little sense of pain, did not share the need for comfort and luxury that the rest of society aspired to; in fact they showed an almost perverse aversion to it. The bookseller James Lackington recalled how a young idiot woman in his Somerset town 'had a great aversion to sleeping in a bed, and at bed time would often run away to a field in the neighbourhood, where she slept in the cowsheds'.[30] 'Savages' were perceived to show the same disquieting impermeability to cold and indifference to discomfort. Dampier noted how the New Hollanders 'lie in the open air without any covering, the earth being their bed'.[31] As he roamed the interior of Canada on behalf of the Hudson's Bay Company, James Isham was astonished that in this harsh climate the indigenous people 'live in tents and for their bedding the cold ground winter and summer'.[32]

Accounts of the habits of native, savage peoples eerily echoed idiot characterizations. A recurring theme of witness testimony in English trial hearings in the eighteenth and nineteenth centuries, when the characteristics of idiocy were being established, was the idiot's animal-like, voracious and disgusting eating habits. At a hearing to establish the legitimacy of the will of John Clopton, characterized as an idiot, one witness recalled his dining habits, which could be compared 'only to a dog with his paws holding and gnawing the bones and meat'. Another witness said that 'his manner of eating was very low, and it was quite disagreeable to see how he put the meat into his mouth voraciously as if he were starved and he did not swallow it half and he did not care where he spit it out.'[33] European travellers recounted a similar discourse of loathsome, 'animal' appetite when they described the eating habits of non-Europeans. Observing a banquet in the royal court of Abyssinia, James Bruce, a wealthy Scottish laird on an early expedition to discover the source of the Nile, described the diners as gnawing on bones 'like dogs'. Each man was hand-fed by two women:

The Hottentots (Khoekhoe people) from southern Africa were depicted as savage and idiotic in appearance and manner, as in this hand-tinted engraving by Jacques Grasset de Saint-Sauveur, *c.* 1797.

his body stooping , his head low and forward, and mouth
open, very like an idiot, [he] turns to the [woman] whose
cartridge is ready, who stuffs the whole of it into his
mouth, which is so full that he is in constant danger of
being choked . . . the more noise he makes in chewing
it, the more polite he is thought to be.[34]

Native Americans were 'naturally gluttons',[35] while Hottentots
ate so fast, using their hands and teeth to tear meat, that they
always appeared ravenous.[36] Isham described the native people
of the Canadian interior as 'tearing the flesh off with their teeth,
grease up to the eyes, . . . spitting upon one another's clothes'.[37]
In Edward Long's 1774 racial diatribe against the 'Negroes' of
Jamaica he reserved particular disgust for what he perceived as
their animalistic eating habits, claiming that they 'tear the meat
with their talons and chuck it by handfuls down their throats
with all the voracity of wild beasts . . . they thrust their hands
all together into the dish, sometimes returning into it what they
have been chewing.'[38] These horrified depictions of a transgressive dissolution of borders between the bestial and the human,
and the taboo-breaking sharing and mixing of ingested food
and bodily fluids, closely mirrored another description of John
Clopton's eating habits:

At dinner he mauled his meat like a pig . . . he poked
his nose down into his plate and the deponent has seen
him ram his fork into his nose and then scoop up gravy,
blood and all, with his knife.[39]

Observers complained that the idiots of England combined
bodily incontinence with a lack of shame. The imbecilic John
Clopton, servants and waiters said, 'made water in the fire place'
and was always 'doing his occasions against the wall of his room
and all about'.[40] Fanny Fust, the young idiot woman abducted
for her fortune in 1787, 'in the presence of men servants pulled
up her petticoats with an intention of making water without

Depictions of
'savagery' presented
idiotic countenances,
as in this depiction
of a man from
Tierra del Fuego
(Argentina) by
William Hodges,
from Cook's second
voyage (1777).

being in the least sensible of the great impropriety of so doing'.[41] Like Fust's servants, male European travellers were astonished when they witnessed such unadorned and naked naturalness. Hennepin observed that in America 'women are not ashamed to make water before all the world', while the captain of the frigate in Baudin's Tasmanian expedition of 1803 encountered a group of Tasmanian women when: 'several of them wished to pass water. The women were sitting facing us about ten feet away so they stood up and legs slightly apart, while still paying attention to us, they obliged their natural needs facing us.'[42] Their menfolk equally bewildered their European visitors by casually doing the same: 'I have seen a native who, while we were speaking to him, needed to pass water, and he merely made a quarter turn to obey the need, and I think this was only on account of the wind blowing the urine on his legs.'[43]

European travellers carried with them from their homelands an idea of idiocy equated with a slothful indifference and incuriosity about the world. Simple-minded, innocent, low-browed, stump-nosed idiots laughed for no reason, appeared insensible to cold and pain, indifferent to warmth and comfort, ate bestially with no conception of manners and attended to their animal needs with no sense of shame or inhibition. These were the people who, back in Britain or France, occupied a position most removed from shared assumptions about the way in which the polite, mannered, enlightened human should conduct themselves. As they reached the shores of America, Asia, Africa and the South Seas they encountered new groups of beings who seemed to them to conform to none of their precepts for 'civilized man'. Bewildered, they sought explanations and rationalizations, and from their speculations began to emerge the idea that they might be encountering idiot races, whole societies whose prospects of mental and social development were as limited and bleak as those of the idiots and imbeciles of the home country.

Ideas of Idiocy in the Travel Narrative

Eighteenth-century traveller accounts began therefore to weave at first a comparative, and then an increasingly interlinked, discourse about the human status of the long-familiar idiot (and imbecile) and the newly encountered savage (and barbarian). The gradual merging of ideas of intelligence and race in European thinking about non-European humans had three extremely important implications. First, travel writing in this period was a highly influential genre, avidly and widely consumed, and the ideas it carried were thus projected swiftly into the public realm. Second, travel, exploration, observation and identification of new physical resources metamorphosed over the century into a system of empire-building, driving acquisition and appropriation of human and material goods, as well as land. As this happened, the human status of the indigenous inhabitants of lands being drawn into these new spheres became significant. What legal status did their human status imply, and what, then, was the legal basis for metropolitan rule and resource exploitation in the emerging empires of Europe? Traveller narratives, and traveller characterizations of the native peoples of the 'new' lands, informed legal thought and played an important role in developing the legal framework that would underpin the establishment of a global colonial system. Third, Enlightenment thinkers and theorists, constructing the 'Science of Man' and theories of society, rarely travelled outside Europe themselves. They relied for their information about non-European societies on the reports and observations of travellers, explorers and the cohorts of naturalists, ethnologists, zoologists and others who were an integral part of voyages of exploration. These accounts, in this way, became deeply integrated into thinking about the origins and varieties of man, the differences between races, and the link between the development of human society and the development of the human mind. The science of man, with its theories about the formation of societies and the development of human minds, was of course closely interrelated, and at times integrated, with theories of law. This was most evident in Montesquieu's 1748 work *The Spirit of Laws*, where he linked the variability of law in different types of society to material and environmental causes.

The popularity of travel narratives, and the voracious seriousness with which they were absorbed by the public throughout the eighteenth century, are well documented. For James Lackington, the self-made bookseller, travel books were an essential part of the prodigious increase in sales he experienced in the last 25 years of the century. If people wanted to know themselves, claimed Lackington, they could only do so by 'possessing a tolerable degree of knowledge of the rest of mankind'. To achieve that, 'the reading and studying of History, Voyages, Travels &c. will no doubt contribute to that kind of knowledge.'[44] The various accounts of Cook's three voyages became a national publishing phenomenon, runaway best-sellers 'anxiously awaited by the reading public . . . by far the most popular travel books of the age'.[45] John Harris prefaced his collection of voyage and travel accounts in 1744 with the assertion that 'The peculiar Pleasure and Improvement that books of voyages and travels afford, are sufficient reasons why they are as much, if not more read, than any one Branch of polite literature.'[46] Collections such as Harris's not only had a wide general readership but enjoyed a specific audience of travellers, explorers and natural scientists, who devoured travel narratives prior to their own voyages. This ensured that a strong undercurrent of pre-formed judgement and concealed assumptions influenced the future reactions and interpretations of travellers before they had even made their journeys. The English travel writer and novelist (and mother of Anthony) Frances Trollope, looking back on these writings from the next century, pointed out how writers would always demonstrate, 'on entering a new country . . . the propensity, so irresistible, to class all things, however accidental, as national and peculiar'.[47]

Joseph Banks possessed John Harris's enormous compilation of travel writing,[48] and when James Burney, brother of the novelist Fanny and a crew member on Cook's second voyage, wrote his own history of expeditions of discovery, he thanked Banks for giving him access to his collection of voyage books.[49] Gilbert White, as well as devouring the news and publications arising from the voyages of his friend Banks, enthusiastically read other travelogues describing journeys to China, North and South America and West Africa.[50] In turn, travellers took White's *Natural History of Selborne* (1789) with them to 'far-flung places, where it served as a nostalgic reminder of home'.[51] White's account of the natural history of this Hampshire village helped to frame those travellers' perceptions of the flora, fauna and people of the places they encountered. Just as White attributed lack of faculty to his indolent and apathetic 'bee boy', so travellers, their copy of *Selborne* tucked in their baggage, gazed on what they saw as the lethargic indifference of savage natives, and wondered if there was a similar cause. Through the travelogue, domestic ideas of idiocy and racial encounters abroad became ever more entangled.

Travel writing therefore reached a wide and growing reading public, while at the same time becoming an essential intellectual tool for travellers themselves, creating new shared assumptions and a body of knowledge about the world and its peoples outside Europe. As well as general readers it also influenced specialist audiences, including legal theorists and lawmakers. Encountering peoples with radically different modes of living from those considered normal in 'civilized' Europe posed legal difficulties. As early as 1625, the Dutch jurist Hugo Grotius, surveying the ongoing devastation of what would become known as Europe's Thirty Years' War, attempted to compose a 'law of nations' that would govern international relations. His *De jure belli ac pacis* (Rights of War and Peace) would become a hugely influential text for eighteenth-century legal theorists. He confronted directly the difficulties caused by variety among peoples. He proclaimed that amid the ruins of states caused by war, 'Europe possessed but one common bond, one vestige of its former unity – *the human mind*.'[52] It was to this shared mind that he made his appeal for a civilizing and unifying law of nations. Rights, he argued, were moral qualities attached to the person and, once perfected, became faculties of the mind 'among rational creatures'.[53] Such rational beings then share, he went on, a repugnance to injustice, such as the deprivation by one man or group of men of what belongs to another, and on this basis an international system of law could be built.[54]

All of this, however, depended on the exercise of reason, which was a prerequisite for the ability to make judgement. At the heart of law lay the ability to promise, which formed the basis of contract, from which flowed trade and commerce. However, Grotius acknowledged, even in Europe, not all people had the gift of human reason: 'The use of reason is the first requisite to constitute the obligation of a promise, which ideots, madmen and infants are consequently incapable of making.'[55] He was referring to the laws of capacity, with their systems of guardianship to govern the lives of those deemed to lack the reason and capacity necessary to govern themselves. In the law of nations, Grotius concluded, there would of course be variations in moral and religious virtue between peoples, and not all humans benefit from 'mental excellence'; these variations would be particularly evident in relations between European and non-European nations. On the whole, none of this should prevent those with lower standards of moral or mental faculty from forming a title to property, and therefore having the right to occupy their own land, as they would still have the fundamental prerequisite of reason.[56] However, what would happen, he mused, if a whole race of people were found who simply lacked reason, and therefore capacity? A lack of reason, he argued, placed a person outside the laws of property and contract:

> Only where a race of men is so destitute of reason as to be incapable of exercising any sort of ownership, they can hold no property, nor would the law of charity require that they should have more than the necessaries of life. For the rule of law of nations can only be applied to those who are capable of political or commercial intercourse; but not to a people entirely destitute of reason.[57]

Grotius conceded that to his knowledge no such race had yet been encountered: 'it is a matter of just doubt, whether any such is to be found.'[58] His argument was clear, however: if an idiot race was to be discovered, they should be subject to a globalized law of idiocy, with a rational race acting as their guardians, allowing them only such necessaries as they needed to survive, just the same as the system of guardianship operated for rational adults to take control over the lives of irrational idiots and imbeciles. The possibility of an intimate link between race and intelligence, where the intelligent race had rights of ownership over the irrational race, was being considered, if not yet claimed.

In 1673 the German jurist Samuel von Pufendorf developed further this idea that the notion of idiocy and irrationality, and therefore incapacity, could be applied to whole races of people as well as to individuals. Building on Grotius' concept of a law of nations, he argued that those who lacked reason, 'the *Natural* light in him as that . . . he might rightly comprehend . . . those general Precepts and Principles which are requisite in order for us to pass our lives here', could not form a nation.[59] Just as idiots were incapable of giving consent, and therefore lacked the right to join civilized society, because of their lack of reason, 'the Contracts and Promises of Ideots . . . are null and void,'[60] so, in the same way, idiot races that roamed, without property and mindless, across 'desolate regions' could make no claim on those lands. The first beings to appear on a territory did not necessarily own it. Ownership should accrue, according to Pufendorf, to the first rational beings who arrived there with the capacity and foresight to settle, make boundaries and cultivate.[61]

These ideas were developed, and bestowed to eighteenth-century jurisprudence, by John Locke, in his *Two Treatises of Government* (1690). Locke affirmed the need to apply the laws of idiocy as an instrument of the law of nations. Discussing the 'new' continent of America, he argued that claims to property could only be made by the rational, because it was from the original law of nature, which consisted of 'men living together according to reason', that the beginning of property had emerged.[62] 'God', he claimed, 'gave the world to the use of the industrious and rational.'[63] Native Americans, he believed, had shown themselves so far unable to exploit the land in the way that rational people would have done:

> Several Nations of the Americans . . . who are rich in Land, and poor in all the Comforts of life; whom nature having furnished as liberally as other people . . . yet for want of improving it by labour, have not one hundredth part of the conveniences we enjoy.[64]

While it was a universal law that 'Man' was allowed freedom of will and liberty of action due to his God-given understanding, if a being, or group of beings, lacked sufficient understanding and therefore the capacity to will, then these functions and understanding would be taken over by a guardian: 'Whilst he is in an Estate, wherein he has not understanding of his own to drive his *Will*, he is not to have any *Will* of his own to follow;

he that understands for him, must *Will* for him too.'[65] Locke's
rhetoric implied that unless Native Americans could demonstrate the intellectual apparatus to break their soil and cultivate
it, thereby indicating the ability to show foresight and understand property and contract, their status was no more than that
of the idiot unable to manage their estate. They would need a
guardian to 'understand' and 'will' for them. A roaming, nomadic,
unrooted life of hunting and gathering implied an inability to
conceive of property, making the land over which the Native
American roamed effectively unoccupied by humans with
capacity, and therefore technically uninhabited. Through lack
of capacity, the Native American could be deemed incapable of
managing their own affairs.

Why did first Pufendorf, and then more assertively Locke,
move from Grotius' somewhat doubtful speculation that there
might be whole nations or races that lacked reason ('it is a
matter of just doubt, whether any such is to be found') to a
more confident assertion that such nations did indeed exist?
By the end of the seventeenth century, travellers were already
reporting that savage nations lacked any form of government,
organized worship or understanding of property and contract.
This apparent inability to form the most basic of social relations
underpinning human society was attributed to a lack of mental
faculty. William Dampier perceived this across the non-European
globe: the Miskito people of Central America 'have no form of
government among them'; the New Hollanders of Australasia
'live in companies of 20 or 30 men women and children. I did
not perceive that they worshipped anything'; while the Nicobar
Islanders of Southeast Asia 'live under no government, every
man rules in his own home.'[66] Hennepin saw it in indigenous
Americans, who had only 'some glimmerings of a confus'd
notion of God' and 'no fixed place of abode'.[67] There was only
one explanation for this, Hennepin explained: savages were
'incapable of the ordinary arguments and reasonings that the
rest of mankind are led by'.[68] The abstract speculation of Grotius
was hardening into agreed knowledge. The idiotic incapacity

of some nations and races was passing from curious hypothesis to assumed fact.

The significance of Grotius' speculation was not lost on those interested in the law of nations or those interested in the law of idiocy. The London jurist John Brydall, writing his summary of idiocy law at the beginning of the eighteenth century, borrowed from Grotius just as Grotius himself had borrowed from idiocy law. He summarized his argument succinctly: 'it being equal that those that cannot govern themselves should be governed by others.'[69] This was now becoming a legal principle applicable to whole nations as well as individuals. Brydall took Grotius' argument to its logical conclusion. People of 'dull apprehension' should be able to govern themselves, but in the case of those who have no reason at all, 'there all right and dominion may be taken from them, yet ought we in charity to make them such an allowance as is necessary for their support and maintenance.'[70] Both the idiot and the savage, if proven to lack reason, needed to be governed and cared for, in the form of basic provisions, by a rational power.

Travellers continued to reinforce the idea of savage irrationality and mental incapacity in their accounts. The British sea captain Alexander Hamilton, who spent thirty years roaming the world, reported that the inhabitants he encountered in African countries were 'lazy, indolent . . . and simple'.[71] Of the Hottentots (Khoekhoe) of southern Africa – a group who were to be much observed by, and attract much opprobrium from, Europeans – the Prussian astronomer Peter Kolben commented: 'A monstrous Indisposition to Thought or Action runs through all the Nations of 'em. Another whole earthly happiness seems to lie in indolence and stupidity . . . [they] never reason but in cases of downright necessity.'[72] Recalling one of the legal idiocy tests in English law, James Isham reported from Hudson's Bay that 'I observe the generality of these natives counting no further than ten,' while John Harris, avidly read by Joseph Banks, remarked of the 'Mohock' Iroquois that 'their ideas are very few, and their words therefore not many.'[73] The idea that the savage was unable to understand the nature of a promise, and therefore a contract giving a notion of property, was reinforced by their portrayal as thieves and liars. There appeared to be no sense of property or ownership: indigenous Caribbean people were 'lazy and thievish', Cherokees 'great pilferers' and the native people of northernmost America 'a crafty sort of people, Cheating, Stealing and Lying'.[74] This directly echoed Fodéré's characterization from the Paris asylums of imbeciles as 'charlatans and rascals' who, lacking the mental faculty to comprehend moral behaviour, transgress all human law simply by having no concept of it.[75]

By the time the Swiss legal theorist Emer de Vattel wrote his *Law of Nations* in 1758,[76] the idea of the idiot nation had become an assumed legal concept and was no longer speculation. The legal, social person must be a rational person, one who enjoys 'such a life as is suitable to a rational being'.[77] Collective rationality would form a moral society, which would enable humans to live together peacefully through mutual understanding.[78] The sign that a group has come to knowledge of itself, is able to exercise its rational faculty, Vattel argued, is when it settles, and 'natural man' becomes 'social man'.[79] The cultivation of the soil is 'an obligation imposed by nature on mankind'.[80] Those who show limited mental faculty by aimlessly roaming over the land demonstrate that they have not achieved full rational status. They must therefore forfeit that land to the rational.[81] Rational man, as he roamed the globe, had become the guardian of idiot man, man unable to conceive of property. European rational man, the king of the new colonies, would own and control all of savage man's land, goods and chattels.

With legal theory now formally proposing the domination of irrational races by civilized, rational European races, it fell to the practitioners of the 'science of man' to explain how this had come about. The science of man was the study of social man, an intellectual exploration arising from the Enlightenment, which sought rational, global explanations for all natural, material and human phenomena and gathered pace from the early eighteenth

Sébastien Le Clerc, illustration of a Caribbean man and woman next to a papaya tree, in Jean-Baptiste Du Tertre, *Histoire generale des Antilles* (1667). They were described as 'savages', lacking reason or any sense of property, like idiots.

century. It was also referred to as 'moral philosophy' and sought to transform moral reflection about human nature into a systematic scientific discipline.[82] Cross-cultural comparisons were essential sources to provide illustrations and explanations of the constitution, and problems, of modern society.[83]

Enlightenment moral philosophers were tireless consumers of travelogues and the reports from abroad of natural scientists. These offered, they believed, for the first time 'authentic', sometimes 'scientifically' validated, eyewitness accounts of the varieties of peoples across the globe. Johann Reinhold Forster, the 'tiresome German botanist-philosopher-church minister'[84] who joined Cook's second Pacific voyage in 1772, emphasized the advantages of these accounts over pre-Enlightenment literature on humankind:

> none of these authors ever had the opportunity of contemplating mankind in this state, and its various degrees from the most wretched savages, removed but in the first degree from absolute animality, to the more polished and civilized inhabitants of the Friendly and Society Isles.[85]

The French social theorist Condorcet acknowledged the debt to travelogues in his *Sketch for a Historical Picture of the Progress of the Human Mind* (1795):

> Our information is based on the tales that travellers bring back to us about the state of the human race among the less civilized peoples, and we have to conjecture the stages by which man living in isolation or restricted to the kind of association necessary for survival, was able to make the first steps on a path whose destination is the use of a developed language.[86]

Montesquieu's *Spirit of the Laws* of 1748 was a key text in establishing the Enlightenment scientific exploration of the origins of society and the development of 'Man'. Montesquieu sought a causal explanation for racial and national variety, particularly what he regarded as the gulf between savage and civilized nations. He attributed environmental causes, chiefly climate and terrain, to national differences, but introduced an important tripartite division of levels of society. As well as civilized nations, there were savage and barbarian nations. Savages were isolated, ranked firmly at the bottom of the developmental scale, while barbarians occupied a space between them and the civilized:

> There is this difference between savage and barbarous nations; the first are little dispersed nations, which for some particular reason, cannot be united, and the barbarians are commonly small nations, capable of being united; the first are generally a nation of hunters; the second of herdmen and shepherds.[87]

Savages as a rule were the indolent denizens of warm climates, and this had a critical impact on their level of mind:

> The heat of the climate may be so excessive as to deprive the body of all vigour and strength. Then the faintness is communicated to the mind, there is no curiosity, no noble enterprise, no generous sentiment; the inclinations are all passive; indolence constitutes the utmost happiness.[88]

Once again, idiot indolence and incuriosity characterized the lowest form of non-white human. For Montesquieu, however, there was also another racial grouping. The barbarians of cooler climates, particularly those of Asia, were more vigorous, and this placed them in a position of mental and physical superiority over the savage: 'In Asia the strong nations are opposed to the weak; the warlike, brave and active people touch immediately on those who are indolent, effeminate and timorous.'[89] These humoral differences created a hierarchy of mind. The inhabitants of warm climates 'are like old men timorous; the people in cold countries are like young men, brave'. Unspoken but implied was the logical third level of mind, the perfect mind of the civilized European in their temperate zone. Thus a link was made between three types of society representing three types of mind: the savage possessed a childlike, enfeebled mind; the barbarian a semi-developed, adolescent mind; and the civilized person a fully developed adult mind.

Montesquieu's work was deeply influential in the Enlightenment search for general causes of social and individual development.[90] The mantle was taken up by the political economist and statesman Turgot, who accepted Montesquieu's mental gradations of three types of 'man', and therefore three types of society, but crucially rejected his spatial division of these variations based on climate, shifting them instead into a developmental process taking place across time. His *Philosophical Review of the Successive Stages of the Human Mind* (1750) made an explicit link between the development of societies through the savage, barbarian and civilized states, and the development of the human mind. 'The succession of mankind', he wrote, 'affords from age to age an ever-changing spectacle.'[91] At the lowest level, some savages simply make no progress at all; 'the original darkness is not yet dissipated.' Barbarians, such as, he suggested, the Egyptians, make some progress but are then 'brought to a standstill by their own mediocrity'. Still others make the journey from barbarism to refinement and civilization.[92] This became known as the stadial, or stage, theory of development, and it established a critical interface between social and mental development. The world displays, Turgot argued,

> at one and the same time all the gradations from barbarism to refinement, thereby revealing to us at a single glance, as it were, the records and remains of all the steps taken by the human mind, a reflection of all the stages through which it has passed, and the history of all the ages.[93]

This stadial development of human society mirrored the childhood, adolescence and adult stages of the human mind, and these in turn reflected the idiot, imbecile and perfect mental faculty division which established levels of human capacity. The savage was a child and an idiot, the barbarian a youth and an imbecile, the civilized person an adult with perfect faculty of mind. As Fodéré would define it in 1792, there was first the idiot group, 'absolute strangers . . . like monsters among the human race', lacking simple ideas and comparable to a seven-year-old.[94] There was then the adolescent-type imbecile group, who with some rudimentary education could form slightly better ideas but who, like impetuous youths, lacked judgement, had no sense of morality and showed a propensity to criminal or cruel behaviour.[95] In Montesquieu's and Turgot's theories, idiots and imbeciles were racialized into savages and barbarians.

The traveller narratives that Montesquieu and Turgot were absorbing had been developing for some time a distinction between the savage and the barbarian, each group operating at a different mental level but both, as far as the European gaze saw it, well below the perfect mental faculties of the European. The problem in trying to present a simple dichotomy between the savage non-European and the civilized European was that travellers were encountering cultures, or evidence of past cultures, in India, China and areas of Central and South America that bore clear signs of what Europeans regarded as civilization: cities, sophisticated architecture, religious worship and systems of law and trade. As Dampier had to admit in 1697, the Chinese were clearly 'very ingenious' people.[96] Hennepin began to make some sort of distinction in North America when he acknowledged that 'barbarians in *North America* have generally a notion of some sort of creation of the world' while 'savages in general have no belief of a deity.'[97]

Certain human groups were identified as distinctively and irredeemably savage and idiotic, unable to progress even to the barbarian stage. These usually comprised the Hottentots and Bosjeman ('Bushmen') of southern Africa, the Fuegians of the southern tip of South America, the Tasmans of Van Diemen's Land/Tasmania and, sometimes, the indigenous people of Australia. Their customs, culture, habits, modes of dress and communication were so far removed from the European way of life that observers could only conceive of them as brutes in human form with radically, and perhaps permanently, undeveloped minds. Turgot saw these groups as irredeemable. Theoretically, he argued, if all people have the same nature, they should progress at the same rate. However, he explained, nature in reality 'distributing her gifts unequally, has given to certain minds an abundance of talents which she has refused to others'.[98] The minds of some races would never develop their 'talents' they would instead 'allow them to become buried in obscurity', and it was from this inequality of mental faculty that inequality in the progress of nations grew.[99]

Travellers consistently characterized certain races as idiotic beyond any possibility of mental redemption. For Dampier, the New Hollanders were the 'miserablest people in the world. They have no houses, or skin garments . . . And setting aside their human shape, they differ little from brutes.'[100] Kolben noted how the Hottentots were 'generally apprehended, throughout *Europe* . . . so brutal a people as to be, in a Manner, incapable of Reflection . . . that they are a nation of Savages, with hardly so much as a Tincture of Reason or Humanity'.[101] As for the Fuegians, Forster, when encountering them on Cook's voyage, pronounced: 'Human nature appears nowhere in so debased and wretched a condition as with these miserable, debased, forlorn and stupid creatures.'[102] Although harmless, their countenance announced that they were 'remarkably stupid'. They compared unfavourably with the imbecile barbarians of the South Sea Islands, who despite their 'lively, brisk temper' and inability to concentrate had progressed to the extent that their minds were 'capable of, and open to, instruction, they have ideas of a supreme being, of a future state, of the origin of the world'.[103] This was all so different from the wretched Fuegians and Tasmans of the frozen southern zones, for whom 'a brutish stupidity is their general characteristic.'[104] To go naked in a bitterly cold climate, concluded John Adams of the Scottish conjectural school in 1789, Patagonians (Fuegians) 'must be very stupid'.[105] (Adams's argument was an offshoot of Montesquieu's climate theory, which claimed that the intellectually weakest humans were pushed into the most 'frigid' or 'tropical' zones by stronger races, who occupied the 'temperate' zones.) These lowest races of savage, according to Adams, were formed, like Fodéré's lowest form of idiot, only of a mass of animalistic bodily sensations, with barely a glimmer of intellectual activity: 'It is very reasonable to infer, that savages, in some of the wildest forms, must be as inferior to civilized man in intellectual abilities . . . as they surpass him in the activity of their limbs . . . and in the exertion of all the meaner functions.'[106]

It fell to Captain Cook's 'tiresome' botanist travelling companion Forster to make explicit the deeply intertwined three-level classification that comprised first the savage, the child and the idiot; second the barbarian, youth and imbecile; and, at its apex, the civilized person, adult and 'perfect mind'. Forster, in his own mind at least, combined the acute observatory powers of the globe-roaming natural scientist with the intellectual depth and vision of the moral philosopher. The

William Wilson, 'Missionary House and Environs in the Island of Otaheite', illustration in James Wilson, *A Missionary Voyage to the Southern Pacific Ocean* (1799). The naturalist Johann Reinhold Forster described South Sea Islanders as imbecile barbarians with semi-developed minds and uncontrolled passions.

stadial process of socio-cultural evolution began with the savage attaining a level barely above the animal: 'From *animality* natives ripen into *savages*, from this state they enter into that of *barbarism*, before they are capable of *civilization*.'[107]

For Forster, the savage/idiot/child type was characterized by harmlessness and innocence, with no understanding of private property.[108] The barbarian/imbecile/adolescent stage featured violent passions and morally outrageous behaviour, but the dawning of reason and understanding.[109] The risk at this stage was that if the mental faculties of reason and morals stalled, the barbarian would remain uncontrolledly 'fiery and violent' for want of education and improvement.[110] Only if progress prevails, and reason and understanding bring the passions under control, does the barbarian pass to '*Manhood* and a *mature age*', which 'are familiar to the CIVILIZED STATE'.[111] So the childlike idiot and the amoral imbecile became entwined with the non-white races labelled 'savages' and 'barbarians' by their enlightened European visitors.

In 1799 Fodéré formally fused the ideas of idiocy and imbecility with ideas of civilization and race as a medical fact. Look across the globe, he claimed, and you would see evidence of successive stages of the development of the human mind in its savage, barbarian and civilized forms:

> There are some nations condemned, throughout the centuries, to a social half-life, just as there are some to whom continual activity is just as necessary as somnolence appears to be natural to those first; some nations are made for unceasing contemplation, while there are others for whom this would be infinitely painful.[112]

Drawing on the 'science of man' and the observations of the great eighteenth-century army of Enlightenment travellers, Fodéré created a global racial hierarchy based on mental faculty. Under the gaze of Europeans, the notions of idiocy and imbecility had been attached to the non-European races of the world and presented as legal, historical, cultural and medical racial fact. The somewhat sleepy idea of the idiot, an enduring but minor feature of law used for the determination of capacity and property rights, and a stock figure of fun and affection in the caricature and the novel, had been globalized. In this process it had become fatally intertwined with the idea of race and a key determinant in the relationship between the masterful, white European parent and what it saw as its newly acquired multi-racial offspring of idiot savages and imbecile barbarians.

And so the world lay before enlightened minds as the eighteenth century closed, a global community of idiots, imbeciles and perfect minds. Those with perfect minds identified, named, and sought to dominate and control those who were idiotic or imbecile. Idiocy was no longer a joke. Skin colour and racial designation had started to become determinants of mental faculty for the people of the world.

PART TWO

New Ways of Thinking, *c.* 1812–70

4

Medical Challenge:
New Ideas in the Courtroom

The nineteenth century would see great changes in how idiocy was understood and how people characterized as idiots, or imbeciles, or simple-minded, were treated. The idiot moved quite rapidly from a person who was seen consistently across most of the eighteenth century as belonging to, and the responsibility of, communities, to a type of person who needed to be detained and treated under medical supervision in institutional settings. In the early part of the nineteenth century there was a steady flow of idiots into the growing network of county pauper lunatic asylums that were built after the County Asylums Acts of 1815 and 1845. Others flowed into the workhouses that proliferated after the passing of the Poor Law Amendment Act of 1834. By mid-century, some 10,000 idiots would be housed in these institutions.[1] In 1855, the world's first purpose-built institution for idiots, at Earlswood in Surrey, would open its doors. This was all part of a wider process of institutionalization involving lunatics, criminals, the poverty-stricken, those with physical disabilities and other disadvantaged groups seen as either vulnerable or dangerous, or both, that occurred across Britain throughout the century. However, what made it possible for idiots as a group to be seen as an object of the institution, when so recently they had been conceived as members, however odd, of their community? A number of diverse factors converged, all related to major shifts in the political, cultural, social and intellectual environment. Important new ways of thinking began to emerge, in particular from the legal world.

Criminal and civil court cases in the eighteenth century demonstrated a decided lack of curiosity from medical professionals about idiocy, which was seen as something that laypeople could discern and make decisions about without the intervention of so-called experts. The major focus of interest in the courtroom was not so much the attribution of the label of idiot, which was believed to be easy enough for any sensible person to discern, but rather the balance between individual freedom and state protection from vulnerability that a lack of capacity brought about. However, something very different was happening from the end of the eighteenth century in France, where idiocy had attracted greater medical interest. Significant institutionalization programmes at the large Salpêtrière and Bicêtre hospitals in Paris had brought idiots, as well as the mentally ill, prostitutes and other disconnected urban groups, under the medical gaze.

The Salpêtrière Hospital, Paris, 18th century.

Medical jurisprudence was already established in France, an area of law where, as the legal writer and physician François-Emmanuel Fodéré happily pointed out, the French were ahead of the English.[2] Phillippe Pinel, known as the founder of psychiatry in France,[3] called in 1800 for the application of medical jurisprudence to the mental conditions of idiocy and lunacy, lamenting that 'in the present state of our knowledge it is the jurisprudence in relation to the different lapses of reason that seems least advanced to me.'[4] Such a move would, he claimed, illuminate doubtful cases, particularly disputes over soundness of mind, where medical men could 'enlighten jurisprudence'.[5] A new cohort of French medical theorists, emboldened by the new scientific authority conferred on them following the French Revolution and later written into the Napoleonic legal code from 1804, set to work.

Fodéré had in fact already produced a medico-legal treatise during the turmoil of the revolutionary 1790s and then published a much-expanded edition in 1813. Claiming he was embarrassed by the quality of medical reports on disordered minds he had seen in previous cases, he promised to codify medical jurisprudence.[6] Medicine would bring to the law a new scientific exactness, a medicalized light shining from the reason of the Enlightenment.[7] He dismissed traditional legal approaches to both lunacy and idiocy as speculative and unscientific.[8] He denounced lay knowledge as gossip and folklore, ridiculing the idea that ordinary people, untrained in medicine, could identify causation, curability or incurability. There could be no comparison, he argued, between the assertions of uninterested 'ignorant people', by which he meant juries, and 'the motivated decisions, given with knowledge of cause by truthful, upright, enlightened doctors'.[9]

To show what this medical authority could bring to the determination of idiocy, Fodéré offered a new classification system which he claimed would bring scientific precision to vaguely defined legal ideas of unsoundness of mind. He described three areas of mental disorder. Alongside 'mania' and 'dementia' lay 'imbecility'. Imbecility, like the other two forms of disorder, deprived a person of the ability to judge and compare, making them incompetent to manage their affairs and naturally excluded from the social order.[10] Imbeciles, from birth, were 'absolute strangers . . . like monsters amongst the human race'[11] and could be further subdivided into three categories. First, those who lacked the simplest association of ideas, parroting words meaninglessly and, by chance, sometimes mouthing something which sounded very rational only to jump immediately to an unconnected triviality. This trait he called 'wondrous divinity' ('divinité fabuleuse').[12] This group was harmless. The second group could manage some simple ideas and tasks, comparable to a seven-year-old. The third group, with some rudimentary education, could form slightly better ideas. There was, however, no connection between their occasionally impressive words and their actions. Lacking judgement, they had no sense of morality; they could appear to talk about abstract moral concepts like injustice but it was, he said, like listening to an automaton.[13] Among these people could be found a misbehaving group of 'pre-pubescent charlatans and rascals' ('les charlatans et les fripons').[14]

The importance of Fodéré's classification was its claim to a new scientific modernity, cutting through the Gordian knot of vague legal musings evolved over centuries of case law, brushing aside the dull stupidity of lay 'common sense' and producing a finely tuned hierarchy of dullness to measure levels of personal responsibility and capacity. It directly challenged the loose subjectivity and assumed certainties of existing legal process, the speculative collaboration between the law and the people to define incapacity. Here was neatly defined, evidence-based fact, driven by the Enlightenment quest for reason, bringing precision and certainty to the administration of justice. Nevertheless, however hard Fodéré tried to excise the past and introduce a new clinical, scientific rationality to legal decision-making, old folk wisdom and beliefs surfaced in his work. He quoted the old adage that we are all mad and should not simply see it in others:

Le monde est plein de fous
et qui n'en veut pas voir,

doit se tenir tout seul
et briser son miroir.[15]

This had in fact appeared in a 1731 English graffiti collection, Hurlo Thrumbo's *Bog House Miscellany*, where it was attributed to a mirror scratching in Paris' rue Boucherie and was translated as 'The world is full of fools and asses / to see them not . . . retire and break your glasses.'[16] When Fodéré wrote about the imbecile's apparent ability to suddenly utter words of 'wondrous divinity', he was incorporating into his scientific medical classification nothing more than the centuries-long running joke about the Parisian cookhouse idiot who solved a dispute through a sudden, random glimmer of insight.[17] His description of a 'new' class of lifelong imbecile, with some abilities but still lacking capacity, added little to eighteenth-century writings on imbecility and his categories offered no causal theory or, indeed, treatment. It was common for French medical men to steal from early *charlatan* or 'quack' medicine and appropriate the wisdom of the laity, which they then re-presented as scientific medical 'fact'.[18] Fodéré's claim was simply that medical men, with their fine observational skills, professional probity and sensibility, would see the idiot more clearly than any layman, including the lawyer.[19] He did, however, introduce one new concept, the idea of the dangerous idiot, linked to natural moral depravity. Unlike the harmless idiot, the dangerousness of this class was their ability to deceive by parroting moral language while not understanding it.[20] In this claim we see the seeds of what would later become the 'moral imbecile', a deceptive being who looked and talked like a fully developed person but lacked morality, reason or any sense of pity.

Fodéré's notion of the moral imbecile as a legal category was now developed by Étienne-Jean Georget, an alienist (a profession that would later become the psychiatrist) at Salpêtrière hospital. In two works on legal medicine and its relation to the mind in 1820 and 1826,[21] Georget came up with four types of imbecile. First, those he described as having no 'mental existence' at all and who would die if not cared for. Second there were those who had some feelings or sensations but could not meet their own needs, acting unreflectively and without purpose. The third group were, he claimed, equivalent to a child of seven: they could recognize some people and objects, had a sense of who might help them and could make their needs known through gestures. Like parrots, this grouping had the ability to assimilate and then perform the words of songs. Finally, there were imbeciles with some feelings and memory, who could judge and perform simple acts but, lacking discernment, could only express themselves in basic language to meet ordinary needs.[22] As well as regarding the imbecile class as criminal, Georget expressed disgust and revulsion for the idiot category. He described them as urinating and leaving faecal matter wherever they were to be found, and as being highly prone to masturbation. They were also short-lived and riddled with disease.[23] The implication of both character-izations – the imbecile as deterministically criminal and amoral; the idiot as helpless, ill and not in control of their bodies – was that both needed some form of long-term custodial medical care. Georget explicitly claimed the superiority of medical truth, accusing both lawyers and the public of being constantly mis-taken in their judgements and strangers to medicine.[24] He argued that punishing imbeciles for their crimes would have no effect because they had no moral understanding and, once released, they would return to crime, the natural impulse of their condi-tion. Only by their lifelong institutionalization could public security be protected.

Analysing a recent arson case, Georget neatly triangulated the intersection of three currents of thought – lay, legal and med-ical – in decision-making on mental capacity, and of course explained the superiority of the medical discourse. Pierre Joseph Deléphine, standing trial in Paris in 1825, was a sixteen-year-old gardener accused of eight counts of arson. Once, he had attached lighted tapers dipped in inflammable liquid to a bird's tail and launched it into a neighbour's garden.[25] Neighbours signed a statement referring to his disordered thoughts, lapses of concentration and habit of running naked around his father's garden. They all agreed that he was not imbecile but rather wicked ('méchant') or evil ('beaucoup de malice').[26] The tribunal agreed with the neighbours' assessment and Deléphine was sentenced to death. Georget dismissed the neighbours' evidence, which he said lacked analytical appraisal, describing surface behaviours but nothing more. Their inability to interpret, signify or understand pathology led them to irrational and superstitious notions of evil and wickedness.[27]

Deléphine's lawyer agreed that the neighbours' demonic claim was absurd. For him this was a matter of mental incapacity caused by monomania, Deléphine's pyromaniac fixation, which he claimed was revealed by his unhealthy pallor and sad eyes.[28] He denounced the stupidity of the neighbours' unrefined views, the propensity of the 'vulgar' to dismiss the whole idea of mental alienation as a fiction used by defendants as a ruse to escape conviction.[29] He issued a rhetorical challenge: 'open the medical annals, consult the tribunal case records, go into the insane hospitals' and there they would learn that nature 'visits the mind just as many misfortunes as the body'.[30] He asked successfully for commutation of the death sentence on the grounds of lunatic irrationality.

For Georget, however, the lawyer's argument was no better than the neighbours'. He was not interpreting evidence; he was simply reporting and labelling behaviours. Georget, in fact, had the necessary evidence in his hands as he wrote, which proved Deléphine to be a miserable and villainous imbecile. What was this evidence? It was the copy of the act of accusation Deléphine had held in front of him throughout the trial. It was covered in his scrawl: endless signatures, meaningless letters, doodles and ink stains. If he had really understood the enormity of his crime, asked Georget, and knew that he was facing a capital charge, would he really give himself over to such infantile pursuits?[31] For Georget this indisputable evidence denoted not only the insensibility of the criminal but also the mind of a child under eight years, which meant stupidity ('bêtise') or silliness ('niaiserie').[32]

This insight was fruitless, Georget added caustically, as at no time during the trial were medical professionals asked to assess Deléphine's mental state.[33] At this point (1826), even French justice was not yet fully ready to accept medicine's ownership claim over imbecility, especially perhaps if it was based on a defendant's doodles.

The importance of this episode lay not in the outcome of Deléphine's trial but in the reasoning of Georget's analysis. He presented a framework of medical truth and scientific analysis and claimed its superiority to what he saw as public superstition and uninformed legal speculation. For Georget, the justice system was corrupt, a synthesis of crude popular 'common sense' and ancient, unscientific legal processes. He proposed a new, enlightened way forward: the medical men would take the imbecile villains and mischief makers who clogged up the courts and fed the guillotines into the lifelong care of the institutions, where many of their peers in fact already lived. The judicial system was wasted on this hidden criminal class, who had no knowledge or understanding of law and morality.[34] Rather than a courtroom there needed to be a statutory process of identification of imbecility followed by dispatch to the institution, where the imbecile would be kept out of mischief and the repulsive idiot cared for. Only in this way would the threat to society posed by these people diminish.[35]

Fodéré had been keen to point out the tardiness of the English law in adopting medical jurisprudence, and in England his challenge was taken up by the physician and apothecary John Haslam in an 1817 treatise on medical jurisprudence and insanity.[36] Haslam suggested that the medical profession could assist lawyers by presenting them with the medical truth about their clients' minds.[37] Haslam certainly had time, and motive, in 1817 to write his book and establish a new, potentially lucrative, field of medical authority. Formerly the apothecary at Bethlem Hospital, he had been called before a select committee in 1814, with the chief physician Thomas Monro, to answer allegations of cruelty and ill-treatment, culminating in his dismissal by the

Henry Dowe, portrait engraving of John Haslam, the discredited former Bedlam apothecary who attempted to classify idiocy in his 1817 treatise on medical jurisprudence.

governors in 1816. The under-employed Haslam embarked on writing his treatise in an attempt to rebuild his career and open up new opportunities as an expert medical witness.[38]

Haslam acknowledged that it was easy enough to identify the average idiot, and even those who could 'whistle tunes correctly, and repeat passages from books which they have been taught by ear' would never fool the medical man, who would know that they could not understand what they were repeating.[39] It was at the borderline between the unsound imbecile mind and the perfect sound mind that medical men could bring scientific certainty. There were some who had inferior, quite dull minds who could nevertheless manage their own lives and affairs, while there were others whose inferior intellects would disqualify them from any responsibility for themselves.[40] Through 'patient examinations and repeated interviews' (implying that the potential imbecile would be under medical supervision for some time), the specialist physician would determine on which side of this divide their patient lay, 'for the mind of any man may be gauged both as to its acquirements and its capacity'.[41] How exactly, and with what evidence, it would be gauged, Haslam did not reveal, as he produced a circular definition of imbecility:

> a state or degree of mental incapacity equivalent to idiotcy, a degree which renders him incompetent to the management of himself and his affairs; and which degree, by observation and enquiry may always be ascertained. The degree, satisfactorily measured, does, in my opinion amount to unsoundness of mind.[42]

In short, imbeciles were imbeciles because a medical expert pronounced them to be so.

Haslam dismissed the lay knowledge of the jury, who in his opinion 'always adopted the popular and floating opinion' through ignorance.[43] He was yet more dismissive of the 'blandishments of eloquence and the subtil underminings of lawyers', which lacked any sort of definition or direction to uncover unsoundness of mind.[44] The medical profession would bring, in contrast, 'sagacity, experience and truth' to the explanation of intellect.[45] Lawyers were interested only in whether a person could count. Medical men could explain the physiological defects of a person and identify whether their counting was mere parrot-like repetition or if they actually understood the abstract concept of number.[46] He concluded that 'knowledge of the human intellect, in its sane and disordered state' could be expected only from medical opinion.[47]

The discredited Haslam, a professional outcast who eventually died poor in 1844,[48] did not have the impact with his treatise that he had hoped for. It was not until the 1830s that other medical men, and lawyers, began to examine the English medical claim to explain and define idiocy in court, and it was done with markedly less enthusiasm than Haslam had shown. Andrew Amos, England's first professor of medical jurisprudence,[49] acknowledged in 1831 that the principal sources of legal authority on imbecility and incapacity were all from the seventeenth and eighteenth centuries, and while this was regrettable, he felt that the only role medical experts should hold in court on matters of the mind would be to detect witnesses making false imbecility claims.[50]

In 1833 the reclusive barrister and legal writer Leonard Shelford was distinctly hostile to the benefits of medical juris-prudence in determining idiocy or imbecility.[51] 'Can no one else do this but a medical man?' he asked rhetorically, and warned that, whatever the limitations of juries and their propensity to 'popular bias', medical evidence was inherently untrustworthy: 'of all evidence in courts of justice, that of medical men ought to be given with greatest care, and received with utmost caution.'[52] The courtroom should beware the opinionated, jargon-strewn evidence of the medical man. Medical evidence about the mind was only acceptable if 'comprehensible to laymen and explicit in facts, tender, slow and circumspect in opinion'.[53] Shelford restated the claim of individual liberty against medicalized encroachment by the state and regretted that vague definitions around imbe-cility in particular would 'invade the liberty of the subject and the rights of the people'.[54] Where imbecility existed, it needed to be determined with great accuracy, because there was no reason why an imbecile person who could remain 'orderly and mannerly' should not retain some self-dominion.[55] Falling into old charac-terizations of the idiot as child, he stated that important indicators of both idiocy and imbecility were childlike behav-iours such as preoccupation with frivolous pursuits, fondness for trifles, shyness, easy submission to control and acquiescence under influence.[56] He argued against the total deprivation of rights for the person deemed to lack capacity through idiocy or imbecility, for even such a person might 'spend his own little income in providing for his wants, as a boy spends his pocket money', despite being vulnerable to exploitation.[57]

A flurry of texts on idiocy and imbecility now emerged on both sides of the Atlantic. British writers remained highly scep-tical towards the claims of the French theorists and Haslam to medical authority in this field. In 1834 the barrister Joseph Chitty mocked the pretentions of the new practitioners of medical jurisprudence to superiority over lawyers in the area of the mind, seeing medical jurisprudence as better employed in clearly scientific fields such as toxicology and post-mortem examination.[58] He warned, 'it is very clearly established that the question whether idiot or not, must be decided by a jury, after hearing all the evidence.'[59] Medical testimony was admissible, but insufficient. All that mattered was whether jurors *thought* the person's mental faculties were 'so enfeebled as to render him incompetent to act for himself', a judgement they could reach through common sense.[60]

In the United States the work of the French theorists was more influential. New York professor of medicine Theodric Romeyn Beck drew heavily on Georget's work in his 1836 treatise on medical jurisprudence, and called for increased use of medical judgement in identifying idiocy and imbecility in criminals and asylum residents. He warned in particular about those whose intellectual functions are quite sound but whose feelings and affections are 'perverted and depraved', another reference to the burgeoning precursors to the 'moral imbecile' class. Only medical men could identify this disguised disorder, Beck argued, and needed the authority to do so urgently.[61]

In 1839, Isaac Ray,[62] medical director of the Augusta Insane Institution, continued the medical assault on the competence of juries and lawyers, arguing that new modes of medical knowledge could offer instead 'facts, established by men of undoubted experience and good faith'.[63] He ridiculed juries as simply 'a number of men, who may have had very little education of any kind . . . [sitting] in judgement on the manner of a man's understanding'. How could the dull, he implied, judge the dull? The law, he complained, was 'greatly behind the present state of knowledge' of idiocy and other conditions of mind.[64] Ray called for the introduction of expert medical witnesses, as employed in France, who would be in a permanent state of readiness to be called by the courts.[65] Such men could settle the complexities of capacity and understanding among the imbecile class, who possessed 'some intellectual capacity, though infinitely less than is possessed by the great mass of mankind'.[66] He added a further complication: the stupid person. Ordinary imbeciles were aware of their intellectual deficit, but the stupid person 'imagines himself equal, if not superior to other men in his intelligence'. Stupid people were consequently far more dangerous, as they were prepared to act 'precipitately and without reflection', while shy, unconfident imbeciles could never make up their minds to do anything for fear of consequences. The stupid person, appearing suspiciously like the moral imbecile, thus joined the increasingly crowded space occupied by persons of dubious capacity between the perfect mind and the perfect idiot. For such imbecile offenders, perpetual confinement in a medical institution was the only sensible course, both to protect society and for their own welfare. It was futile to expect courts and juries to act correctly in these puzzling cases.[67]

Towards the mid-nineteenth century, therefore, there were strong currents of thought in France and America – each only recently emerging from wider social revolutions – advocating a revolutionary medicalized modernization of judicial process, whereby expert witnesses would set scientific fact against the fanciful opinions of juries and the arcane meanderings of the lawyer. In France this was driven by a new faith in scientific evidence and medical testimony as enshrined in the recent Napoleonic Code and a growing medical assertion of power.[68] The Revolution had spawned a new class of 'citizen doctor' who saw themselves as 'a saviour in the battle against . . . pathology' and as 'fulfilling a national mission'.[69] In Britain there was deep suspicion of this new medical knowledge of the mind, even within the medical profession; medical jurisprudence focused more pragmatically on forensic science, with its poisons, knife wounds and fake life assurance claims, than on the speculative art of fathoming people's minds.[70] There was greater concern also about the personal liberty implications of state intervention in the name of protection.

Despite, however, this strain of legal resistance in Britain to medicalizing the idea of idiocy, the population of idiots seemed to be growing exponentially as old, loose categories of unsoundness of mind hardened into notions of the lifelong imbecile, sometimes harmless but sometimes dangerously amoral, threatening the fabric of society from below. There was then the full-blown or 'perfect' idiot, mostly helpless and pitiable, sometimes disgusting and repulsive. From some parts of the medical world arose an insistent call for a judicial process that would bypass mainstream courts and create a direct route into lifelong medical supervision, offering care for idiots and protection both for and from imbeciles. Whether institutionalized for care or protection, idiots and imbeciles would experience a complete and final separation from their original community.

Idiocy in the Nineteenth-century Courtroom

How did these changing ideas play out in court cases over the nineteenth century? In the criminal courts there was a discernible shift, part of a wider social turn against the poor and those marked as deviant by reason of abnormality of behaviour, mind or body. Idiot defendants became, from the late eighteenth century, less likely to be acquitted, more likely to be punished harshly, and prone to be seen as dangerous rather than hapless or harmless. There was also a sharp diminution in the number of idiots appearing for trial in criminal courts as the nineteenth century progressed, no doubt linked to the increasing numbers finding their way to incarceration in institutional settings. The trend in the civil courts was less marked, with idiot defendants' individual freedoms and right to live a life independent from state interference continuing to be an important feature of lawyerly argument, jury decision and public opinion. Medical expert opinion did, however, start to insinuate itself into trials that concerned idiocy in some ways, and the argument for the need for such testimony was made strongly by some parts of the profession. There was a clear class element driving the distinctive directions that criminal and civil processes took. The hapless, lower-order idiots appearing at criminal trials were seen as

Thomas Rowlandson and Augustus Charles Pugin, 'Old Bailey', colour engraving from *The Microcosm of London* (1808–10). A harsher tone developed in Old Bailey trials from the early 19th century.

suitable objects for punishment and the institution. The wealthy sons and daughters of the upper and middle classes appearing before the civil courts, meanwhile, were seen as entitled to a more individualized and sympathetic legal hearing.

Class was not the only factor. At the Old Bailey criminal court, the perceptible change in courtroom attitudes towards idiot defendants from the early nineteenth century was partly brought about by a professionalization process as the discretionary, amateur ethos of the eighteenth-century criminal trial was slowly replaced by a new professional culture led by aggressive and challenging lawyers.[71] What had previously been effectively an amateur altercation between the victim and the accused, presided over by the judge, became an adversarial procedure with professional standards, conducted by paid advocates.[72] This brought with it the advent of the expert witness – surgeons, chemists, doctors – and barristers began to equip themselves with a modicum of medical knowledge.[73] For the idiot, until now supported by character witnesses who would testify to their naivety, good nature and harmlessness, this represented a turning point. The implications for the medicalization of their condition and replacement of the informal discretionary mercy available to them previously was clear. The first 'expert' physician appeared in an idiot trial in 1789.[74] This reduction of the discretionary, informal character assessment process typical of the earlier trials led to a hardening climate of reduced tolerance around idiocy.

When sixteen-year-old John Leck, known as 'Foolish Johnny' and also extremely deaf, appeared in 1800 charged with stealing metal, there was little sign of any form of discretionary mercy. A hostile judge instructed the jury first to determine whether Leck was of sound mind by pronouncing whether they believed he knew right from wrong, for which they needed to be satisfied that he had the understanding of a child aged fourteen. If so, the judge opined, then he was 'answerable to the laws of his country'. He warned the jury not to indulge or excuse him on the grounds of his idiocy,

> for nothing can be more mischievous than that sort of character . . . this half-witted man, going by the name of Foolish Johnny, should be suffered to go about, and committing depredations of this sort; and therefore however the neighbourhood may be inclined to indulge him, or soften his actions by calling him Foolish Johnny, if he is of that kind of understanding as to know when he is doing wrong, he ought to be amenable to the law.

He added that 'it is the duty of the Parish, where they have idiots, to lock them up.' The Jury found him fit to plead, and he was found guilty, fined one shilling and imprisoned in the House of Correction for six months.[75]

This was a quite sudden and dramatic change in courtroom tone and content, which directly challenged 'neighbourhoods' not to 'soften the actions' of idiots through indulgent nicknaming and tolerance of deviance. The message was that idiots must either take responsibility for their actions and be judged by the same standards as others, or be 'locked up', institutionalized and kept separate because they could not understand, let alone play by, the rules of society.

From this period a hardening of attitudes from both public and legal professionals is evident, and a pattern of harsher punishment for low-level crimes can be discerned. The judge in the trial of Foolish Johnny Leck had intimated that despite being half-witted he was capable of using this to evade responsibility for his actions, when he knew well what he was doing. The judge even cast doubt on the authenticity of Leck's deafness.[76] All this was an echo of the characterization of the amoral, rascally imbecile that Fodéré was describing in Paris at around this time. At the trial of Conrad Frederic in 1807 for a minor theft, similar aspersions were cast by the judge. Frederic was idiotic, profoundly deaf and unable to speak since an attack of childhood fever.[77] Nevertheless, he was accused by the judge of having a great deal of cunning, his lack of hearing compensated for, in the old trope about the compensatory faculty, by an advanced capacity for duplicity. The punishment was harsh: six months' imprisonment and a public whipping. Frederic's disabilities were seen as the driving force behind, not an excuse for, his behaviour.

Witness testimony developed a similarly harsh tone. In 1819 Charlotte Lawrence was accused of stealing a frock from a six-year-old child as she walked to school, her confusion clear as she testified, 'I picked it up in the shape of a doll.'[78] There was, however, no tolerance shown by the child's mother, who asserted 'I never heard of her being an idiot,' or by the court, who imprisoned Lawrence for two months. A similar refusal to accept idiocy as mitigation for defendants was evident six years later in John Battle's trial for horse theft. The horse owner's response to the lawyer's question 'Is not the prisoner an idiot?' was: 'I know nothing of him – he was wise enough to take my horse.' The testimony of Battle's brother to his good character, ability to work hard and weak intellect was not enough, and Battle was hanged, despite evidence that he had been teased and manipulated into taking the horse by a group of passing gentlemen. One witness stated, 'I thought him an idiot, and did not notice him.' Another referred to him as 'an old fool'.[79]

Generally, a sense of dangerousness and premeditation surfaced – that idiots concealed their true motives beneath a cunning mask just as they were concealing the goods they had stolen. In the courtroom, the idiot was now sarcastically described as 'wise enough' to have committed their crime and was no longer an indulged figure of amused toleration. In criminal trials at least, a hardening of tone from judges began to displace the inclusiveness and acceptance that had characterized trials of idiots for most of the eighteenth century.

In the civil courts things were somewhat different. The important case of *Ingram v. Wyatt*, which meandered through the ecclesiastical courts of Canterbury and London between 1824 and 1832, influenced the 1830s English theorists and offers a window on to the enduring strength of eighteenth-century notions of capacity, and resistance to medical encroachment.[80]

John Clopton (who had changed his name from Ingram) inherited a considerable estate from his brother. When he died in 1824 he left everything to his solicitor and executor, Henry Wyatt. Clopton's sister Barbara Ingram, the sole beneficiary in Clopton's earlier will, disputed Wyatt's inheritance on the grounds that her brother was an imbecile, lacked capacity and had been imposed upon and defrauded by Wyatt.[81] The Court of Prerogative found in favour of Clopton's sister, ruling against Wyatt and awarding her the inheritance. The judge concluded that Clopton had always been treated as a child and was very weak, inactive, indolent, torpid and had below-par understanding. Therefore his attorney, Wyatt, had exploited him.[82] However, in 1831 the Court of Delegates reversed this judgment and awarded the will to Wyatt. They argued that although there were clearly grounds for suspicion against Wyatt, Clopton's capacity had been satisfactorily established.[83]

A number of factors make this a significant case in the legal framing of idiocy and imbecility. First, although later reversed, the judgment that Clopton was imbecile and imposed upon, and the judgment of what constituted imbecility, were used as case law in subsequent cases of suspected imbecility.[84] Second, despite the campaign from some physicians, there was not one instance of medical testimony in the eight years of the dispute. Finally, significant weight was attached to the lay opinions concerning imbecility expressed by the 28 witnesses from all social levels who spoke during the case. Each was asked their opinion of Clopton's imbecility and each confidently expressed their diagnosis. Their language and characterizations of imbecility then passed into the judge John Nicholl's judgment, which in turn passed into the subsequent series of 1830s legal treatises.

Witnesses included Clopton's cousin, waiters, housemaids, his laundress and an apprentice hairdresser. His cousin complained about his frivolity, how he would say 'the same things over and over', his extremely shy and indolent disposition and his dirty habits.[85] Servants repeatedly alluded to his childlike vulnerability. Flourishing his stick out in the street he would pretend to ride a horse and carriage, shouting 'yehep yehep yehep' while gangs of boys 'made game of him', calling him Mad Ingram or Old Yehep.[86] Most importantly, he was vulnerable to exploitation: 'he could be persuaded out of anything and into anything,' commented the laundress.[87] A tailor with whom he lodged constantly had to persuade enraged members of the public not to strike Clopton, explaining that he was 'not right in his mind'.[88] One witness even described how, many years earlier as an apprentice hairdresser, he had dressed Clopton's hair each day at a coffee house in Fleet Street. Seeing that Clopton was 'half-silly' and talked a 'pack of nonsense', he would deliberately do ridiculous things with his hair, 'tying up his tail behind so as to make it stand up like a stick or curl it up in some ludicrous form'. The result was that Clopton 'used to strut around the Coffee Room and everyone laughed at him'.[89]

As each witness completed their testimony, they were asked their opinion of Clopton's understanding and capacity. For one waiter, he was 'not of proper understanding', while for another

he was 'of very weak understanding'.[90] To the laundress 'he was
... wicked rather than weak.'[91] She did not believe that he was
at any time 'capable of any act that required thought, judgement
and reflection, because he never remained in his right mind'.[92]
A housemaid felt that he behaved 'like a man who was not right
in his mind' but that 'it proceeded more from madness than
from weakness of mind.' He could certainly not, in her opinion,
manage any concern or business because of his derangement.
Even the practical-joking apprentice hairdresser was asked his
opinion and pronounced Clopton 'half silly and not in his right
mind'.[93] It is clear from this that the opinion of the layperson,
their cultural understanding of imbecility, was sought and given
validity in the court process. In this case, 'lay' did not mean the
'intelligent sort' of the propertied jurymen but comprised male
and female members of the lowest serving class, young and old.
Also striking was the confidence with which they gave their
judgments.

When Judge Nicholl summed up, he outlined the 'childish-
ness . . . frivolous pursuits, fondness for and stress upon trifles,
inertness of mind, paucity of ideas, shyness, timidity, submission
to control, acquiescence under influence and the like' that characterized the imbecile John Clopton.[94] This neatly summarized
the comments put forward by the witnesses. His conclusion,
that Clopton showed 'considerable weakness of mind, and
exhibits a character much exposed to fraud and imposition',[95]
as well as comments on Clopton's inertia and torpidity, also
reflected the confidently delivered assessments of the public.
His conclusions, including his characterization of the childish imbecilic characteristics, passed verbatim into Shelford's
1833 treatise[96] and then onwards through the rash of works on
legal idiocy that followed, which drew on the case of *Ingram
v. Wyatt* to form and develop the legal concept of the lifelong
imbecile. In this way the opinions of the public passed into legal
theory about imbecility, just as much as any abstract theorization by academic jurists. Medical opinion in *Ingram v. Wyatt*
was entirely absent.

However, a hearing in 1832, the same year as the Lord Chancellor rejected a final appeal on *Ingram v. Wyatt*,[97] was characterized not by an absence of doctors but by an overabundance of them. Twenty-three-year-old Rose Bagster, described by her schoolmistresses as an exceedingly slow and stupid scholar prone to violence, was heiress to several fortunes from her mother and other relations. On a visit to the London Zoological Gardens a Mr Newton, who was part of her group, persuaded her to join him in his cabriolet to Camden Town, where a carriage with four horses was waiting. She was conducted to Gretna Green, where a parson was awakened to conduct a marriage ceremony.[98] After locating her daughter, now Mrs Newton, her mother fetched her from a Carlisle hotel and brought her back to London, whereupon she instigated a commission of lunacy to have Rose declared of unsound mind and the marriage consequently annulled.[99]

Witness testimony was dominated by the medical profession. Twelve doctors in all testified, some of them among the most prominent names in London's mad-doctoring world.

The young imbecile Miss Bagster was abducted by Mr Newton during a visit to the London Zoological Gardens in 1832, which are depicted here in a hand-coloured lithograph by George Scharf, 'The Giraffes with the Arabs who brought them over to this Country', 1836.

They included John Haslam, the disgraced former Bethlem apothecary and author of the medico-legal treatise; Sir George Tothill, visiting physician at Bethlem;[100] Dr Monro, the former Bethlem chief physician, sacked at the same time as Haslam;[101] and Sir Alexander Morison, author of *The Physiognomy of Mental Diseases* (1843) and later to be physician at asylums in Hanwell and Surrey.[102] Each had visited Miss Bagster (as all called her) at home, some on several occasions, to assess her level of imbecility, if any. At one point Miss Bagster, when asked a question by the jury, replied, 'I am so afraid of making a mistake that I dare not say . . . I have seen about two dozen doctors, and I cannot reply.'[103] She was perhaps unconscious of the irony of her words when she told Morison of feeling unwell, 'from the effect of seeing so many doctors'.[104]

The medical witnesses did not, however, present the unified, scientific demonstration of truth that the theorists claimed they would bring to legal process. They divided into two acrimonious camps, half believing Miss Bagster to be imbecile and half diagnosing mere ignorance and lack of education. Some of the differences could be attributed to personal rivalry. Monro declared 'the state of her mind as extreme imbecility', evidenced by her lack of judgement and her demeanour.[105] Haslam, whom Monro had betrayed and blamed at the select committee inquiry into Bethlem eighteen years earlier,[106] concluded the exact opposite: 'her countenance bore no mark of imbecility whatever . . . she is not a lunatic, she is not an idiot, she is not of unsound mind.'[107]

The medical evidence bore little of the stamp of science, focusing almost entirely on arithmetical weakness and, in the eyes of the medical men, Miss Bagster's sexually transgressive predilection for fighting and willingness to talk openly about her sexual experiences. Twice the judge had to ask all females present to vacate the court while doctors repeated what Miss Bagster had told them 'without hesitation or embarrassment' and in the 'plainest and grossest terms' about the familiarities that had passed between her and Mr Newton. These had occurred not only in hotels after the marriage but also, shockingly, in the carriage on the way to Gretna Green.[108] However, despite all this, and the threats that she posed to notions of gender and propriety, it was her lack of mathematical ability that was decisive in the judgement of those doctors who declared her imbecile. She did not know how many pence there were in a shilling and thought there were six days in a year.[109] In a post-trial editorial the *London Medical Gazette* ridiculed this obsessive questioning about numbers, particularly the 'byzantine questions' of Dr Root: 'no doubt if she had answered his question about the four percent, he would have given her something more knotty, such as the extraction of roots or the solution of cubic equations.'[110]

The doctors who considered Miss Bagster non-imbecile, led by Morison and Haslam, questioned their fellow doctors' reasoning. They argued that the constant medical interviews had lessened her sense of modesty and her arithmetical problem was due to ignorance rather than innate imbecility. Both scorned using arithmetical questions to determine a person's capacity.[111] Despite these arguments that ignorance did not equate to imbecility the jury took just one hour to declare her of unsound mind.[112] Rose Bagster lost her rights over her goods and property, and her marriage was annulled.

Medical involvement in the Bagster case contrasted starkly with *Ingram v. Wyatt*, where a claim for medical authority could equally have been made but was entirely absent. There was no systematic process whereby medical authority was invoked in such cases. Lay testimony in the Ingram case was given just as much credence in court as medical testimony in the Bagster case. Legal concepts of idiocy, and the burgeoning arena of imbecility, were still uncertain ground for medical practitioners, who encountered strong and enduring beliefs that these conditions were easily discernible by the layman through appearance and common-sense notions of behaviour. The fact that medical men were so clearly divided themselves about what constituted imbecility did not aid their claim to indisputable scientific truth. There seemed to be no 'scientific' proof of the condition, simply

observation of appearance and behaviour and mathematical tests
that appeared no different to what the layperson, even indeed a
servant, could discern themselves.

The *London Medical Gazette*, in a shrewd editorial, recognized the damage caused to the credibility of medical testimony
by the divided opinions and often risible testimony of the
doctors in the Bagster case. The paper attacked the elasticity
surrounding notions of 'unsound mind', an increasingly obscure
and 'bottomless' phrase 'that swallows up . . . all the proofs and
facts of whatsoever kind offered to its undistinguishing appetite'.[113] It was a phrase 'on which no two professional persons,
be they lawyers, physicians or divines could agree'. The editorial
highlighted the absurdity of considering arithmetical ability an
indicator of soundness of mind, resulting in the description of
someone as rational in the morning and then imbecile in the
afternoon because she could not complete a sum.[114] Lost amid
the doctors' squabbles and posturings, complained the *Gazette*,
was the injustice of the verdict. Miss Bagster's problems were
due to a monstrously mismanaged education, not unsoundness
of mind, and the *Gazette* dissented unreservedly from the verdict.[115] Doctors had allowed the prejudices of jurors, 'mainly
commercial men', to take the place of reasoned medical testimony by bamboozling them with conflicting medical evidence.
Naturally, therefore, the jurors had taken matters into their own
hands to deliver this 'extraordinary verdict'.[116] The failure of
medicine to present a united front and a coherent rational
explanation of imbecility had allowed the old irrational and
opinionated ignorance of the layman to win the day.

The medical profession was still fighting the same battle
thirty years later when the sensational case of William Windham
came to court. Windham, from an eminent Norfolk family, had
inherited a very large capital sum, property and substantial
income on coming of age in 1861. Three weeks later he had
married a woman of 'worthless character', Agnes Willoughby,
with whom he was allegedly obsessed and who until recently
had been a 'kept woman' with another gentleman. Windham

had given her a very large settlement. In the same month he had bought her jewellery worth £14,000.[117] Two months later his new wife had left him, allegedly becoming involved in sexual misconduct with various men. Windham petitioned for dissolution on these grounds in 1862.[118] He was widely perceived, however, to be an imbecile, with eccentric habits, limited understanding and considerable communication deficits. His family brought a Commission of Lunacy in an attempt to protect his inheritance from what they saw as his imbecilic vulnerability to exploitation and fraud, and to annul his marriage. In the days before the hearing, a furious correspondence erupted in *The Times* between 'an Eastern Counties Traveller' and the management of the Eastern Counties Railway. The terrified passenger was complaining that he and his fellow travellers were convinced that Mr Windham, dressed in the livery of the railway staff, was being allowed to drive trains while unqualified, having unlimited resources with which to bribe the staff. Passengers were aware

W. F. WINDHAM, Esq.

William Windham, a wealthy imbecile whose court case caused a sensation in 1860s England.

MRS. W. F. WINDHAM.—FROM A PHOTOGRAPH BY MAYER BROTHERS, REGENT-STREET.

Agnes Willoughby, the 'kept woman' whose marriage to Windham precipitated the scandal in 1861.

that Mr Windham was about to be examined by a Commission for Lunacy and expressed the hope that he would, from now, be closely monitored.[119]

The commission opened on 16 December 1861[120] and with its salacious undertones and Windham's wealth, eccentricity and suspected imbecility proved irresistible to the public. Prince Albert had died two days earlier, on 14 December, and yet between his death and the report of the conclusion of the Windham case on 31 January 1862 the Windham commission received more coverage in *The Times* than the Prince Consort's death.[121] The jury concluded, after a very lengthy hearing, that Windham was of sound mind and capable of managing his affairs, swayed by the powerful arguments in favour of liberty of the subject and the right to eccentricity advanced by his defence. Medical men had offered evidence to support the arguments of both sides. *The Times* supported the verdict, saying that the jury 'must have been as insane as Mr WINDHAM himself was asserted to be if they had come to any other conclusion'.[122] However, they issued a lurid and prophetic warning, acknowledging that liberty of the subject carried a price for the vulnerable:

> yet for the next few years this Mr Windham will, in all probability, be a pauper . . . the sharks of society, the borrowers and the users, the toadies and the swaggerers, the procuresses and the courtesans, the keepers of dens of infamy, and all the parasites which feed upon the corrupt parts of the social body, have their prey marked out to them.[123]

Windham was continually pursued through the courts in the following years by his wife and various debtors until his bankruptcy was declared in 1864. In 1866 he died of heart disease aged just 25, his fortune squandered.[124]

In 1887 Dr John Langdon Down, author of the *Ethnic Classification of Idiots* (1867) and former superintendent of the world's first idiot asylum at Earlswood in Surrey, looked back on the Windham case with a certain grim satisfaction. 'It is now several years since this city was excited by the trial before a Master in Lunacy of a young man whose ability to manage his own affairs was doubted.'[125] He recalled that at the time he had written a paper for *The Lancet*[126] demonstrating a link between the condition of the mouth and the idiot: idiots tended to have vaulted palates, which caused dribbling and betrayed the presence of congenital idiocy.[127] Down had written, 'the flow of water from the mouth is universally associated in the popular mind with the condition of idiocy. The slavering may vary in degree. It may occur only at periods of excitement, and at meal times, or with scarcely any intermission throughout the day.'[128] At Windham's commission his lawyer had convinced the court it was wrong to consider him feeble-minded because he had mouth deformities that caused his 'defective utterances'.[129] Down's paper was published too late to refute these claims in court, and was eventually only referenced in counsel's final address. By then it was too late to alter the opinion of the jury, 'who supported the doctrine of the liberty of the subject'.[130] Down, now in the twilight of his career, gazed back and condemned the catastrophic consequences of uninformed laymen clinging to outmoded concepts, when medical science warned of the consequences of considering imbeciles and idiots to have the same rights as others. 'The poor congenital imbecile', he wrote, 'was allowed to go his own way to destruction, with the result of becoming speedily bankrupt in fortune, ruined in health, and a scandal to an honoured ancestral name.'[131] Wealth, person, bloodline, all were destroyed. Medicine, in the person of Down, had warned them it would be so, but foolishly they ignored it. It was time for society to properly understand, Down argued, the prerogative of the medical man over the idiot and the imbecile.

The Windham case captured important ambiguities surrounding idiocy in the 1860s. The idea of the idiot remained recognizable from the figure that was theorized at the beginning of the eighteenth century. They were isolated, struggling to managing their affairs, failing in relationships and everyday transactions, vulnerable to exploiters, a group apart from common humanity, sometimes pitied, sometimes loathed. Yet another version of the idiot endured, loved and protected by families, known in communities, protected from exploiters and invested with a status far from dehumanizing. There were strong popular notions at all levels of society about what constituted idiocy, and these forms of knowledge passed into both law and medicine (the drivelling idiot, for example, a notion medicalized by Down) rather than passing exclusively downwards from elite theoreticians. The population that could now be described as idiotic continued to swell considerably, joined by growing ranks of ingeniously constructed imbeciles, the eccentric, the promiscuous, the criminal and the transgressive; sometimes dangerously invisible, usually threatening to social order. The medical profession was divided over both the nature and the extent of its claim to authority in these areas. In France and America there were strong claims for medical authority as a repository of indisputable scientific fact that should not only drive legal decisions but even bypass them, creating a direct route to the asylum. Yet in Britain, this challenge to existing legal authority faced important resistance from a deep commitment to the principles of individual liberty and protection from state interference, even if these carried exploitative risks for individuals. This thinking too was backed by some medical men. Imbeciles, and sometimes even idiots, should be able to live their own lives if they wished, presiding over their own small lives where possible.

In both the criminal and civil courts intellectual currents, of which they were largely unaware, swirled around the idiots and imbeciles who found themselves in the public, and legal, gaze. For some, like Foolish Johnny Leck and Conrad Frederic at the Old Bailey, the consequences of new modes of thought were only too real: harsh physical punishment and incarceration. Others, particularly those from the wealthier classes, continued to live their lives, unchanging, often to the exasperation of those around them, who wished them to be educable and improvable, to become rational, orderly and mannerly. When the apparently imbecile Miss Rose Bagster returned home to London after being spirited away to Gretna Green for marriage, a friend reported that she 'spoke of the elopement as a lark and said she would like to run away'.[132] William Windham, even at the height of his miserable pursuit through the courts and as his fortune dissipated, continued to terrify *Times*-reading Eastern Counties passengers by dressing as a guard, carrying a bunch of keys and appearing to be in charge of trains rumbling across eastern England.[133] The law was slowly tightening its grip on, and control over, those it deemed idiotic or imbecile, but there was, thankfully, at least some room for individuality, eccentricity and non-conformity yet.

5

Pity and Loathing:
New Cultural Thinking

When the revolutionary young poet William Wordsworth introduced a new form of idiot with his lyrical poem 'The Idiot Boy' in 1798,[1] he provoked some strong reactions. He also turned his back firmly on the amusing, dull-witted 'bottle heads' who had bumbled their way through the challenges of everyday eighteenth-century life, and who still held sway in the caricatures and jokes of his time. Who was this new type of idiot?

The severely idiotic and deeply rural Johnny Foy is sent by his doting mother Betty on a horse late one night to fetch a doctor from the nearby town, to treat their ailing old neighbour Susan Gale. Fretting in their isolated forest cottage, Betty knows this is a risk as Johnny has no sense of direction and little language, but she relies on the 'mild and good' pony to get him there. Johnny fails to return; sick with worry, Betty eventually finds him, safe and mindless in a glade on the grazing pony. She hugs him tearfully: 'Oh! Johnny, never mind the Doctor; / You've done your best and that is all.'[2] On the way home they encounter the miraculously remobilized Susan Gale, who has overcome her bodily pains to search for Johnny.

What was Wordsworth saying about the idiot? Johnny Foy mostly communicates through meaningless 'burring' sounds. Although loved by his mother and neighbour he shows no love or affection in return. Who, or what, is it that they love? In

Wordsworth's characterization he is an unreachable 'solitaire', cast adrift on the remote island of his imbecility, a simple, unthinking child of nature. The horse seems to think more than he does: 'But then he is a horse that thinks!'[3] It is the horse that is expected to accomplish the mission of getting to the doctor. While all around him experience strong emotions, the idiot boy seems to feel nothing other than a general meaningless happiness, revealed in his laughter and burring sounds. It was pointless and foolish expecting him – a human type that cannot think, feel or do – to accomplish a task. He was, however, both a loveable and pitiable type: someone on whom feelings could be expended, but only as an object of feelings and not in any shared, reciprocal way. Wordsworth was at pains to point out that Johnny Foy was not meant to be the loathsome form of idiot: 'my idiot is not one of those who cannot articulate, or of those that are unusually disgusting in their persons.' Indeed, he wanted to challenge 'the loathing and disgust which many people have at the sight of an idiot', which he saw as attached to 'a false delicacy'.[4]

His intentions were not realized. Wordsworth's collaborator on the *Lyrical Ballads*, Samuel Taylor Coleridge, criticized him for not having taken care to preclude 'the disgusting images of ordinary, morbid idiocy, which yet it was by no means his intention to represent. He has even by the "burr burr burr" un-counteracted by any preceding description of the boy's beauty, assisted in recalling them.'[5] Furthermore, when the idiocy of the boy was combined with the folly of his mother, Coleridge felt, the whole thing became 'a laughable burlesque'.[6] Her folly, of course, was to love and care about her idiot son, and to imagine him capable of anything. Others concurred. The young critic John Wilson complained, 'I have seen a most excellent painting of an idiot, but it created in me an inexpressible disgust.' Furthermore, said Wilson, it was inconceivable that 'a person in a state of complete idiocy should excite the warmest feelings of attachment even in the breast of his mother'.[7]

Here was an irony. Coleridge and Wordsworth, fired by the sentiments of the French Revolution, wanted to bring a new

Romantic sympathy to the representation of the common man and woman. Their collaboration on the *Lyrical Ballads* would sentimentalize, that is to say bring feeling and authenticity to, the lives and personalities of the ordinary people to be found in every village. Yet when the Romantic gaze was projected onto the idiot it found only the empty shell that was Johnny Foy, slumped listlessly on his horse and carried haplessly in whatever direction the horse happened to go. He could not feel, and the only feelings worthy to project onto him were either unreciprocated pity or, given his lack of capacity for human feeling, loathing of his unnaturalness. As the idea of Romantic sensibility took shape, the idiot began to be defined by a new focus, and was ceasing to amuse.[8] In 1796 Fanny Burney had described, in *Camilla*, the trickle of drool on the chin of the handsome idiot girl that caused a fleeting disgust in Eugenia.[9] Burney's disgusting idiot girl was now joined, two years later, by Wordsworth's pitiable idiot boy. Was the idiot ceasing to be a cause for amusement and becoming an object of sorrow or disgust? Was a new morally and physically repellent type emerging, replacing the more indulged, if odd, idiot type of the eighteenth century?

Other significant cultural shifts, with underlying implications for the idiot, began to take place around this time and in the ensuing early decades of the nineteenth century. Slang changed, both in name and nature. It ceased to be 'cant', the disguising language of the criminal underworld and the roguish poor, and became 'flash', the stylish 'slick lingo of London's ultra-fashionable world'.[10] It moved from something that people wanted to keep secret to something that people wanted to be known.[11] The turning point for this upper-class appropriation of low-life language was the publication of Piers Egan's edition of Grose's *Classical Dictionary of the Vulgar Tongue* in 1823.[12] Egan was the author of *Life in London*,[13] which featured the men-about-town adventures of the rakish swells Tom, Jerry and Logic, who liked to descend on both high- and low-life venues in late Regency London. They took an anthropological delight in mixing with the lowest as well as the highest circles in London and adopting the 'flash', the hybrid of lower- and upper-class slang that was derived from these mixings.

However much Egan and his characters delighted in London's low life, they brought the moralizing judgement of their class to its depiction. This was evident in Egan's edition of Grose's originally explicit work where he pronounced that 'when an indelicate or immodest word has obtruded itself for explanation, [I have] endeavoured to get rid of it in the most decent way possible.'[14] As well as introducing the upper-class, intellectual-ized slang of Oxford and Cambridge, Egan bowdlerized, either through omission or euphemism, sexual and other offensive terms. A pushing-school was no longer defined as a brothel but as a 'Cyprian lodge'. The clap became not venereal disease but 'a delicate taint'.[15] The muff was no longer the 'private parts of the woman' but simply 'the monosyllable'. The same cleansing and euphemistic turn affected terms related to idiocy. In Egan's version of Grose, as well as the glossary of terms helpfully appended to *Life in London*, a new breed of clever in-jokes denot-ing stupidity appeared, with lengthy explanations of their meaning and origin. A 'garret (or upper story)' was 'The head. His garret, or upper story, is empty, or unfurnished i.e. he has no brains, he is a fool.' A 'canister' was 'the head, with a sly allusion to its emptiness'.[16]

Other slang and flash dictionaries adopted the same more allusive, intellectual, verbose style, displaying the cleverness of the authors to their literate peers rather than reproducing the raw, direct language of the streets. In the *Sportsman's Slang* dic-tionary of 1825 the term 'FRS' was introduced, meaning 'a Fellow Remarkably Stupid (not a Fellow of the Royal Society)'.[17] 'Jerry wags', clearly derived not from the streets of St Giles but from the *Life in London* stories of the arch-wags Tom and Jerry, were 'half-drunken, half-foolish fellows, mostly bumpkins, newly town-rigged, seeking for a spree'.[18] This was far removed from earlier definitions by Grose and others of the idiot bumpkin as 'an awkward lout or country fellow'. A fresh mode of talking about idiocy was appearing in the new-style slang lexicons which shifted away from simple, vivid one-liners, addressed directly to the idiot on the street, to witty conceits exclusively shared and understood at the idiotic class's expense by educated, rakish men about town. The 'buffle head' was replaced by the 'deadly lively: one who is half stupid but pretending to his wanted activity and *nous*' – in other words, somebody trying to operate above their intellectual level. Much of the old idiot slang was ejected from the new line of flash dictionaries that flooded the booksellers, whose names betrayed their high-class modishness, to make way for infusions of university slang[19] and the jargon of the sporting rake's favourite pastimes, horse racing and boxing. *The New and Comprehensive Dictionary of the Flash Language*, *The Flash Dictionary*, *Sportsman's Slang* and *The Modern Flash Dictionary* oversaw a move to the exits by the dull, stupid idiots who had loomed so large in the lexicons of the previous century.[20] Interest in them declined fast and was replaced by new butts for derision from the social circles of the arch-wags. In the everinventive world of street argot, the idiot was shifting from a directly addressed being, however demeaning and ridiculing that address might at times be, to a type spoken about from a distant sphere by their betters or, worse still, ignored. Changes in language signalled a changing social status and visibility.

Jestbooks, and the humour within them, were changing also. There was a radical reduction in idiot jokes, and a new cast of characters took their place. Driving this was a newly racialized strain of humour in the form of a sharp increase in the number of jokes about Jews and the introduction of the buffoonish, simpleminded, comedy-accented 'Negro'. Jews started to be presented as unpleasant, bungling tricksters. 'Negro' jokes entered the jestbook from 1790 and from the 1800s were a much-used stock character. The protagonists, like idiots before them, blundered their way through life misunderstanding what was going on around them and calling out to 'Massa' for help. They gulped down grog too quickly and found it was 'too 'trong Massa'; and they worried that in the dark the Devil might 'take away de poor negro man'.[21] They took on the idiot's role of wise fool: 'the *hog*, he eat, he drink, he sleep, he do nothing all day. The *hog* he the only *gentleman* in England.'[22] They were even characterized as humorous when about to be flogged, seemingly as impervious to pain as the previous century's bone-headed yokel in a cudgel fight and pleading with their 'Massa' to get on with the whipping and stop the moralizing: 'Massa, if you flogee flogee; or if you preachee preachee; but no preachee and flogee too!'[23]

As jokes that had appeared throughout the eighteenth century were recycled in nineteenth-century publications, the idiot protagonists lost their place to new objects of derision. Whereas in 1721 it was an idiot who lay on his death bed and assured friends that he would make his own way to the graveyard, by 1832 a 'poor man' had taken his place.[24] By 1865 it was the menacing working-class factory hands of industrializing Birmingham who had 'not heads to think, nor hearts to feel',[25] rather than the dear old country simpleton. Sly Jewish tricksters got their comeuppance through 'distributive', or mob, justice or wrote laughably illiterate notes, their bumbling incompetence

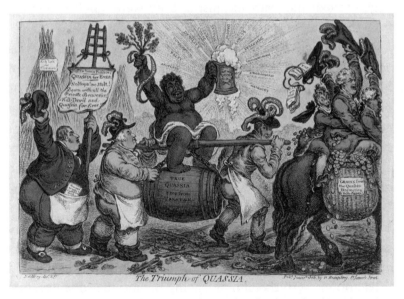

James Gillray, 'The Triumph of Quassia', 1806, hand-coloured etching depicting the procession of a 'hideous negress' symbolizing Quassia, a drug obtained from the Quassia tree, which is supposed to have supplanted hops in brewing. One of the rays coming from her frothing tankard is inscribed 'idiotism'.

observed not with amused indulgence but vitriolic detestation.[26] Very occasionally, an unconvincing idiot would reappear, telling a preacher with a dozing congregation: 'I should have been asleep too if I had not been an idiot.'[27] These last vestiges of the joke idiot were too self-aware, too knowing and witty in their replies to be the accidentally wise fools of earlier: 'I know some things sir, and some things I don't know sir,' said a 'youth of weak intellects' to a thieving miller. 'I know that millers have fat hogs, sir . . . I don't know whose corn they eat sir.'[28] They had become a convenient plot device to lead to the joking punch-line, no longer related to any discernible idiot type encountered in daily life. New classes of 'joke object' were appearing in new forms: Jews or urban workers who needed to be put in their place, or the light-brained, child-like 'Negro', a source of amusement if controlled under the watchful eye of 'Massa'. As Vic Gatrell has written, 'in and after the 1820s low life was increasingly represented as a terrain of anxiety and didactic moralisation; it became less and less funny.'[29] The displaced idiot, barely noticed, began to exit the jestbook, just as they were quietly creeping from the realm of slang.

This radical shift in the content and object of jokes was accompanied by a wider conceptual change in the idea of humour, of what was suitable to make people laugh. Gatrell has observed that although there were of course continuities in what constituted humour, there was a 'significant change that happened quite quickly' around the end of the eighteenth century and beginning of the nineteenth. This included the emergence of taboos about sexual and scatological humour and squeamishness about the lower body parts in particular, and disorder in general.[30] External decency of behaviour was now more generally assumed, and a drive for improvement in manners and morals was linked to a campaign for a more disciplined urban order, with the aim of leaving behind the rude excesses of the Georgians.[31] This was a distinctly unpromising new environment for the morally and physically incontinent, undisciplined and often uncomprehending idiot, who now faced what has been called a general 'cleansing process' sustained by 'a deepening wish to control, moralise and marginalise those who defied that process'.[32]

Caricatures changed in the same way. This change was radical and noticeable enough to be commented on by contemporaries who lived through it. It is worth quoting the novelist William Makepeace Thackeray's observations in a tribute in 1840 to the caricaturist George Cruikshank at some length. Looking back at the satirical prints and print shops of his youth, he lamented:

> Mr Cruikshank may have drawn a thousand better things since the days when these were, but they are to us a thousand times more pleasing . . . there used to be a crowd round the window in those days of grinning good-natured mechanics, who spelt the songs and spoke them out for the benefit of the company, and who received the points of humour with a general sympathising roar. Where are these people now? You never hear any laughing at HB [John Doyle, a modern lithographic caricaturist[33]]: his pictures are a great deal too genteel for that – polite points of wit which cause one to smile in a quiet, gentlemanlike kind of way.[34]

This shift from the roaring laugh of the streets to the smile of the 'gentlemanlike kind of wit' was a 'transformation of both aristocratic and subculture values into . . . "polite" assumption'.[35] It signalled an exit from the jestbook of not only the idiot but a whole cast of other characters: bawdy prostitutes, urinating drunks, comic cripples and dwarfs, bamboozled deaf and blind people and lusty women. It meant, in the end, the demise of the jestbook itself, the jokes 'consigned to oblivion or cleaned up as children's literature'.[36] Joe Miller's jestbook of 1836 dropped its most tasteless jokes 'in deference to the greater delicacy observed in modern society and conversation'.[37] Few jestbooks were published after it in the Victorian period.

New Cultural Ideas of Idiocy

What were the implications of this quite startling change in the cultural practice of humour for the representation of idiocy? As the joke book, the slang lexicon and the biting satirical caricature no longer offered the idea of idiocy a home, how did new ideas of idiocy form? There were three significant cultural arenas, from the 1830s, in which the idiot appeared in radically new guises. First, there were the new 'amiable humorist' magazines that provided gentle amusement and genteel satire on events and themes of the day for the literate middle class. Second there was the increasingly popular literary form of the novel, often serialized in weekly or monthly publications prior to full publication, offering a new hybrid sentimentalist-realist perspective on the world. Novelists took up Wordsworth's call for the writer to 'keep his eye on the subject' and speak 'in the real language of men'.[38] Finally there was a new narrative, practised both by enthusiastic amateurs and medical men, which portrayed the idiot as an observed object, not only of clinical and scientific interest but of refined amusement and titillation.

Punch, from its launch in 1841, epitomized the new form of genteel humour. A co-founder was the humorist Mark Lemon, who produced one of the last, and certainly the most sanitized, jestbooks of the nineteenth century.[39] It was underpinned by the cult of the so-called 'amiable humorist'. This form of humour turned its back on the satire, ridicule and brutal exposure of eighteenth-century (and earlier) comedy.[40] Instead, by the mid-nineteenth century, it became the norm that 'the best comic works present amiable originals, often models of good nature, whose little peculiarities are not morally instructive, but objects of delight and love.' This represented a rejection of 'ill-natured' wit and the promotion of 'cheerfulness and innocent mirth'.[41] A mode of humour of this nature left no place for the raucous, incontinent, buffoonish, somewhat edgy idiot of the previous century.

In the pages of *Punch* the idiot became from the very beginning not an eighteenth-century jestbook-type individual, blundering their way through the complexities of urban, or indeed rural, life, but an anonymous type who functioned as a comic device to pass sardonic comment on the rest of society. The right of the monarch to appropriate the land of idiots simply became a joke vehicle to express the ironic concern that the sovereign would make idiots of all the lords and thus appropriate all their assets.[42] The appellation 'idiot' became a catch-all term to deride those of whom *Punch* writers disapproved, one rooted in its original form but now transmuted into a form of insult aimed at the non-idiot. Labelled as idiots by *Punch* were campaigning humanitarians, judged to be in need of the very charitable support to idiots for which they had campaigned. When the Earl of Shaftesbury (an early campaigner for idiot asylums) presented a petition in 1855 from teetotallers to prohibit brewing in the United Kingdom, 'Mr Punch' trusted that 'the names of the unfortunate creatures have been obtained from the clerk of the House by the Idiots Friend Society'.[43] Similar derision was directed at the National Temperance League, with *Punch* expressing surprise that its members were not 'cared for in any asylum for idiots'.[44] The very idea of an idiot asylum, from its beginnings in 1847,[45] was seen by *Punch* writers as a perpetual and ever-giving comic gift. The whole editorial staff of the *United Irishman* should be transferred there and 'put under kind medical treatment', they jibed, as should 'the correspondents of the *Morning Advertiser*'.[46] A shambolic piece of work on local drains by the Board of Works brought the asylum for idiots to Mr Punch's mind,[47] while some assistants from the Idiots' Asylum needed to be brought in by the Humane Society, claimed Mr Punch, to stop idiotic members of the public from skating on dangerously thin ice.[48] News that idiots from the asylum were being taught music was an opportunity to swipe at foreign musicians 'of limited intellect'.[49] After a four-part song called 'The Idiot Boy' was sung at an Earlswood Idiot Asylum fundraising dinner, *Punch* suggested that 'The Cork Leg' should be sung at surgical hospital dinners.[50] Any egregious performance by a politician was greeted by the call: 'will the Secretary to the Asylum for Idiots inform us whether there is a vacancy at Earlswood?'[51]

All this presented the idiot not as a living being on the streets, in homes and in communities but as a distant category, an object of charity and institutionalized care and an easy catalyst for genteel humour at others' expense. The idiot in this way was not thought of as an individual at all but became a descriptor for any person or group of people that excited the disdainful pity, irritation or loathing of the writer. Their new status as barely considered charitable object was neatly summed up in an 1877 *Punch* cartoon where a monocled, top-hatted young man addressed an elegant young lady:

'Going to the Throat and Ear Ball, Lady Mary?'
   'No—we are engaged to the Incurable Idiots.'
   'Then perhaps I may meet you at the Epileptic Dance on Saturday?'
   'Oh yes—we are sure to be there. The Epileptic Stewards are so delightful!'[52]

The cleansing process of the moral drive for urban discipline and order had relegated the idiot to a hidden site for incurables, while those who made them an object of their fashionable philanthropy were barely aware of their existence. In its first edition in 1841, *Punch* referred to itself as 'an asylum for the millions of perishing puns which are now wandering about without so much as a shelf to rest upon'.[53] It was an apt metaphor, as, in the words of Gatrell, 'humour itself was beginning to be taught good manners.'[54] As jokes were brought into the new reforming and well-mannered asylum of comedy, so idiots began to gather, or be gathered, within the containing, improving and reforming walls of their own institutions.

Gathering pace also was the new form of the novel, adopting a realist construction and leaving behind the picaresque, digressive, rambling eighteenth-century productions of Henry Fielding, John Cleland, Tobias Smollett, Laurence Sterne and the army of more obscure 'ramble' fiction writers. The novel became a new arena for idiot characterization. These new characters were far

An upper-class couple discuss their fundraising efforts for the 'incurable idiots', illustration in *Punch; or, The London Charivari*, 23 June 1877.

more integrated into the plot than the occasional idiot character who cropped up for comic effect, then just as rapidly disappeared, in Smollett and Fielding. They were more ideologically meaningful than the handsome, fornicating Tom Fool or Will and Dick in *Fanny Hill*. Most notably, Charles Dickens introduced a new sentimental, piteous, good-hearted but ultimately doomed form of idiot in the character of Smike in his novel *Nicholas Nickleby*, first published as a monthly serial aimed at the widest possible market in 1838.[55]

Smike, the dog-like idiotic youth, is first abused by the appalling Squeers family at their brutal Yorkshire school, where he is used as their servant. He is, as Wackford Squeers puts it, 'a nasty, ungrateful, pig-headed, brutish, obstinate dog'.[56] Rescued by Nicholas, he responds with the canine qualities of blind affection and loyalty, following Nicholas 'with an ever-restless desire to serve or help him . . . content only to be near him. He would sit beside him for hours looking patiently into his face.'[57] The 'poor creature' Smike, with his 'unmeaning stupefied gaze',[58] becomes doomed at the point when, in an unfamiliar environ-ment of kindness and pity, those feeble thoughts are able to turn to himself, who he is, and how he relates to others. The change in him is noticed first by the portrait painter Miss La Creevy, who of course has acute insight into Smike's physiognomy and in whom he excites strong feelings of pity: 'I have watched him and he has brought the tears into my eyes many times.'[59] She has noticed that the effect of the environment of kindness in which he is now nurtured is that:

> since he has been here, he has grown . . . more con-scious of his weak intellect. He feels it more. It gives him greater pain to know that he . . . cannot understand simple things. Not three weeks ago, he was a light-hearted busy creature . . . as happy as the day is long. Now he is another being – the same willing, harmless, loving creature – but the same in nothing else.[60]

When he becomes loved, Smike reacts by feeling love himself, for Kate, Nicholas's sister. This is, however, a death sentence, for Smike has enough capacity to understand that this love cannot be reciprocated: his is the human love of a man for a woman, but utterly futile because it comes from one who is not a full man. Kate's is the tender pity of the sentimental being for the poor creature. Smike allows himself to die, pining away until, on his final day, he is carried, childlike, by Nicholas to a beautiful spot and laid down to breathe his last: 'there was little pain, little uneasiness, but there was no rallying, no effort, no struggle for life.' Kate marries, as does Nicholas, and they and their chil-dren are able to enjoy Smike in his most palatable form, as a tender memory. His death was just and necessary, as Charles Cheeryble, the archetypal amiable humorist, assures Nicholas:

> Every day that this poor lad had lived, he must have been less and less qualified for the world, and more unhappy

H. K. Browne, 'Nicholas instructs Smike in the art of acting', drawing for Charles Dickens's novel, *Nicholas Nickleby* (1839). Smike was presented by Dickens as an imbecile character with dog-like qualities of affection and loyalty.

in his own deficiencies. It is better as it is, my dear sir. Yes, yes, yes, it's better as it is.[61]

Nicholas can only agree: '"I had thought of all that, sir," replied Nicholas . . . "I feel it, I assure you."'[62]

There is the suggestion here from Dickens that the idiot who knows himself can only wish for death. Better to be the unaware, grinning, fatuous idiot than the imbecile who knows just enough to understand their place in the world; abused or pitied according to happenstance, but even in the tenderest of environments unable to know real human feelings and relations. It is the duty of the knowing idiot to take themselves out of the society of others, for the pity they excite is only a burden to the good, the loathing they draw from others a misery for them and a degradation of the social fabric. Dickens acknowledged and developed this thinking fourteen years later in his *Household Words* periodical. He recalled his own childhood encounter with idiocy:

> a shambling knock-kneed man who was never a child, with an eager utterance of discordant sounds which he seemed to keep in his protruding forehead, a tongue too large for his mouth, and a dreadful pair of hands that wanted to ramble over everything, our own face included.[63]

What should be done with these human creatures? Dickens pondered. Was each idiot simply 'a hopeless, irreclaimable, unimprovable being'?[64] Consigning such human types to lunatic asylums or workhouses would not alter their place in the imagination. They would still be 'wallowing in the lowest depths of degradation and neglect: a miserable monster, whom nobody may put to death, but whom everyone must wish dead, and be distressed to see alive'.[65] Without proper intervention, the idiot 'must always remain an object of pitiable isolation'.[66]

As Dickens expressed what he saw as a universal wish for the death of the idiot in the public mind, he strongly interwove notions of both pity and loathing. He described the familiar common assumptions about idiot appearance and the incontinence of the idiot body, with the flexed knock-knees, the sloping forehead, the uncontrolled mouth, the protruding tongue, uninhibited rambling hands and of course the jabbering, nonsensical sounds. Such a being was pitiable, but the effect of the pity they excited was distressing. It was the irredeemable hopelessness of their disgusting body and way of being that united pity and loathing in a desire for the death of the 'pitiable object'. Smike, when first observed by Nicholas, was filthy, ragged, lame, with 'nervous wandering fingers' and a vacant look.[67] Even when cleaned up, tenderly treated and under the pitying gaze of Nicholas and his circle, his death was still the most merciful solution. However, Dickens now proclaimed, in the face of a merciful death there had arisen a chance of redemption. His *Household Words* article of 1853 promoted the idea of the specialist idiot asylum, inspired by the work of Seguin in Paris and recently established in Britain as small experimental institutions in Highgate and Essex from 1847 (precursors to the much larger Earlswood Asylum for Idiots from 1855). He listed the remarkable discoveries that had emerged from this practice of removing the idiot from the society where they caused so much distress, to the controlled, educating and reforming space of the specialist institution.

According to Dickens, some long-suspected attributes of idiocy had been established as 'truths' through the study of the idiot class that these closed sites had enabled. Idiots 'suffer less from physical pain than beings of a finer organisation' and 'are found below the average sensitiveness to the electric battery'. Moreover, 'the contemplation of death does not distress them.'[68] However, new things had been learned also. Some idiots had remarkable gifts – for copying designs, rhyming, performing music and sewing buttons, for example. They had enough dim religious impressions to have some 'instinctive aspirations' towards God. An approaching thunderstorm could disorder the stomachs of a whole asylum.[69] Dickens thought, at least, that these were new 'discoveries'. Yet in fact the wise fool with special talents; the ape-like imitative fool; the fool with unmediated access to God through their simplicity; the incontinent idiot over-influenced by nature: all of these were enduring and long-lasting myths and representations of idiocy. They had, however, been repackaged and re-presented as new expertise and knowledge, from inside the asylum walls. As Patrick McDonagh has noted, 'occasionally, older concepts of idiocy resurface within newer frameworks, or simply refuse to disappear. Indeed these older concepts often determine the shape taken by newer ideas.'[70] The dominant new idea was that segregation was the answer to the idiot 'problem'.

At the heart of the redemptive salvation that Dickens believed the specialist idiot asylum could offer the doomed and dying idiot lay the doctrine of improvement. Here the wildness of the savage idiot could be colonized, tamed and safely pitied. Young men who could not read books or talk coherently learned to mend watches to a high degree of skill. Others became builders of fine model ships.[71] As 'improvement' set in, under a regime of order, discipline, training and culture, even the loathsome appearance of idiots would transform into something of beauty:

> Although this poor creature had been gradually becoming more dwarf-like and deformed ever since her birth, she now advanced rapidly towards a perfect development . . . Her muscles strengthened with her growth, the skin became elastic, and attained the usual degree of warmth, the wrinkles of the face vanished, the old-woman expression disappeared, and the pleasing traces of youth became apparent.[72]

The specialist asylum solved the idiot paradox, protecting society from idiot dangerousness and protecting the vulnerable idiot from the dangers of the sophisticated, trickstering, huckstering world of the mid-nineteenth century. It was a place of transformation, where loathsomeness was removed, function restored, talent inspired and separation from the corrupting world maintained.

The need for such a protecting and transforming institutional vehicle had been laid out in Dickens's characterization of Barnaby Rudge, the eponymous hero of his 1841 novel. Written just two years after the novelization of *Nicholas Nickleby*, *Barnaby Rudge* portrayed a very different sort of idiot. The book was Dickens's imagining of the eighteenth century, via the tumultuous anti-Catholic Gordon Riots of 1780. Barnaby, caught up in the riots, is an idiot, but of what sort? From the beginning, for all his loveable innocence and naivety, he carries an underlying menace with his unnerving, wild, restless energy. 'If only I could but tame down that terrible restlessness,' complains his benighted and suffering mother.[73] There is a hint of deception behind his innocent presentation. Gabriel Varden, the kindly, deeply bourgeois lockmaker and protector of the Rudges, speculates: 'take care, when we are growing old and foolish, Barnaby doesn't put us all to the blush.' Barnaby's pale face is 'strangely lighted up, by something which was not intellect'.[74] This rumbling sense of threat is exacerbated by the one deep relationship that Barnaby holds: not with a human but with his faithful, if sinister, talking pet raven, Grip.

Barnaby oscillates between a pitiable, permanent child and a frightening, unfathomable, threatening presence. His potential for cunning is constantly stressed, even as a baby, when he was 'so ghastly and unchildlike in its cunning . . . old and elfin-like in face'.[75] A subtle narrative of both pity and loathing for Barnaby is threaded through the novel. As Barnaby is manipulated to join the riots, he demonstrates awesome violence and becomes admired by the mob. He is only fighting because he sees those he thinks are friends under attack. He has no understanding of the riot's politics. At the end he walks bravely, but uncomprehendingly, to his execution, only to gain a last-moment reprieve secured by Gabriel Varden. Bourgeois respectability rescues him from the consequences of his calamitous involvement with wild mob disorder. Dickens's message is both a paradox and very clear: the world is too dangerous a place for the idiot, and the idiot too dangerous a person for the world. Barnaby, we are told after his reprieve, would never set foot in London again, his inner wildness and the city's turbulence too toxic a mixture. An invisible but controlling spatial boundary has been placed around him.

There is a salutary parallel between *Barnaby Rudge* and Tobias Smollett's novel *The Adventures of Roderick Random*,

J. Yaeger, engraving
of Dickens's Barnaby
Rudge, 1841, shown
as simultaneously
vulnerable and
dangerous.

published in 1748 and greatly admired by Dickens despite what he called its 'lack of tenderness'. In one incident, Random and his faithful, if dense, sidekick Strap, while asleep in an inn room, are terrified by a monstrous raven, followed by a very old white-bearded man who cries inhumanly: 'where is Ralpho? where is Ralpho?' Strap and Random are both left quivering in fear, convinced they have seen ghosts. They find the next morning that the old man is an idiot who lives at the inn and was trying to reclaim his pet raven, Ralpho.[76] The episode has no real point other than to ridicule all involved – Random, Strap, the idiot and the raven. There is certainly no tenderness, no pity, and yet the idiot remains, a part of the inn and daily life, laughed at but not despised or loathed. Perhaps Ralpho gave Dickens the idea of a raven companion for Barnaby, but Barnaby and Grip were a very different pairing. There was much tenderness and pity for this uncomprehending idiot, only able to communicate with a bird, but also a constant drumbeat of menace, danger and wild loathsomeness. Barnaby's wildness is tamed following his escape from execution; he becomes neutered and fit for pity. Grip, quieter also, stays by his side. For Grip the cage beckons, for Barnaby the asylum. The ridiculing but tolerant insouciance of one hundred years earlier had disappeared. Idiocy had become a disturbing and serious business. A long distance had been travelled from the clean-limbed, stout and pretty Will and Dick of Fanny Hill's acquaintance.

In his later visit to the small Park House Asylum for Idiots in Highgate, London, which inspired his *Household Words* article, Dickens found just the place for Barnaby. It would also have suited Smike, who could have passed his days there happily learning skills and being helpful, without harbouring dangerous notions of love across the unfathomable divide between the sound and unsound mind. The *Household Words* article ended with a stirring call: 'We hope, through the instrumentality of these establishments, to see the day, before long, when the pauper idiot will be similarly provided for, at the public expense.' Then, speculated Dickens, we may be able to change the oft-quoted line from *Macbeth*, 'a tale, told by an idiot ... Signifying nothing'. In future, he predicted, the tale of an idiot will tell *something*.[77] The asylum will have transformed what was useless into something useful.

Idiot characters fascinated Victorian writers, who conceived them as a problem, transforming the harmless figures of fun of eighteenth-century fiction and coding them with heavy symbolic meanings. In George Eliot's novella *Brother Jacob* (1860) the eponymous Jacob, a 'very healthy and well developed idiot', is a classically ambivalent Victorian portrayal.[78] He inadvertently foils the plans of his brother 'Zavy' (David), who has stolen money from their parents, established a booming confectionary shop under a false name and arranged to marry into a wealthy merchant family. Jacob, an archetypal, ever-hungry yokel idiot wearing a smock and carrying a pitchfork, bursts into David's shop one day, hugging him tightly and gorging on his pies and sweets. He never lets go of his pitchfork. David's deception is unmasked as a result and he is jeered out of the town, his business ruined. Like Barnaby, Jacob is endearingly innocent and gullible but simultaneously dangerous, evident in his menacing pitchfork and his propensity to violence if thwarted in his animal desires. His innocence and truthfulness unmask the lies and manipulations of his evil brother. Yet Jacob also represents something else. David's confectionary business has changed the town. Housewives and maids no longer cook but buy luxurious prepared foods instead. This leaves them, dangerously, with time on their hands as a new consumer-oriented capitalist spirit threatens the social order and challenges assumptions about women. The actions of the simpleton Jacob restore the old order, the shop closes and the women start to cook again. For Eliot the danger of this idiot was that while he may have represented a lovable traditional past, he was also a threat to progress with his timeless, unchanging ways.

Elizabeth Gaskell's Will, in her short story 'Half a Lifetime Ago' (1855), is another idiot laden with deeply symbolic meanings. Always simple, he lapses into full-blown idiocy after an attack of fever. His put-upon, androgynous hill-farming sister Susan, who in her father's words had 'more of a man in her than her delicate little brother ever would have', sacrifices everything to care for him. She loses her fiancé, never marries, does not have the children she longed for and lives a formidably tough and isolated life with her idiot charge, deep in the inhospitable hills. Lancaster Asylum beckons: 'they've ways there both of keeping people in order and making them happy,' a doctor suggests. Susan resists, doggedly retaining her care of her idiot brother while she loses all else from her life. The emasculated idiot is again presented as a sluggish obstacle to progress. His presence in the family home brings to an end a bloodline, prevents new birth and blocks the agricultural progress Susan's fiancé would have brought. The fiancé has plans for the farm but cannot bear even the presence of Will: 'of late he had absolutely loathed him. His gibbering, his uncouth gestures, his loose shambling gait, all irritated Michael inexpressibly.' The modernizing Michael presses for Will's admission to an asylum, but in vain, and so he takes his modernizing ways elsewhere. Susan's pity for her helpless brother fuels Michael's loathing and a family is consigned to history, pushed under by the weight of their 'great lunging clumsy' offspring.[79]

Over the nineteenth century, therefore, the idiot was at the heart of new sites of concern and anxiety, seen as a disconcerting symbolic threat by fiction writers and marginalized in magazines as a distant occupant of institutions. The same process was evident in visual representation. As the raucous, shambolic street life of Georgian caricature, in which the idiot had played a small walk-on part, disappeared, new realms of public concern were given visual form. Racial and class anxieties, sometimes combined, came to the fore. The low type, representing inferior classes in general, was represented with prominent cheeks and large nose, mouth and jaws, but also 'a darker skin which emphasises the white of the eyes and teeth . . . a prognathous Africanoid type'.[80] Henry Mayhew, in his 1840s studies of the London poor later published as *London Labour and the London Poor*, viewed London street people in 'specifically anthropological terms . . . [as] a vagabond "race" whose physiological and psychological characteristics distinguished them from the respectable ranks of society'.[81] The poverty of these 'nomad' people became inextricably linked with criminality and low intelligence in a newly racialized paradigm.[82] Political anxieties also intruded into this complex mix. As agitation for Irish home rule grew, particularly when fuelled by extra-political violence, the caricature of the innocent if simple-minded 'Paddy' of eighteenth-century comic art became first a visibly degenerate man and then 'an ape-like monster bent on murder or outrage'.[83]

This creation of a general idiot type imbued with menacing class and racial characteristics displaced the earlier specific comic idiot, harmlessly present but detached, as depicted by Gillray, Rowlandson and Cruikshank. New, very specific idiot characters now appeared, not at the margins of the representation but very much at its heart. The first was as a problematic group who had come to public attention as a result of political and social changes, and therefore required some sort of socio-political response. In William Heath's 'Canvassing' of 1830, reflecting the pressure for wider electoral participation that was to result in the Reform Act two years later, a clearly reluctant politician woos the vote of a grotesque washerwoman. With her are her two children, one of them 'an imbecile',[84] an overweight, slope-headed child, hands dangling in front of his belly, gazing vacantly at the visiting politician. The other child is a bawling baby. 'How are all your sweet darling children?' the politician asks his potential constituent. The anxiety expressed in this satire – apart from the obvious point about the duplicity and mendacity of smiling politicians – was the accumulation of rights by the degenerate poor, including

William Heath, 'Canvassing', 1830, hand-coloured etching of a politician wooing the vote of an obese washerwoman with an imbecile child.

W. Ridgway, after Thomas Webster, 'Schoolboys arriving at school, showing different attitudes', 1862, engraving depicting idiotic-looking children waiting to go into school amid fears about widening access to education.

their idiot offspring, and the damage that this would inflict on the political and social fabric. Thomas Webster's print 'Going to School' (1862) contrasts a group of children on their way into a schoolroom. The critic in the *Art Journal* noted the intelligent look of one boy, sitting by the door with a well-formed forehead and cranium, and contrasted him with the boy about to enter, head sloped over a primer, 'whose half-idiotic countenance testifies to his mental calibre; he is poring over his allotted task, but it is clearly beyond his grasp.'[85] The critic also noted his 'bull-dog' physiognomy, his low forehead, poor cranium and heavy lower jaw.[86] The underlying anxiety caused by the idiot here was that widening access to education for the poor would create the problem of attempting to improve the unimprovable mind. This took place within the context of the build-up to the 1870 Education Act, which created a framework for the education of all children aged between five and twelve. In such an environment, idiots could no longer be left to themselves to muddle through on the streets. The gaze of the concerned political and middle classes fell on them as political and educational reforms brought them into focus. They did not like what they saw.

Greater public focus produced the third new cultural arena to which the idiot migrated, that of the observed object of clinical and scientific interest. This was expressed in visual form by ostensibly anatomically correct drawings of idiot types, particularly Cretins from the Alpine region (people with congenital hypothyroidism, who were particularly concentrated in the Swiss Alps region at this time). Gentleman travellers brought back and displayed their drawings like any exploring ethnographer. As can be seen in the engraving of a Cretin by the alpinist, artist and explorer Edward Whymper, there was a dual purpose to these representations. They were ostensibly to inform, through close clinical observation and reproduction, scientific classification of idiot types. They also had the deliberate effect of shock and titillation as they laid bare the abject, loathsome deformity of the cretin and other types for a curious public.

Medical men began to construct narratives about idiocy that gave a foundation to their claim to control, manage and treat these idiot types. These improvement narratives always involved 'wild', repellent, abject idiots being brought into the asylum environment and transforming as they responded to the disciplined institutional regimen, which sparked activity in their dull, unutilized brains. In his *Household Words* article of 1853 Dickens recounted stories from Johann Guggenbühl, the medical man who had created an asylum in the mountains for the Swiss 'Cretin' population and remarkable transformations that had occurred at the Paris Bicêtre.[87] His stories were redemptive, involving miserable, filthy and physically repugnant idiots brought in from the brink of a lonely death on the outside, and miraculously transformed inside. The Christian underpinnings of these parables were sometimes overt. According to Dickens it was Guggenbühl's observation in 1839 of 'a poor Crétin muttering a prayer before a crucifix' that convinced the Swiss physician to devote his life to the study and care of the Cretin population.[88]

Edward Whymper, 'A Crétin of Aosta', 1871, wood engraving
of a thyroid-deficient physically 'cretinous' beggar.

The improvement narrative reached its apotheosis in *The
Mind Unveiled*, a work published in 1858 by the American asylum
superintendent Isaac Newton Kerlin.[89] The introduction set out
what the book would reveal: 'Among the greatest discoveries of
the present century is the fact that Idiots may be redeemed, from

their sorrowing night of ignorance and degradation, to enjoy the light of knowledge, and become co-laborers with their more favoured fellow-men.'[90] The redemptive parables that followed were very clear about the necessary ingredients for improvement, but also showed how limited that improvement would be. It would take place only within the calming, secure walls of the asylum, where previous mischiefs and degradations would be confronted and eradicated and replaced with compliance and the ability to apply menial and practical skills. This could only happen with high levels of control and submission. The first chapter, featuring the journey of Beckie, 'our little mute girl', and the wild, crippled Bessie, is entitled 'Our Household Pets'.[91] Both have become compliant, domesticated and submissive from wild beginnings, captured, tamed and trained. The narrative is of Beckie the wild half-child, half-animal, captured by the intrepid explorers of medical science:

> She was in the grove, alone; and carried in her little clenched fingers, a quantity of sticks and stones . . . her form was crouched, and she moved about among the leaves, apparently in search of something. But on our approach, she bounded away with the grace and lightness of a startled gazelle. We followed her and after much coaching and many manoeuvers, succeeded in getting her to approach.[92]

Violent, slapping, biting, mute and with foetid breath, she is brought into the asylum. Within months, the transformation has occurred, and 'our little prodigy' is now 'more gentle and obedient, answering with a smile, when before she gave a pitiful contortion of countenance'.[93] She knows her alphabet, can read some words and count to fifteen. But Kerlin made the limitations clear: 'mentally she is a progressing child of four years, instead of eight.'[94] He made his readers aware that, despite the miraculous salvation achieved by the asylum, full transformation to ordinary human status could not be managed. The 'household pet' would remain just that, safe in the comforting hands of its owners, at risk if allowed back out into the wild.

Kerlin's narratives of 1858 marked a new resting place for the idiot in the long cultural journey they had made since the easy-going eighteenth-century characterization as the amusing, buffoonish characters of joke, slang and caricature. That idiot, however boneheaded, stupefied, drooling or rambling, had been largely tolerated and indulged. They caused amusement and invited affection in eighteenth-century society, and if they did attract hostility, abuse and violence this was neither universal or even habitual. Hostility was always counterbalanced by those who saw them differently and were protective towards them. Sometimes, if handsome, they could even be objects of desire. To be laughed at and ridiculed was not an experience exclusive to idiots in the eighteenth century, when everyone including the over-educated, genius and pompous was a target for satire. Laughter was a human transaction that marked a person's belonging rather than their marginalization, however unpleasant and distressing it could undoubtedly be at times. The idiot was most definitely there, in the heart of communities, even if peripheral and sometimes barely noticed. As the era of the nineteenth century began, all this started to change, a change signalled most markedly by Wordsworth's 'Idiot Boy' in 1798. The idiot started to become no longer a laughing matter but an object of pity and loathing, sometimes simultaneously.

These changes, discernible in the late eighteenth and early nineteenth centuries, accelerated from the 1830s. What happened? Certainly humour changed in a radical way, from the roar at the ridiculous that characterized most of the eighteenth century to 'the polite points of wit', as Thackeray called them, 'which cause one to smile in a quiet, gentlemanlike kind of way'.[95] As idiots departed, barely noticed, from the joke book, street slang, caricature and the comic corners of long-forgotten ramble fiction, they were adopted into new cultural codes. They reappeared in the 'amiable humorist' magazines such as *Punch* as much more distant figures, a formalized grouping, inhabitants of unseen asylums who provided good fuel for a joke at the expense of politicians and other civil wrongdoers. They occupied a more central role in novels but were now imbued with heavy symbolic meanings, signallers of nineteenth-century anxieties about rapid social change and disorder and a 'deepening wish to control, moralise and pathologise those who defied that process'.[96] Idiots in fiction became usually an object of pity, and certainly not an object of laughter. Yet the pitiful feelings exerted on them by the sentimental went unreciprocated, causing a growing sense of loathing for these insensible, unthinking, morally and physically deformed beings. They began to be subject to the curious, somewhat surprised stare of politicians and educationalists who now found themselves entangled with the lower orders, including its dullest members, to a greater extent than they had previously anticipated, as wider suffrage and universal education loomed. At the same time the medical gaze, keen to cure everything, and seeking new objects of control and treatment, slowly turned on them. This placed the idiot in yet another cultural arena, the discovery and improvement narrative of the scientific study. What the laissez-faire, parochial, corrupt and disorderly eighteenth century had been unable or unwilling to achieve, the new scientific professionalism and orderliness of the nineteenth century would accomplish. The idiot would be taken off the streets, cleaned up, confronted and transformed into a compliant creature of the asylum.

Why did these changes happen? The idiot was caught by a convergence of factors that radically shifted their place in the collective consciousness. First, manners changed, and with them the criteria for social acceptability became more complex and demanding. Bodily control and the control of emotions became the accepted social norm. This did not mean that everybody transformed into a polite, mannerly, morally upright citizen, but most understood what was expected of them and could choose whether to comply. For the small group who could not understand the expectations, this transformation in manners became an alienating and marginalizing process.

Second, the humanitarian, universalist spirit inspired by both the Enlightenment and the American and French revolutions had some unexpected consequences. As the liberating gaze of young revolutionaries like Wordsworth fell onto the hitherto peripheral idiot, they expected to find beauty, heroic simplicity, unsullied natural innocence and an inner sensibility that belied the stuttering, burring exterior. When they looked, as Coleridge pointed out, these things were not there, certainly not in the form they wanted them to be. Where, Coleridge asked in exasperation, was the idiot boy's beauty?[97] The idiot would pay dearly for this perceived lack of heroic inner beauty in the eyes of the Romantic humanitarian. They became people who could not live with the rest, lacking the inner self that conveyed personhood, trapped in their loathsome bodies and limited minds. This meant either death, as understood and chosen by Dickens's Smike when he became aware of his fundamental human inadequacies, or separation. Only in the parallel, closed, artificial world of the asylum could the idiot realize those few small bodily skills that they possessed and become the tamed, loveable if limited household pets described by Isaac Kerlin. The idiot became defined by their suffering and pain, which caused revulsion in the pitying observer. Looking at an idiot, a monstrous cretin, became almost an act of titillating pornographic taboo.[98] The wild, degraded idiot, discovered wandering in the glades and forests of the improvement narratives, was a titillating sight indeed, a savage needing to be seized, controlled and dominated.

In summary, the change in manners, the widening of the franchise, the extension of education and the humanitarian impulse all led to idiots and those like them becoming seen as a problem. From living unseen and accepted in communities, they became topical, of interest, and the effect of this formal scrutiny was to classify them as different and then distance them from the communities within which they had hitherto lived. Idiots became seen as a threat to both the Enlightenment ideal of the free and reasonable citizen and the Romantic ideal of simple inner beauty, a problem and no longer a laughing matter.[99] The high walls of the asylum offered an alluring solution for this disturbing group and the unease they caused to the modern sensibility.

6

Colonies, Anthropologists and Asylums: Race and Intelligence

Enlightenment thinkers, obsessed with trying to 'define' the peoples they were encountering beyond the shores of Europe, had initiated a raft of false ideas that, by the beginning of the nineteenth century, starkly conflated race and intelligence. Intelligence was now located on a sliding scale from the 'perfected' mind of the white European down to the lowest form of dark-skinned, 'savage' human. Practitioners of the so-called science of man linked those they saw as savages to those they saw as idiots, and those they saw as barbarians to those they saw as imbeciles. As the British Empire expanded, a new concept of 'racial intelligence' began to emerge. This provided explanations for a host of puzzling phenomena, such as modes of living that differed radically from European norms, global cultural and moral variations, and the indifference of non-Europeans to European values and belief systems. To differ in these ways from the European was, many Europeans believed, to display a lack of mental faculty, the degree of mental deficit determined by the degree of 'strangeness' that separated the savage or barbarian from the European. This linking of racial variation to mental deficit also, of course, validated European legal claims to non-European territory and resources and justified domination of native peoples by European interlopers. Further, it confirmed the superiority of European civilization as the highest stage in a global process of mental and social development that placed the white European male at its apex.[1]

This newly racialized idea of the savage idiot and the barbarian imbecile rode on the assumption that non-white people lacked reasoning power, which deprived them of the powers of abstraction, idea formation or moral behaviour. This meant that they had no capacity to govern themselves. Like idiots, they were perceived as slothful, indolent, indifferent and impervious to pain and discomfort. Some, those designated savage, were seen as irredeemably idiotic, even in appearance, and were thought to live naked, animalistic and aimless lives. Others, those designated barbarian, were defined as more advanced imbeciles. Such people showed some signs of basic reasoning, government, affective relations and practical ingenuity, but their fierceness, recklessness, cruelty and inability to control their passions left them in a semi-civilized, half-brained developmental space between the savage and the civilized person.

From the early nineteenth century, as trade and colonial empires grew, the number of Europeans encountering non-Europeans grew. What had been largely observational and speculative (if highly influential) thinking in the eighteenth century strengthened into harsher, more politicized and increasingly moral framings of the populations under the European gaze. The observers themselves changed, from wide-eyed, relentlessly curious explorers and natural scientists on voyages of discovery, to world-weary administrators, moralizing missionaries and settlers bedding in for the long term. A new 'high moral tone' began to suppress any discernible 'relaxed co-existence' between the newly arrived and the indigenous.[2] The attitude to idiocy at this time also became harsher and more politicized. Groups not previously considered problematic were drawn into the sphere of public policy, under an increasingly intense medical and political gaze. Medico-legal theorists identified loathsome helplessness in the idiot and dangerous amorality and criminality in the imbecile. In this way two sets of ideas, newly formed myths, began to converge into a single belief system. The link between helpless idiots and indolent savages, and amoral imbeciles and unrestrained barbarians, was becoming embedded in the European mind. Theorists of the science of man and mental scientists reinforced one another's beliefs about race and intelligence and began to present those beliefs as certain scientific fact.

Travellers had observed what they viewed as a lack of foresight, a tendency to live for the moment, in indigenous populations, characteristics which they claimed distinguished them radically from Europeans. A general 'unconcern for futurity' was attributed to a lack of reasoning power: 'to forego present ease for future advantage . . . can only be suggested by cultivated reason.'[3] At the end of the eighteenth century, Watkin Tench complained from Sydney that 'like all other Indians, the impulse of the moment is alone regarded by them . . . one day must be very like another in the life of a savage.'[4] This idea of the listless, live-for-the-moment idiot-savage persisted and began to carry with it a threat of impulsive dangerousness. When James Hingston Tuckey led a naval expedition to explore the Zaire River (now the Congo River) in 1816, he warned his crew that in 'that state of savage nature which marks the people of . . . newly discovered countries . . . the impulse of the moment is the only principle of action.' For this reason, the crew would need to be 'guarded in our intercourse with them . . . showing we are prepared to resist aggression'.[5] There was also an expectation that any savages encountered would be 'addicted to theft'.[6] This unmeasured, unplanned existence became an indicator of a permanent absence of any moral system and therefore a godless and irredeemable life. John West, chaplain to the Hudson's Bay Company, wrote in 1824: 'generation after generation have passed away in gross ignorance . . . all is gross darkness within them as to futurity, and they wander through life.'[7] The idiot-savage came to be perceived as outside time itself as conceived by the European: 'time is of no value for an African,' wrote the Franco-American explorer Paul Du Chaillu in 1861.[8] To stand outside time implied absence from any fixity in place, and from the claims of ownership and entitlement that this could bring.

All this conformed with uncanny exactness to the developing Euro-American medicalized notion of the idiot, as described by Isaac Ray in 1839: 'nothing leads them to act but the faint impressions of the moment.'[9] Idiots, Ray explained, 'are particularly deficient in forethought'.[10] They lived what he described as an 'automatic life . . . utterly unchanged by external circumstances, and scarcely indicating the species to which they belong'.[11] This unthinking sensuality carried the danger of amorality: 'various propensities, such as the sexual feelings, cunning and destructiveness, they often manifest in an inordinate degree of vigour and activity.'[12] In such ways, savagery and idiocy became locked together, both human types imagined to have no sense of time, eternally wandering, always threatening to unleash a set of violent and sexual passions untouched by any moral code. This perception removed non-white peoples so far from the so-called civilized person, fixed in place and cognisant of time, that their very status as a human was in doubt. Maria Nugent, wife of the governor of Jamaica, recalled a 'coloured lady' attending her, who 'told me that she was twenty-four years old, and shewed me her grand-child. I found afterwards that she was fifty-four; they have no idea of time and distance.'[13] When, in Harriet Beecher Stowe's *Uncle Tom's Cabin* (1852), the fiery, uncontrolled young slave girl Topsy is asked about her origins by Miss Ophelia, she replies that she has no age and no mother and, indeed, denies having been born. Idiots and savages were regarded as outside time and space, strangers to the conceptual universe of developed whites.[14] It was what Fodéré called 'the obliteration of ideas'.[15]

This characterization of idiots and imbeciles, and of savages and barbarians, as dangerous proceeded in parallel, with a shared language and assumptions. For the missionary West, in the wild untameability of the Native American child was seen 'the secret spring of his character. He is a murderer by habit, engendered from his earliest age.'[16] Early encounters painted a picture of non-white people as simple, amiably grinning innocents; and this now came to be seen as a deception, masking an unpredictable and pitiless violence. In Jamaica, Maria Nugent, while observing 'the short-lived and baby-like pleasures' of the slaves during their Christmas Day celebrations, also noted nervously the news seeping in from Haiti of atrocities against the white population, and the restless bustle of the local slaves at this news. Their childlike characters were no longer innocent but indicative of a dangerous, immature addiction to turbulence: 'like children they are fond of fuss and noise and have no reflection.'[17] John West (a different John West to the one working as a missionary among Native Americans) in his 1852 *History of Tasmania* mocked the early colonists who found their 'new acquaintances . . . peaceful, light-hearted and obliging' and were charmed by their simplicity. They would eventually discover, he crowed, that they were 'improvident, importunate, and intrusive . . . rapacious and mischievous . . . treacherous and blood-thirsty'.[18]

The same drumbeat of dangerousness pervaded medical writing on idiocy; the same transition from amiable simpleton to amoral criminal. Fodéré's 'charlatans and rascals' became, for Georget, an entire hidden criminal class, with 'only vague or imperfect notions of social duties and justice . . . a group of limited beings supplying the courts, the prisons and the scaffolds'.[19] The danger lay in the impetuosity of the unreflective mind: 'the stupid person acts precipitately and without reflection,' wrote Ray. They were subject to 'gusts of passion' and had a 'propensity to . . . misanthropy' coupled with 'an advanced sentiment of cunning' and a 'ferocity of disposition'.[20] Their lack of foresight excluded all sense of accountability or consciousness of wrong.[21] The savage idiot, said Beck, was possessed of 'feelings of irresistible violence leading to criminality'.[22]

Who should be defined as an idiot-savage and who as an imbecile-barbarian became more concerning for Europeans as undeniable evidence of the advances of civilization in lands such as India and China emerged. Explanations of how 'lower' races could achieve such a level of human development were needed. James Mill's *History of British India* (published in 1817 and written without Mill ever visiting India or knowing any of its languages) acknowledged that Hindus had made some intellectual advances to some form of political system and 'passed through this first stage in the way to civilization'.[23] For Mill these advances were essentially a mental journey, 'instructive to those who would understand the human mind, and the laws, which, amidst all the different forms of civil society, invariably preside over its progress'.[24] Like imbeciles, who could show some early aptitude to learning which would then stall as they approached adulthood,[25] the Hindu people of India had, he claimed, shuddered to a halt, after their early promise, at an intermediate stage of mental development. Noting the classic imbecile characteristics of the mixture of 'great violence, as well as great gentleness of manners' that Hindus displayed, and their propensity to 'dissimulation and falsehood',[26] Mill pronounced them semi-civilized. The people of Hindustan, with their great cities, cultivation of the soil and 'artificial systems', compared favourably against the idiot-savage people of America, who lacked fixed habitation or any form of government. Ultimately, however, 'the progress of knowledge, and the force of observation, demonstrate the necessity of regarding the actual state of the Hindus as little removed from that of half-civilized nations.'[27]

The notion of imbecility helped to explain the developmental progress of some 'lower races' without threatening the elevated status of the European, and also minimized the importance of anything they had achieved. Such 'intermediate' races were described, like imbeciles, as being educable early in life, possessing a good capacity for imitation, more advanced mentally than the idiot, but very short of the perfect mind. They were capable therefore of a certain amount of education and able to acquire some rote learning. As Ray put it about the imbecile, they had 'some intellectual capacity, though infinitely less than is possessed by the great mass of mankind'.[28] This would allow them, however, to learn to read, write, count and make some progress in music.[29] Fodéré agreed that 'some, especially those whose education has been cultivated, are capable of more composed ideas.'[30] The problem was that this imbecile learning was achieved not through reflection but through what Fodéré called 'the blind drive; the impulse of imitation'.[31] An imbecile could acquire facts and knowledge but never attain the capacity to form ideas, which required rational capability. Ray noted the example of 'one who learned many dates, numbers, history and repeated them all mechanically, but was destitute of ideas, all power of combining and comparing'. They 'can repeat but not understand', which allowed for only particular, strictly limited, mechanical talents such as 'music, drawing, painting and machinery'. Whatever practical accomplishments they might have, they would never understand the purpose of them.[32]

The same characteristics were applied to the 'semi-civilized' races. The bishop of Calcutta, Reginald Heber, observing young Indian students in Calcutta schools, noted that 'many of them write beautifully and are excellent accountants . . . they exhibit . . . considerable quickness, and a good memory; but are deficient, when compared to English boys of the same age and rank . . . in common sense, courage and honesty.'[33] They lacked, according to Heber, the shared ideation ('common sense') and the moral qualities arising from it which those inhabiting the highest mental sphere possessed. Imbecile-barbarians possessed mediocre, imitative, mechanical habits, none of them requiring reflection or abstraction. As Mill remarked dismissively about Indian buildings and sculpture, there was nothing in the mechanical arts of this 'manufacturing people' that 'any set of men, in a country so highly favoured by nature, might not have discovered'.[34] The Chinese, he added, though also imitative and derivative, were superior to the Hindus in manufacture.[35] People could pass, it was agreed, from the lowest form of savagery to a higher form of barbarity, but this was a move from childlike idiocy to adolescent imbecility rather than the attainment of mental or civilizational maturity. To achieve a state of full mental development, many European observers believed, was beyond most non-white people. Attempts at education, they claimed, simply failed, even if native children learned something in their early years. E. W. Landor noted from Australia that:

> Those of mature age . . . appear to be incapable of eleva-
> tion above their original condition. Considerable pains
> have been bestowed . . . upon the native children . . . in
> the hope of making them eventually useful servants to the
> settlers. Most of them, however, betake themselves to the
> bush, and resume their hereditary pursuits, just at the age
> it is hoped they will become . . . permanently civilized.[36]

This dismissal of the mental capacity, or willingness, of indigenous people to learn was echoed even by civilizing evangelists,
who resorted to a theory of ineducability to explain the failures
of their own educational initiatives. A report from the Religious
Society of Friends lamented that, in the case of the Native
American peoples of Jersey, of whom they had once nurtured
high hopes: 'there is little encouragement to be exhibited. Much
of the good that was contemplated was never realised . . . there
were several who still pleaded for a return to their former barbarous and wandering habits of life.'[37] Barbarians, like imbeciles,
could only be educated to a certain level, and even then were
likely to regress to their former state.

This led to a view held by European administrators of the
limited functions that semi-civilized barbarian people could
perform, which closely mirrored the roles assigned to imbeciles
within the burgeoning asylum systems of Europe and America.
In Paris, Georget had described the useful menial and mechanical roles that the imbecile could offer, for a small reward, within
the confines of the asylum. They could function as servants,
domestics, commissionaires, cleaners and porters.[38] Ray described
imbeciles as the group who, among the lower orders of society,
perform 'in menial and mechanical jobs'.[39] Non-white races
were also classed as suitable for imbecile-level menial jobs only.
The Jamaican 'negro' was described, in a notorious racial diatribe by the Royal Navy officer Bedford Pim in 1866, as a born
'hewer of wood and drawer of water', a phrase from the Book
of Joshua.[40] Four years before Pim, John Langdon Down, who
had become the superintendent of the world's first purpose-built

idiot asylum at Earlswood in Surrey, made the explicit link between localized imbecility in his asylum and globalized racial imbecility, using the same biblical reference: 'Just as in the outer world there is a graduated series from the most commonplace intellects – who are the 'hewers of wood and drawers of water' – up to the giant minds . . . so is there amongst an imbecile population a gradual shading in an inverse direction.'[41] Such imbeciles could, he added, 'perform mechanical work with system and order'.[42]

In contrast to these pessimistic and bleak, racially charged accounts of irredeemable idiocy and imbecility, the doctrine of 'moral treatment' was pioneered by William Tuke at the Retreat, a Quaker 'institution for insane persons' in York founded in 1796. It rejected the punitive regimes 'calculated to depress and degrade' that had characterized approaches to mental disturbance and deficit previously.[43] Its aim was, instead, to 'awaken the slumbering reason' through 'gentleness of manner, and kindness of treatment'.[44] Under this system, which largely rejected methods of physical restraint or punishment, the disordered mind would learn to acknowledge the moral authority of those who were treating them, first learning 'respect and obedience' and subsequently attaining a level of 'rational and orderly conduct'.[45] Doctors working in idiocy were quick to appropriate and apply this new moral treatment theory, with Phillippe Pinel enacting reforms at the Bicêtre and Salpêtrière asylums in Paris, subsequently developed further by the psychiatrists Jean-Étienne Esquirol and Édouard Séguin.[46]

If moral treatment was an approach that could improve the minds of the disordered, the idiot and the imbecile, then it could of course be applied to those non-white races perceived as possessing such minds. Frances Trollope made the connection explicit in a discussion of the 'negro-slave' population of America in 1832:

There seems in general a strong feeling throughout America, that none of the Negro race can be trusted, and . . . fear . . . is the only principle by which a slave can be actuated . . . But I am persuaded that were a different mode of moral treatment pursued, most important and beneficial consequences would result from it. Negroes are very sensible to kindness, and might, I think, be rendered more profitably obedient by the practice of it towards them, than by any other mode of discipline whatsoever.[47]

Moral treatment, she argued, could be applied as a method of training the savage or semi-civilized mind towards improved rationality and therefore greater obedience to, and respect for, moral systems of governance. The advantage for Europeans of manufacturing such a shift in a slave society was that it entailed a move from a regime of physical domination and control to one of mental self-control, which could eradicate dangerousness in an enlightened way. The same advantages were espoused by Tuke for the application of moral treatment in the asylum system. This doctrine of order and discipline through kindness became a common thread in European speculation about the way forward for relations between colonizing whites and indigenous peoples. The relationship should become effectively that of the kind asylum-keeper enforcing moral discipline among their mentally deficient charges. Maria Nugent decided that the reason her Jamaican slave servants demonstrated a 'want of exertion' when working in the house was the cruelty of the slave system.[48] She acted decisively: 'assemble them together after breakfast, and talk to them a great deal, promising every kindness and indulgence. We parted excellent friends, and I think they have been rather more active in cleaning the house ever since.'[49] The same optimism that enthused the asylum movement about the powerful effects of moral treatment on mind and conduct enthused those, particularly missionaries, who were concerned with the 'improvement' of dark-skinned indigenous peoples. The Reverend John Philip wrote of the Bushmen of southern Africa: 'they are susceptible of kindness; grateful for favours . . . disposed to receive instruction; and by the use of proper means, could be easily brought to exchange their barbarous manner of life for one that could offer more comfort.'[50] In Jamaica, the Baptist missionary and abolitionist James Phillippo argued that it had been brutal and degrading treatment, 'a system that reduced them to the level of the brute', that had left its people 'the dwarfs of the rational world'.[51] Through instruction and improvement, from which they had hitherto been excluded, and with their remarkable faculties of wit and imitation, these 'simple-minded villagers' would be able to live an orderly, moral life.[52] All that was needed was the introduction of a 'liberal and enlarged scheme of sound education'.[53]

This was the sort of benign moral treatment regime noted by the adventurer Du Chaillu when he encountered a missionary school near the Gabon river, an orderly settlement where the children began with prayers, then cleaned their dormitories,

The Shepherds first view of his Flock – The Picnic.

H. G., 'The Shepherds first view of his Flock – The Picnic', 1860, engraving of four missionaries and a child looking at an African tribe from a distance. Moral treatment was advocated for savages and barbarians, as well as idiots and imbeciles.

attended breakfast where they were 'taught to eat after the manner of civilized people' and then spent the day under instruction.[54] Séguin's regime for his idiot charges at the Bicêtre involved an identical mix of instructional group prayer, cleanliness, correct eating habits and industry. The prayers were specifically written (by Séguin) to encourage morally improving occupational tasks and purposeful, mannered eating habits. Imbeciles and idiots would ask God to bless their food and to ensure that all unfortunates would have bread to eat.[55] This purposefulness was designed to eradicate the disgusting, mindless eating habits which idiots (and savages) were believed to have. They would then implore God to bless the work they were about to do, 'to improve us and to make us useful to society'.[56] This conduct, ordered within an imposed moral framework, would encourage the imbecile to embrace the civilized world and its codes.[57]

Moral treatment as applied to both the idiot population and non-white populations was not seen as an approach that would achieve equality or indeed full 'recovery' and attainment of reason. It was, rather, a utilitarian method to achieve discipline and control over troubled, and troubling, populations, who would then live orderly, regulated and unthreatening lives. It required the internalization of a particular form of obedient consciousness in those seen as having a moral deficit or disorder. As Tuke did for the lunatic in York, so Séguin did for the idiot and imbecile in Paris, engaging in a process of 'actively moulding the idiot to the social world'.[58] Medical practitioners were imposing a regime of training, reward and punishment (the withdrawal of favour, rather than physical beating or seclusion) in order to impose their will on the idiot:

> Moral treatment consists of the implementation of all appropriate moral methods to corroborate the health and educational prescriptions to which the idiot refuses more or less to submit himself, and to make him pass, from the exceptional state in which he languishes, to the social state.[59]

The intention was not kindness for its own sake, or to accord the idiot or imbecile full human status, but to find the most effective method of making them orderly, and to eradicate the thirst for revenge or violence that harsh physical treatment might cause. It was the 'hatred . . . vengeance and fanaticism' of the imbecile that Séguin believed moral treatment could tame. Imposition of will was all, and the Parisian medical men no more expected their idiot and imbecile charges to become morally responsible for their own actions than they would believe a trained dog morally culpable.[60]

Those advocating the moral treatment approach to savage and barbarian peoples thought along the same lines. The Society of Friends in London reported in 1844 on the 'Native Indian' tribes to whom they were applying their mission:

> These aborigines have often been treated as though they were wild and irreclaimable savages . . . but how seldom have Christian dispositions been recommended to them by example? How seldom has the attempt been made to win them over, not by force, but by love?[61]

The savage would be 'won over', made tame, by the imposition of a moral will that would enable them to take control of their own selves and accept social obligation to others.

However, with disillusioned missionaries reporting that natives were returning to their 'wandering habits' despite education,[62] the Quaker Friends began to doubt their own methods. Simultaneously, a scornful anti-liberal narrative developed deriding the idea that moral treatment could improve 'degraded' races:

> Kindness and indulgence have never yet been able to eradicate the generic character of deceit, ingratitude and cruelty. To the philanthropic mind, ignorant of the African character, this may appear an uncharitable assumption; yet . . . those who better know that

unfortunate race from habitual observation, will confirm the fact.[63]

These remarks by the anti-abolitionist George Wilson Bridges, rector of a parish in Jamaica, represented a vitriolic riposte by conservatives to the moral treatment approach, even if conservatives and liberals shared to a large extent assumptions about the natural inferiority and mental incapacity of non-white peoples. For conservatives, only total colonial domination of the savage would do. Among the most degraded of all idiot-savage tribes, argued the missionary William Buyers, no amount of kindness or attempt to inculcate a moral system was possible, and only death would bring an end to their misery: 'the almost entire incapacity of such tribes for amalgamation with the higher civilized races, render their extirpation, at least as distinct races, almost certain.'[64]

There were similar diatribes against practitioners of moral restraint in relation to the idiotic, the imbecilic and the insane. When the psychiatrist John Conolly announced in 1840 that all forms of restraint and physical discipline would be removed from the Middlesex County Asylum at Hanwell, the move was denounced in *The Times* as 'a piece of contemptible quackery and a mere bait for the public ear'.[65] Echoing the warnings of Bridges about the dangerous consequences of moral treatment for Jamaican slaves, and his fulminations against the folly of do-gooding philanthropic reformers, Conolly was warned that:

> Nothing can be more absurd . . . than the attempts of theoretic visionaries, or candidates for popular praise, to do away with all restraint . . . it can never prevail without much danger to personal security, and a useless waste and dilapidation of property.[66]

Non-white races and those designated idiot or imbecile found themselves locked together in an unwelcome embrace. Should they be overtly controlled within a harshly punitive disciplinary system, or willed towards self-control through a regime of moral treatment? Either way, their perceived incapacity meant that the imposition of some form of control was inevitable.

Idiots, Savages and the Anthropological Move

Throughout the nineteenth century, theory concerning both idiocy and savagery continued to emphasize the link between the idiotic mind and the savage mind that had been first posited in the previous century. However, this was no longer framed as a matter of curiosity but became a much more ideological debate about treatment, control and governance, both at home and abroad. The asylum movement grew in tandem with the formation of systems of colonial governance, and specialists in both drew from each other.

Eighteenth-century legal theory, which drew on idiot and imbecile capacity law to define limitations of rights to property and self-management for indigenous people, now became a central plank of colonial governance. Native peoples were seen as not in possession of the land over which they roamed because they lacked the capacity or the desire to manage it. John West of the Hudson's Bay Company justified colonial expansion in northernmost America on the grounds that the Native Americans 'form no arrangement, nor enter into calculation for futurity. They have no settled place of abode, or property, or acquired wants and appetites, like those which rouse men to activity in civilized life . . . [where] they keep the mind in perpetual exercise and ingenious invention.'[67] In the same way as the idiot or imbecile could be within human society, but not a part of it, the savage could be in a land, but not of it. It was in Australia that the use of capacity to deny indigenous peoples' possession was most overt. The other John West, writing about Tasmania in 1852, clearly outlined the application of legal assessments of capacity of mind to savage tribes, alluding to capacity law: 'the assumption of sovereignty over a savage people is justified by necessity – that law, which gives to strength the control of weakness'.[68]

This applied not only to savages but to semi-civilized bar-barians, who, in consequence of their imbecile minds, could not understand contract and must therefore submit to the will of those who did: 'the barbarian that cannot comprehend laws or treaties, must be governed by . . . force.'[69] This rendered unfea-sible the very idea of concluding treaties with groups of savages or barbarians, particularly those who wandered and did not cultivate. By so doing they demonstrated that they had no reason, foresight or capacity: 'The legal recognition of rights in the soil, pertaining to the native inhabitants of colonised regions, is attended with some difficulty . . . the parliamentary committee, in a review of the whole question, did not recom-mend treaties with savages.'[70] Emer de Vattel's *Law of Nations*, particularly his notion that some lacked the mental capacity to cultivate and settle, and the concept of *terra nullius* ('land belonging to nobody'), was used repeatedly in legal judgments to deny indigenous peoples rights to property.[71] These became staples of the settler idea that indigenous peoples existed outside the laws of property because of their perceived inability to con-sent. It was argued that the aimlessness of their wandering implied that they had no notion of ownership or value.[72] As in idiocy law, those who were deemed irredeemably idiotic were denied all ownership. Those perceived to be imbecilic and there-fore to have a certain amount of capacity were allowed limited, regulated ownership. John Philip remarked on what he saw as the strange anomaly that in India, native people were allowed to own a certain amount of land, while South Africa's native populations had virtually no rights over land at all.[73] Remarkable it may have seemed to him, but an understanding of the law relating to the property of idiots and imbeciles at home would have revealed to Philip the logic that underpinned what he saw. The British colonial system divided its lands, and peoples, into idiots and imbeciles.

The debate continued about the supposed link between race and intelligence. In 1802 a study emerged not of faraway exotic savages but of an intriguing French savage, Victor 'the Wild

Coloured engraving of Victor, the Wild Boy of Aveyron, 1805.

Boy' of Aveyron. Captured (for the third time) in 1800, this wild boy had been seen by peasants, or so they claimed, running on all fours through the mountains and forests of the Tarn region for a number of years.[74] He was moved to the National Institution for Deaf-Mutes in Paris in late 1800, where a young medical student, Jean Marc Gaspard Itard, was officer of health. Itard was allowed to take the child into his home, aided by his house-keeper, to conduct experiments into his psychology.[75] As with previous discoveries of wild children, such as Peter the Wild Boy and Marie-Angélique Le Blanc in the eighteenth century, a discussion emerged about the condition of 'Man' in the natural state and whether the unsocialized savage child could provide answers about innate ability and learned behaviour. Were people born with natural cognitive and social skills or was the human mind formed by external impressions, leading to the formation of ideas though uniquely human social interactive processes?

The reaction to Victor, however, was radically different to that which had surrounded earlier wild children. Peter the Wild Boy was taken first to the Hanoverian court in London as a curiosity and then, when people tired of him, to live out a quiet life in a family home in the Hertfordshire countryside. Marie-Angélique Le Blanc went first to a general hospital and then to a succession of convents.[76] Victor was different. He became an immediate subject of medical observation and was swiftly pronounced an idiot by Pinel.[77] He then became the subject of an experiment, as Itard took him into his home with the aim of socializing him and proving that he was not, as Pinel believed, an idiot, but a 'being highly interesting'.[78] Itard and Pinel did, however, share assumptions about what characterized Victor. He disappointed by showing indifference rather than astonishment when introduced to the sights of Paris. He was a 'disgusting, slovenly boy' with no affective feelings and with 'convulsive motions', incapable of attention and lacking memory.[79] With his disgusting eating habits, insensibility to pain, unwillingness to lie on a bed and 'aversion from society', Victor matched the prevailing characterization of both the idiot and the savage.[80] Where Itard differed from Pinel was in his belief that Victor was an educable savage who could be 'cured' of these habits and traits, rather than an ineducable idiot who could never develop full understanding. His salvation would come about through a treatment programme of 'moral medicine . . . lately introduced in France by . . . Pinel'.[81] Itard would work with Victor to attach him to social life, expand the sphere of his ideas and lead him to the use of language through imitation.[82] While expressing cautious optimism in his first report, by the time he wrote his second report in 1806 Itard was resigned to Victor's lack of progress and expressed disillusionment with the limitations of 'moral medicine'.[83] Victor was transferred, first back to the Institution for Deaf-Mutes and then, his frenetic masturbatory habits causing offence, to the annex of a hospice, where he ended his days.[84] The importance of the Victor of Aveyron episode was in underlining that, whether the person was perceived as a savage or an idiot, the need for treatment under a moral regime was undisputed. Itard began with the 'progressive' belief that a natural savage, while sharing a range of characteristics with the idiot, could be trained and coaxed towards full rationality. He ended with the pessimistic conclusion that a savage was no more capable of acquiring reason than the permanent idiot.

Itard's early optimism was reflected in the work of James Cowles Prichard, a British physician and ethnologist who devoted himself to researches in both mental abnormality and racial variety. Prichard espoused in 1813 the same optimistic view that whatever the evident differences in mental faculty across different peoples in the world, 'the same inward conscious nature and the same mental faculties are common to all in the races of man.'[85] All humans were derived from the same family rather than separate species. He acknowledged that his readers would find this difficult to accept when faced with 'the African Negroes . . . the New Hollanders, the Hottentots, the Esquimaux, the Papuas or the woolly-headed tribes who are scattered through the Indian and Pacific oceans'.[86] However, Prichard maintained that racial variety was caused by environmental factors such as climate and social influences and that 'constant and immutable' distinctions between races did not exist. He drew the analogy of common humanity in idiots and imbeciles, detecting the 'first glimmerings of intelligence' in idiots and noting that the imbecile, like the barbarian, was 'susceptible to improvement'.[87]

There was, however, strong opposition to this progressivist theory of intellectual and social development. From the 1850s a radical racist perspective arose from a group of theorists who believed in the permanent and unalterable inferiority of non-white races. They believed that the variation in mental faculty that they perceived among different races was such that separate human races had separate origins and belonged to different species, a view known as polygenism, in opposition to the common origin theory, or monogenism, of Prichard and others. This 'scientific racism' accepted as fact the equivalence of idiocy and the mental capacity of non-white races, and applied this to their theory of a hierarchical global social order. The Scottish anatomist Robert Knox set out this deeply racialized credo in *The Races of Men* in 1850, attacking the idea of a common origin for all humans: 'look all over the globe, it is always the same; the dark races stand still, the fair progress.'[88] This was due to 'a psychological inferiority in the dark races generally'.[89] His diatribe was relentless. Knox derided the 'Hottentots' as a 'simple feeble race' and the indigenous American as 'a half-civilized barbarian'.[90] He disparaged the 'Chinese, Mongol, Kalmuc and Tartar . . . tribes and races' as derivative peoples whose 'mechanical art is no proof of high intelligence'.[91] None of this was new (it was, ironically, highly derivative). However, Knox was the first to explicitly contend that the idiot, imbecile and perfect mind status of the different races of the world was a frozen, permanent, unchanging global fact of life.

Two years after Knox, the French aristocrat Arthur de Gobineau made the fixed mental and racial division of the world explicit. There were three races, said Gobineau: 'the White, the Black, the Yellow'.[92] The savage black races were of the lowest level of mental development and had the idiot characteristics of 'monstrous indifference' and 'dull, or even non-existent mental faculties'. The 'yellow man' had imbecile traits: 'he tends to medi-ocrity in everything . . . he does not dream or theorise, he invents little, but can appropriate and take over what is useful for him.'[93] The white race stood at the top. Education or social change would make no difference: racial mental faculties were fixed and unalterable. Writing as the burgeoning asylum movement in Europe began to bring growing numbers of the idiotic and imbe-cile into its sphere, Knox, Gobineau and their supporters saw confinement and control for the non-white races as the only future.

Such debates were part of a vigorous public discourse in mid-nineteenth-century Britain. Were the savages encountered across the globe, and increasingly brought back to Britain as part of ethnological exhibitions and displays, irredeemable idiots, or did they simply have early, childlike minds that would advance over time from a state of innocent mental simplicity to fully developed enlightenment? Was the savage noble or depraved? Was the idiot a trainable innocent or a loathsome sub-human? Dickens, writing in *Household Words* in 1854, mocked the idea of the noble savage, and the pious philanthropists who espoused it: 'There are pious persons who . . . claim for . . . every savage born to the woods and wilds all innate virtue. We believe every savage to be in his heart covetous, treacherous and cruel.'[94] Dickens noted that in observing a group of Zulus at an ethnological exhibition, he saw only a savage, nothing noble, and commented: 'I call a savage a something highly desirable to be civilized off the face of the earth.'[95] For Dickens the savage was an object of detestation with no moral feeling, and he believed that 'the world will be all the better when his place knows him no more.'[96] In his very similar tirade several years later Dickens described idiots as 'wallowing in the lowest depths of degradation and neglect, whom nobody may put to death, but whom everyone must wish dead, and distressed to see alive'.[97] The wish was the same for both the savage and the idiot: that they should be civilized through moral treatment, or bred off the face of the earth.

All this took place in the context of the development of the emergent disciplines first of ethnology and then of anthropology. The Ethnological Society of London was established in 1843, with its own journal from 1848.[98] Formed from the Aborigines Protection Society, it now focused on the 'pure science' of studying 'Man'.[99] Members, such as James Cowles Prichard, broadly shared the more liberal, progressive, monogenist view of a common origin of humanity and the potential for advancement of savage and barbarian peoples.[100] The society was as much interested in the brains and intelligence of different types of human as in their habits and cultures and saw as its field of study 'the condition of the existing families of mankind; their physical characters, their intellectual capacities; their moral qualities, their habits of life'.[101]

The focus on the brains as well as the cultures of different peoples made the society of great interest to medical professionals, particularly those working in the field of mental abnormality. Twenty-seven asylum medical superintendents or doctors joined either the Ethnological Society or the Anthropological Society between 1843 and 1867. They were prominent participants.[102] A direct link was formed between 'degraded' people at home and abroad:

> The tests by which we recognise the claim of the outcast and degraded of our own, or of any other highly civilized communities, to a common humanity, are the same as those by which we should estimate the true relation of the negro, the Bushman or Australian, to the cultivated European.[103]

One of the most prominent medical men to join the Ethnological Society was John Conolly, who was president from 1854 to 1856. Conolly, a pioneer of moral treatment in public asylums, was superintendent of the large lunatic asylum in Hanwell, Middlesex, opened in 1831, where he took a particular interest in the small patient population of idiots.[104] He visited the Bicêtre and Salpêtrière in Paris in 1845 to study the work of Pinel and Séguin[105] and became convinced that 'congenital idiots, such as are found encumbering the wards of all our asylums', needed some sort of specialist institution that separated them from lunatics.[106] He was then instrumental in establishing first the small Park House Asylum for Idiots in Highgate in 1847, followed by the temporary premises of Essex Hall in Colchester as demand for places grew, and finally the Earlswood Asylum for Idiots in Surrey, which opened in 1855.[107] Conolly was a mentor to John Langdon Down, the young physician who became Earlswood's most influential medical superintendent.

Conolly drew together medicine and ethnology, commenting on the 'Aztec Lilliputians', young siblings brought to London from Central America for exotic ethnological display as the alleged last degraded specimens of an ancient Aztec priestly caste:[108] 'My own attention having . . . been particularly directed to the characters of idiocy, in the asylum for those afflicted beings at Highgate, I was at once struck with the remarkable resemblance of those little Aztecs to some of the lowest types there observable.'[109] He made a claim for the authority of mental scientists like himself in matters of ethnology, deriding the strange theories proposed about the 'Aztec children' by 'anatomists, physiologists and men of science', who had all missed that the children represented the state of arrested development brought on by microcephaly.[110] For a mental scientist like Conolly, this was immediately apparent: he was already familiar with an eleven-year-old boy at the Highgate asylum with a brain of a similar size.[111] Conolly readily acceded to the stadial theory of development, accepting also, in common with most members of the Ethnological Society, the theory of the common origin of man. He also agreed with the universalization of the hierarchy of intelligence to link the progress of societies with the progress of the faculties of the human mind. He described 'the gradual development of man's higher faculties and his gradually changed condition', the transition from the 'savage man' to barbarian and later 'emergence from barbarism and want to refinement and enjoyment'.[112] His optimistic account conceded the different levels of mental development apparent in races across the globe, but opportunities for improvement were discernible, driven by the mind common to all people 'all over the wide earth'.[113] Medical treatment of 'debased' idiotic and imbecile minds at home, according to Conolly, offered a prescription for the treatment and improvement of the savage and barbarian races elsewhere.

In 1863, the Anthropological Society of London was formed as a breakaway group from the Ethnological Society. There had been tensions for some time between the humanitarian-inclined Ethnological Society and a new, radically racist current of thought represented by Robert Knox (author of *The Races of Men*) and James Hunt, a speech therapist and anti-abolitionist who had joined in 1854.[114] Hunt, who became the first president

The 'Aztec Lilliputians', identified by John Conolly as a 'low form' of idiot, seen here in a lithograph by G. Wilkinson.

of the Anthropological Society, was clearly seeking a platform for his racist views, but gave a scientific justification for the establishment of the new body. Ethnology was simply the history of races, while anthropology was 'the science of the whole nation of man'. He condemned the obsession with what he called the 'article of faith' of a common origin of 'Man' and argued that instead anthropology would study, irrespective of origin, 'all deviation from the human standard of organisation'.[115] He was particularly interested in study of the 'negro', whom he regarded as the most inferior of all species. The creation of the Anthropological Society marked a broad split between more liberal monogenists, who believed in the common origin of all humanity, and radically racist polygenists who believed that different races were different species and that non-white humans lived in a state of fixed mental inferiority.[116]

Given their deep-seated belief in the intellectual inferiority of the non-white races, members of the Anthropological Society were as interested in the study of intellectual deficit at home as they were in the study of other races abroad, and were keen to make comparisons and links. Their journals reported eagerly on Paul Broca's comparisons of negro and idiot skulls in Paris, British-born microcephalics, a large idiotic family in Norfolk, the educability of idiots, and female microcephaly.[117] Such reports nestled comfortably alongside accounts of 'Esquimaux', 'Hottentots' and the exotic savages of the South Sea islands. In an intellectual world that was coming to define race solely in terms of a hierarchy of intelligence, why would they not?

Into this milieu, from 1864, strode the medical superintendent of the Earlswood Asylum for Idiots, John Langdon Down. Down's interest in the study of race and human development was no doubt stimulated by his close friendship with his mentor Conolly, but he chose to join the far more racialized environment of the Anthropological Society rather than Conolly's more trad-itional Ethnological Society, a surprise given his historical reputation for liberal views.[118] The Anthropological Society was, however, the place to be, growing with 'amazing rapidity' in its first two years, gaining five hundred members and a Manchester branch.[119] For an ambitious, relatively young (37-year-old) medical superintendent, keen to make his mark in public life but working in the unfashionable field of idiocy in a Surrey backwater, the Anthropological Society seemed to offer more opportunities than its fading ethnological counterpart.

Down was a regular attender and enthusiastic participant in Anthropological Society meetings. What he heard and read directly influenced his own research interests and writings. In 1864 a meeting on consanguineous marriages (between close relations)[120] prompted him to conduct his own research into the parentage of 1,138 idiots at his asylum and conclude that statistical reports of the dangers of diseased offspring from such marriages were grossly exaggerated. In 1867 he informed a meeting that the shape rather than size of the brain was of overriding importance in intellect: sometimes a smaller-brained person could be quicker and shrewder than a larger-brained person.[121] By this time, Down had measured the skulls and dissected the brains of over 150 idiots who had died at his asylum.[122] He was at home in this anthropological world, where links between the skull measurements and cranial capacity of microcephalics and other idiot types were consistently measured against those of different racial types in the quest to prove the new anthropology's racial assumptions. The German polygenist Karl Vogt lectured to the society that the idiot was a halfway stage between primates and the lowest form of human, by which he meant a female Bushman (San). He 'proved' this by measuring the skulls of an ape, a microcephalic idiot and a 'negro woman', and pronounced the idiot as having passed the simian stage, but nowhere near yet even the lowest human stage.[123] For Down the medical man, interested in theories of race, neither Vogt's findings nor his methods were particularly startling.

Down's liberal, monogenist views have been stressed by historians, although the anomaly of his belonging to James Hunt's racially charged Anthropological Society has also been noted.[124] However, the racial views of those who believed in monogenism and human unity could be as extreme as those of polygenists.[125] Certainly a warm relationship existed between Down and the society's racist polygenist leader James Hunt. Hunt praised Down for his scientific observation of facts when Down intervened in the discussion about the importance of brain quality over size in 1867.[126] Nor did Down desert Hunt during one of the Anthropological Society's darkest racial episodes. In 1863, Hunt had delivered a vitriolic paper to the society in which he classified the 'negro' as a distinct species from the European, with the male negro's brain equivalent to a child's brain and the female's brain approaching that of an ape.[127] Following the 1865 Morant Bay rebellion in Jamaica, which resulted in the deaths

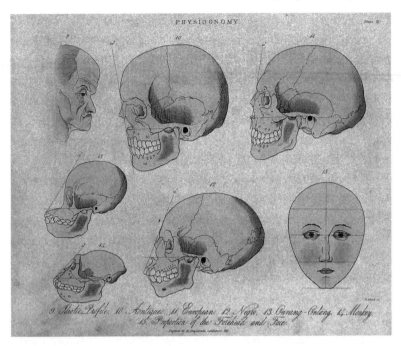

H. Adlard, 'Physiognomy', 1824, coloured engraving. Comparisons of idiotic, monkey, orangutan and 'perfect' skulls were common in 19th-century anthropology.

of twenty white settlers, and subsequently five hundred black Jamaicans killed in retribution by the Jamaica militia on the orders of the governor, Hunt's response was to invite the eminent naval commodore Bedford Pim to deliver an extreme racial diatribe against black people and in defence of the governor's actions.[128] Amid a furious national debate in Britain over the events in Jamaica, demand for tickets from Anthropological Society members was so high that the venue for Pim's speech had to be moved to St James's Hall to accommodate the audience. One of those who managed to secure two tickets was Down.[129] He listened, with the large crowd, as Pim denounced the 'negro' as one who 'remains a child, and is never capable of a generalization . . . he is naught but self'.[130] This was an archetypal description of the idiot type. The negro, Pim went on, 'in slavery was incapably better off than he is a freed man'.[131] His oration was 'frequently interrupted with applause and loud cheers', and as Hunt closed

THOSE THEY CALLED IDIOTS

the meeting three cheers for Governor Eyre were called.[132] After the meeting a small number of members resigned from the society, nauseated by the vitriolic racist tone, but Down was not one of them.[133] Hunt's approval of Down appeared to strengthen from this point, as Hunt supported him in meetings and groomed him in society committees for higher office. Late in 1866 Down was elected to the council under Hunt's chairmanship. He remained a member until 1869, when Hunt nominated him to be his vice-president, clearly attempting to position Down as his successor (Hunt died several months later). The nomination was, however, rejected by the rest of the council, and Down resigned his position in the same year. Down's alienation from the extreme racist views of Hunt appears nowhere near as complete as has been portrayed.

Down's intensive involvement with the Anthropological Society and his particular interest in race help to explain his paper 'Observations on an Ethnic Classification of Idiots', published in 1867. Shortly after his move to Earlswood in 1858, Down had promised that he would take advantage of the opportunity afforded by the large concentration of young idiots being brought together within the 'spacious walls' to establish a classification of the pupils, based on their degree of intelligence and capability.[134] He was true to his word, yet the classification system he produced in 1867 was quite unexpected and novel. Down announced that 'among the large number of idiots and imbeciles which came under my observation . . . a considerable portion can be fairly referred to one of the great divisions of the human family other than the class from which they have sprung.'[135] He meant by this that he had observed, among his idiot charges, the five races of the world as defined by the early anthropologist Johann Friedrich Blumenbach in 1775: Caucasian (or European), Mongolian, Malay, Aztec (or American) and Ethiopic (or African).[136] What was intriguing about the ethnic classification system he had developed was, he claimed, that although all the idiots in his asylum were of Caucasian parentage they appeared to spring from all five of the world's racial divisions, and had not all been born Caucasian as one would expect.[137] His theory was that the puzzling emergence of alien ethnicities among the idiot offspring of Caucasian parents was the result of an atavistic degeneracy that, because of some external or internal influence (he speculated that in the case of what he called Mongolian imbecility it might be tuberculosis in the mother), caused ancient, degenerate racial types to emerge in a more advanced population.[138] This was known as recapitulation theory, which Down had borrowed directly from his anthropological sources. This theory argued that as embryos, higher animals, including 'Man', pass through stages that represent in sequence the adult forms of the ancestral creatures that preceded them. According to recapitulationists, one could also see in white children the savage manifestations of the lower races. They further argued that 'abnormal' adults in 'superior' races represented atavisms, or 'throwbacks', 'the spontaneous reappearance in adults of ancestral features that had disappeared in advanced lineages'.[139] Down's mentor Hunt had stressed the great importance of the concept of 'reversion to type' to the Anthropological Society in 1863,[140] and it would be these discussions that would set him on his path to his recapitulation theory of idiocy in 1867.

To derive his theory, Down had walked the wards of Earlswood, sometimes with Conolly, studying the faces of his idiots and imbeciles to identify their racial type.[141] As well as the expected Caucasians, he saw the 'prominent eyes, the puffy lips ... retreating chin ... [and] woolly hair' of the Ethiopians, the prominent upper jaws and capacious mouths of the Malays (South Sea Islanders) and the deep-set eyes and slightly apish nose of the American. Most of all, however, he discovered 'the great Mongolian family' with their flat, broad faces, oblique eyes, wrinkled foreheads and large thick lips. There could be no doubt, he claimed, that these extraordinary racial resurfacings of primitive groups were the result of degeneration.[142] The classification was hierarchical, as was Blumenbach's, with savage African and Native American types at the bottom, barbarian Mongolians and Malays on the next level and, of course,

Caucasians at the top. However 'liberal' this monogenist theory, the white Caucasian ruled supreme.

Down's short paper was the culmination of a two-hundred-year process that began with ideas of the idiot-savage and the imbecile-barbarian. Now idiots and imbeciles were being reconstructed as savages and barbarians. The legal concepts of idiocy and imbecility had been applied to non-white races to justify colonial domination and control, and had now been reimported in a racialized form to claim institutional ownership over those very same idiots and imbeciles. It was not just appearance that drew Down to his conclusions. His most detailed description was of the 'Mongolian imbecile' type that he had identified, who would of course later be labelled as people with 'Down's syndrome'. He had fortuitously correctly identified a category, but incorrectly attributed a racial origin to it.[143] Almost a century later, in 1959, Jérôme Lejeune, a French human geneticist, would identify that those labelled 'Mongolian imbeciles' by Down possessed 47 chromosomes rather than the usual 46, a genetic anomaly known as trisomy 21. There was nothing racial about it – it was present in all populations across the world, including the population of Mongolia. It did not have evolutionary origins but was passed down in a single generation. Any resemblance of people with the trisomy 21 anomaly to Mongolian people was more in the mind of Down than in any observable reality. Lejeune and other geneticists argued that the racially tinged label of Mongolism be dropped and, in 1965, after representations from the government of Mongolia, among others, the World Health Organization dropped the term. Dr Down, despite his bizarre and mistaken explanation, gained his place in medical history and Mongolism became Down's syndrome (later also Down syndrome) in the English-speaking world ('trisomie 21' in France).[144]

In his 'Observations on an Ethnic Classification of Idiots', Down described the characteristics of 'Mongolian imbeciles': 'They have considerable powers of imitation, even bordering on mimics. They are humorous and a lively source of the ridiculous often colours their mimicry.' It was natural, for Down, that a

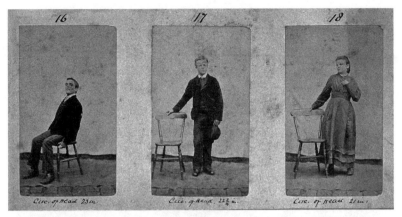

Down's syndrome in two young men and a young woman, three photographs by George Edward Shuttleworth, *c*. 1900. Down invented the category of Mongolian Imbecility, later to be known as Down's syndrome, in his ethnic classification.

barbarian race such as the Mongolians should be good at imitation and mimicry. This, as many writers had pointed out, was how such races made up for their shortfalls in reason and mental faculty and achieved some degree of civilized life. As Fanny Parks had remarked in India in 1850, 'in the evening the native mimics came to perform before us; they imitated Europeans very well, and mimicked the gentlemen of the parties.'[145] And it was this strange, supposedly ancient racial facility, this native 'remarkable facility for wit and imitation',[146] that had mysteriously re-emerged, according to Down, through the recapitulation process in these Mongolian children of Caucasian parents. It was a perfect merger of race and mental capacity. For Down, the five races of the world came together in the idiot population and were slowly civilized by the asylum, a microcosm of the colonial system.

Both inside and outside his asylum, Down mounted displays of what he now theorized as the races of empire. Large crowds would attend public fetes in the asylum grounds where young patients performed 'acts of agility' and there was then a 'procession of the patients, rendered gay by flags and banners', with evolutions performed to 'the sound of merry music'.[147] The civilizing effect of the Earlswood regime on its idiot 'savages' was evident. A report in the local paper complimented the civilized

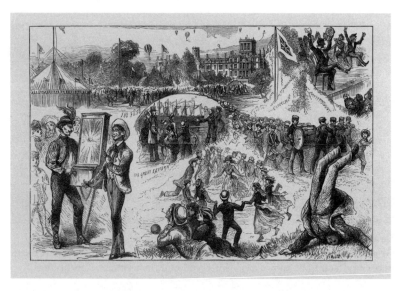

Sketches at the Summer Fete of the Earlswood Asylum for Idiots, 1876,
engraving. Down put on display the young patients at the Earlswood Asylum,
whom he theorized as belonging to the five races of the world.

behaviour to be found in the asylum grounds: 'the noise and
rough element generally attending fetes are at Earlswood con-
spicuous by their absence.'[148] As Down's Aztecs, Africans,
Mongols, Malays and Caucasians paraded before them, the
British public could be assured they were witnessing the taming
of the four corners of empire. A fully uniformed asylum band was
introduced by Down, becoming known as the asylum military
band.[149] Marching was also introduced (for the male patients)
and drills took place throughout the week, accompanied by the
band with their drums, brass and pipes. Any event, including
visits from the Lunacy Commission,[150] was accompanied by
the band and the marching of the inmates both inside and outside the asylum. In 1869 a group of 273 young idiots was escorted
to Brighton by train, where all the males marched behind the
band along the sea front. In the same year the band accompanied
a party of 213 who marched to Redhill to see a menagerie. They
even accompanied a group who marched off for a local picnic.[151]

These public displays plugged into the deep national feelings
about empire, Britain's place in the world, military power, race

and humanity that had developed during the past two centuries. This was not an isolated, cut-off asylum; it echoed to the constant daily playing of the military band and displayed to the people of Britain its parades and spectacles, well-formed lines of idiot pupils marching through the towns and countryside. Down's presentation was of the five races of empire coming together in the idiot population, slowly civilized by the asylum: a microcosm of the global power held by the empire over its idiot and imbecile populations around the world. The idiot had been removed from society to the institution, but was now re-presented as something strange, exotic and exciting. The savage idiot, and the barbarian imbecile, had come home.

7

Into the Idiot Asylum:
The Great Incarceration

Thinking about idiocy in general, and idiots and imbeciles in particular, changed rapidly, and in radical ways, from the early years of the nineteenth century. The image of the harmless, if odd, community idiot figure that had largely prevailed in eighteenth-century thought came under new and hostile scrutiny. The criminal law process became more vindictive, more severe and less understanding. In the civil courts, particularly in France and America, but also in England, medical experts jostled for position with lawyers and juries to assert their authority in idiocy cases. In wider cultural representations, including in poetry and novels, the idiot became either a helpless shadow person, not really fit to live a human life, or a dangerous threat who warranted confinement. In some respects the idiot disappeared from public consciousness altogether, no longer even a recognizable character in jokes or street slang. A new, genteel form of humour saw them simply as far-off denizens of the institution. As ideas of race and intelligence were intertwined in a gigantic intellectual fabrication across the 'science of man' and 'mental science', the idiot was invested with new characteristics of barbarianism and savagery. There was a general drift towards a characterization of marginal threat or of helpless obscurity on the periphery. It was inevitable that such a shift in opinion and modes of thought about idiocy would bring real-life social consequences for those who found themselves labelled as idiots and imbeciles.

There had been a growth in institutions during the eighteenth century, but not on a huge scale. By the century's end there were a small number of charitable hospitals, including Guy's and St Bartholomew's in London, which were largely aimed at the poor, and a small number of voluntary asylums for the 'lunatic'. There was a small network of fairly informally run workhouses for the destitute and the indigent, and a few dozen, mostly small-scale, private madhouses where the well-heeled lunatic could be kept from public view by their embarrassed families.[1] Punishment for the criminal tended to be physical, from whipping or branding up to execution, sending an exemplary message to others who might be contemplating a criminal life, rather than attempting reform of the individual through imprisonment. Transportation, first to America and then to Australia, was the solution for those spared execution but deemed unfit to remain in British society. The small number of eighteenth-century prisons, such as London's Newgate, were largely holding centres for those awaiting trial rather than centres of long-term incarceration. 'Bridewells' were classified as hospitals, putting the idle to work, training the young destitute and providing temporary detention for the most incorrigible criminals. The locus of care, and of correction, remained in the community, in the family home, an informal realm where accountability, if it existed, was to the highly localized parish rather than the state. This meant that communities on the whole were obliged to adapt themselves to accommodate and live with those who might be regarded as deviant, disturbing or different.

All this changed radically over the nineteenth century, which would become the period of Britain's 'great incarceration'. As we shall see, a huge programme of asylum building from 1808 (accelerating from 1845), punitive workhouses from 1834 and an exponential growth in prisons transformed the landscape and led to a transcending shift in the numbers of people institutionalized in some form and separated from their communities. Beginning with nine voluntary institutions, the asylum movement transformed both the physical and psychological landscape of Britain. The 'mentally unsound' were moved in ever greater numbers from their communities to these proliferating institutions. From 1815 Parliament authorized, through a County Asylums Act, publicly funded asylums for 'pauper lunatics', and twenty were built. From 1845 a new County Asylums Act made it compulsory for counties to build asylums, and a Lunacy Commission was set up to monitor them. New buildings sprang up at breakneck pace. Similar exponential growth took place in workhouses and prisons.

Idiots were caught up in this general institutional move of the helpless, the dangerous and the vulnerable. They occupied 'an inferior position in the psyche of Victorian lunacy reform'[2] and, in the early decades of the century, drifted into workhouse care.[3] This was an unintended, or at least unforeseen, consequence of the 1834 Poor Law Amendment Act. The Act promoted a shift from 'outdoor relief', or financial support for the vulnerable to remain in their own homes, to 'indoor relief', requiring that they move to institutional workhouse provision. Consequently, thousands of idiots found themselves in workhouses by 1837. As we shall see, by 1856 many workhouses had become asylums in all but name, resources and expertise. Thus the idiot became a problem within the new state institutional system. They were deemed unfit for the community, but they were also incurable, ineducable and largely not dangerous, and therefore unfit for the asylum. Subsequently, pressure to establish a separate asylum for idiots in England was exerted by a small group of physicians who, in partnership with a group of wealthy charitable donors, eventually opened in 1855 the five-hundred-bed Asylum for Idiots at Earlswood in Surrey, the world's first purpose-built asylum for idiot children, entirely charitably financed.[4] Between 1859 and 1872 further charitable idiot asylums were established in the east, north, west and Midlands of England.[5] In 1870 the first large state-run 'asylums for chronic imbeciles' were established at Leavesden in Hertfordshire and Caterham in Surrey, each housing more than 1,000 of the idiotic poor from London.

Early drawing of the Earlswood Asylum in the *Illustrated London News*, 11 March 1854.

Why did this move to incarceration of those deemed unfit to live in society take place, and why were those labelled idiot or imbecile caught up in it? There were significant changes in public opinion, across a range of ideological standpoints, that came sharply into focus following the events of the French Revolution on the other side of the Channel. The revolution, which began in 1789, unleashed unprecedented, competing ideological and social forces in Britain. A maelstrom of new opinions and ways of looking at the world and its social structures ensued.

Radical groups, beginning with the London Corresponding Society and culminating in the Chartist movement of the 1830s and '40s, met – first in alehouse rooms and later in their thousands on the streets – to advance the new causes of a more equal social order, an expanded franchise and full civic participation.[6] A febrile political atmosphere prevailed, in which the poorer classes were major protagonists. As war broke out with the revolutionary government in France, there was serious British unrest in 1794 over food prices and impressment, and in 1795 some 12,000 rioters besieged 10 Downing Street.[7] Radical writers such as Thomas Paine and William Godwin identified themselves with these protests of the impoverished classes and advocated universal rights. The radical call for universal rights demanded a new type of person: the active citizen. If political and social rights were to be extended to those who had not previously held them, these new citizens would need to respond in kind, by exercising responsibility, participating in public discussion and debate and contributing to society as its necessary agents. This would have profound implications for those deemed unfit, or incapable, to take on such responsibilities.

A socially conservative counter-reaction to this new radicalism, built on fear of the terrors that were being unleashed in the name of revolution on France, and anxiety that the spread of revolutionary ideas could cause the same to occur in Britain, quickly materialized. This took both secular and religious forms. Politically, an apparatus of repression and surveillance was constructed, creating an intense atmosphere of political oppression of 'revolutionaries'.[8] Even in private taverns, conversations were spied upon by government agents, with those involved reported and prosecuted.[9] In 1792 a proclamation was issued against 'tumultuous' meetings and seditious writings; *habeas corpus* was suspended in 1793, 1798 and 1817; and ever more restrictive libel acts and prosecutions proliferated from 1792 to 1819.[10] From the accession of George IV in 1820 there occurred what has been called 'the silencing', whereby satire, such a feature of eighteenth-century life, was denigrated for its unacceptable moral carelessness and legislated into temporary quasi-oblivion.[11] Edmund Burke's *Reflections on the Revolution in France* (1790) provided the ideological justification for the counter-revolutionary measures. A prevailing atmosphere of paranoia and intolerance caused threats to be discerned in all parts. To be different, to stand out, at this time became a dangerous status.

Fuelling and sustaining this antithetical conservative response to the new strains of social radicalism was a renewed evangelical moral drive, the so-called 'second awakening'. From the 1780s, evangelical and messianic societies proliferated, attracting patriarchal reformers such as William Wilberforce. In the 1790s, while supporting humanitarian anti-slavery and child welfare movements, evangelicals also supported repressive legislation against what they saw as the ungodly radicals with their threats to the social order. In 1802, the Society for the Suppression of Vice was formed, which included in its membership Wilberforce and the moral reformer Hannah More. Under these leaders was launched a radical sanitizing and remoralization mission across British society, aimed at restoring and maintaining godliness, social order and clean living among the lower classes.[12]

Neither of these strong currents of opinion – the radical movement towards universal citizenship or the reactionary remoralization campaign – augured well for the idiot population. Each faction demanded of the poor and the incapacitated an active commitment to self-improvement and social participation. The vehemence of the ideological contest left little room for those whose minds resisted, or were impervious to, moral or intellectual betterment. This put those designated idiots or imbeciles at risk of being identified as a social problem, and then slipping into exclusion and, once out of sight, irrelevance. As new in-groups were formed, out-groups fought for status and inclusion, as was the case with Mary Wollstonecraft's struggle for the rights of women and the Corresponding Societies' battles on behalf of working men. Those unable to speak for themselves were pushed to the margins, either incapable of making the transition from harmless dullard to dutiful citizen demanded by the radicals, or to become the passive objects of the social cleansing campaign of the reactionary moral evangelists. They were in danger not so much of becoming the subject of negative opinion as of disappearing from the realm of opinion altogether, drifting into a sphere in which, unnoticed, they lost all status.

Radical opinion, therefore, however much it was framed as progressive and leading to a utopian future, did not augur well for the incapacitated. When Thomas Paine wrote his *Rights of Man* (1791–2), Paine, himself originating from the lower orders of British eighteenth-century society, argued that 'a great mass of mankind are degradedly thrown into the background of the human picture.'[13] While a revolution such as the one that had just taken place in France precipitated the initial liberation of this mass into the foreground, a second revolutionary phase, of instruction and improvement, was necessary to fulfil revolutionary aims of equality, liberty and citizenship. This initial stage of revolution would inevitably entail outrages (such as carrying heads on spikes and summary executions) because of the as yet unformed minds of the newly liberated: 'These outrages were not the effect of the principles of the Revolution, but of the degraded mind that existed before the Revolution, and which the Revolution is calculated to reform.'[14] The job of a revolution, therefore, is to improve the minds of the people so that the essential unity of Man can be achieved: 'By which I mean that men are all *of one degree* and consequently that all men are born equal, and with equal natural right.'[15] Only it was quite clear that in Paine's mind all men (he referred to only one gender) were not born equal. For Paine, the absurdity of the hereditary aristocratic principle was its system of '*mental levelling*', which 'indiscriminately admits every species of character to the same

John Dalrymple, after James Gillray, 'We explain de Rights of Man to de Noblesse', 1798, hand-coloured etching from the *Consequences of a Successful French Invasion* series. Revolutionary excesses were seen as the consequence of the unformed minds of lower-class revolutionaries.

authority'.[16] Accordingly, with ignorance put on a par with wisdom, 'kings succeed with each other, not as rationals but as animals. It signifies not what their mental or moral characteristics are.'[17] His objection to the hereditary principle of monarchy was that kingship is 'an office which any child or idiot may fill'.[18] While it 'requires some talents to be a common mechanic . . . to be a king, requires only the animal figure of a man – a sort of breathing automaton'.[19]

Paine was arguing less for a universal system of social equality than for a new hierarchy of mind, a meritocracy in which talents, both innate and learned, were recognized. He talked about men having what he called pre-existing 'intellectual rights, or rights of the mind', which were linked to the civil rights they would enjoy by being members of society.[20] The assumption was that to enjoy rights, and therefore to enjoy citizenship, a person's mind needed to be capable of forming and understanding those intellectual rights which transmuted into civil rights: citizenship was not a given, but earned through mental faculty. This vision of rights linked to inbuilt mental capacity has been described as 'the shadow language of inequality paralleling the much more visible rhetoric of republican equality in France and America'.[21] The social contract was not a matter of simple equality but a new hierarchical reordering of society based on vague and undefined, but commonly 'understood' and approved, ideas of 'merit' and 'talent'.[22] The greatest absurdity of the old hereditary system, for the radicals, was that under it an idiot could rule. Under the new meritocratic system, with its hierarchy based on intelligence and talent, the idiotic and the dull would never rule again: indeed, their ability to participate in citizenship at all was under question. What place could there be for them in this new society of new men?

For Paine, government's only claim to legitimacy was that 'the *individuals themselves*, each in his own personal and sovereign right, *entered into a compact with each other* to produce a government.'[23] To become a proper, civilized Man, engaged and participating in society, men must be able to understand and make a contract. Thus, as rights became increasingly formalized and defined, any group perceived as lacking the capacity to exercise the contract implied by them, and carry the responsibility for them, became equally sharply identified as part of an incorrigible out-group. Such out-groups were visibly separable from the mass advance and progress of humanity that a 'universal' system of rights would bring. Paine denounced absolutist regimes, 'the attempt to govern mankind by force and fraud, as if they were all knaves and fools'.[24] He could scarcely avoid feeling 'disgust at those who are thus imposed upon'.[25] To be governed without rights, to play no active role in citizenship, was only for the fool. The rational mass of humanity could, with instruction, achieve full human citizen status. In this radicalization of political thought, the out-group of idiocy had suddenly narrowed significantly and was becoming isolated. Paine talked of 'that great chain of connexion' which holds a civilized community together through 'mutual dependence and reciprocal interest', but where now was the idiotic or imbecile person's link in that chain?[26]

In 1793 the journalist, novelist and political philosopher William Godwin, fired up by the revolutionary victories in France, advanced in a very pure form the idea of the progressive perfectibility of the human race which he felt the revolution heralded. His *Enquiry concerning Political Justice* denounced the prevailing conservative belief of the eighteenth century that 'everything in the universe is for the best' and should not therefore be changed because it expressed God's will.[27] Humankind was not only improvable, he argued, but actually perfectible: 'By perfectible, it is not meant that he is capable of being brought to perfection. But the word seems sufficiently adapted to express the faculty of being continually made better and receiving perpetual improvement, and in this sense it is here to be understood.'[28] The capacity for continual improvement, in Godwin's vision, was infinite and would never end.[29] The human mind would make 'perpetual progress' because of its facility to assimilate, store and combine impressions into ideas, thus transforming experience and ideas into knowledge and wisdom.[30] Many men might currently be what Godwin called 'a clod of the valley', but these rural dimwits would, with education, advance to the highest level of civilization.[31] His language recalled Grose's slang dictionary, published a few years earlier, with its references to the 'clod hoppers', 'clod pates' and 'clod poles' that comprised the dull, brainless peasantry.[32] Godwin concluded with an astonishing, utopian, anarchistic depiction of a world in which 'men' would live for ever, therefore not even needing to propagate, and where there would be no war, no crimes, no need for justice or government. Disease would be abolished, as would anguish, melancholy and resentment, in a society of perfect humans.[33]

Though struck with this vision of utopian perfection, Godwin nevertheless saw the history of the human race up to this point as very imperfect, going so far as to call it 'one vast abortion'.[34] He drew attention to the 'traces of stupidity, of rooted insolence' on the faces of most people. But this was as they were now. Human capacity for improvement and advancement should not be doubted. With a philosophy of skilful education of the masses, even the most 'stupid and inanimate dolts' could be improved and eventually fulfil their citizenship duties in a spirit of unrestrained freedom of enquiry.[35]

There was, however, an exception. Godwin defined a citizen's duty as 'the application of capacity in an intelligent being'.[36] It followed that, if citizenship was a matter of capacity, then it could not quite be universal, and nor could the march to perfection. There were some human beings 'palpably and unequivocally excluded by the structure of their frame'.[37] What was to become of those who were 'palpably and unequivocally excluded' from this progressive world, built on reason and sound understanding, of perfection and excellence, where morbidity and even mortality would be abolished? What would become of those with diseased minds, perpetually imperfect, unimprovable or lacking reason? On their fate Godwin was silent, but his use of the word 'excluded' was prescient.[38]

In this way radical opinion, though promoting the benefit of the many, saw no place for the mentally enfeebled in the new utopia. The proclaimed new world of active citizenship, rights, duties and infinite mental improvement seemed to pay no attention to what place they could occupy. The progressivism of radicalism was no friend to the idiot, for whom it seemed unable to conceive a place.

However, the countervailing currents of conservative opinion after the French Revolution also offered little hope for those consigned to the category of idiocy. Edmund Burke's *Reflections on the Revolution in France* in 1790 denounced the takeover of France by 'a handful of country clowns . . . some of whom are said not to be able to read and write'.[39] He warned that if people sought to move and operate outside their allotted role this would destroy social order.[40] His reaction to what he saw as the seizure of power by the dull-witted was consequently apoplectic: 'What sort of a thing must be a nation of gross, stupid, ferocious, and at the same time, poor and sordid barbarians . . . possessing nothing at present and hoping for nothing hereafter.'[41] For Burke, the stupid, potentially 'good and useful' in their allotted sphere, were, like barbarians, violent and terrifying if they sought to move out of it.

The writer, moral reformer and educator Hannah More, a friend of Burke, moved rapidly from initial support for the Revolution into the anti-revolutionary camp after reading Burke's *Reflections*.[42] More was a prominent activist along with the reformer William Wilberforce and their friends in the so-called Clapham Sect, who led the second wave of the evangelical revival that swept the country in the 1780s and '90s.[43] Between 1795 and 1798 she published the 'Cheap Repository Tracts', a series of evangelical chapbooks aimed at the poor, over a million of which had been distributed by the end of 1795 and which sold continuously into the 1850s.[44] The tracts were political propaganda, counter-revolutionary, socially conservative and loyalist in tone, and have been described as an 'ambitious concerted attempt to change people's minds . . . part of a continuing upper class endeavour to reform and moralise the poor'.[45]

James Gillray, 'The Republican – Attack', 1795, coloured engraving depicting idiot-countenanced revolutionaries attacking King George III. Fear of revolution influenced public opinion in the 1790s.

More's tracts saw literacy among the poor as essential, but not for personal advancement or class betterment, as neither of these would make them good or happy. Its purpose was to enable the simplest of people to read and understand God's word, and thereby achieve grace and salvation.[46] She constantly stressed the message of personal responsibility for learning and self-improvement through parables and moral homilies. Beggarly boys with 'mean and low minds' who refused the assistance of the kindly middle classes were 'dull and distrustful lads' who deserved their impoverishment. They were sinners turning from God. Their failings were caused by 'continual absence of mind . . . false reasoning . . . seeming dullness . . . and insensibility'.[47] The dull have a personal responsibility for self-improvement, she wrote, and to carry a disproportionate amount of natural imperfection is no excuse. The tone towards those dullards who do not take responsibility for the moral improvement of their minds was punitive and retributive.

More set out a philosophy that required the rich and enlightened to teach the poor and dull, but laid an equal onus on the dull and poor to accept the teaching and improve their minds. The consequences, for both sides, of failing to fulfil their duty were, literally, damning. The dull were educable, and it was therefore their choice if they failed to respond to the moral education and manners that the 'great' must give them. The duty of the middle and upper classes to eradicate dullness of mind was a great movement: 'an increasing desire to instruct the poor, to inform the ignorant and to reclaim the vicious, is spreading among us,' More pronounced.[48] In More's tract *The History of Hester Wilmot*, a Sunday school teacher explains that the only way to ensure the attention of her children is to demand constant repetition of the scriptures they have heard until they achieve understanding: 'Those who had weak capacities would, to be sure, do this but very imperfectly: but even the weakest, if they were willing, would return something.'[49] Learning was an act of volition that even the weakest could turn their minds to, if they were only willing. To be unable to learn was no longer a misfortune, it was a sin.

In More's allegorical tale of 'Parley the Porter', the dim-witted, gullible Parley, porter to the well-fortified castle and grounds of a great master, allows 'robbers' to overwhelm the castle and commit 'rapine, murder and conflagration'.[50] This is allowed to happen because Parley is a 'soft easy fellow', echoing witness descriptions of idiot defendants in eighteenth-century courtrooms.[51] The master represents God, the robbers the forces of evil, and Parley the dull-witted part of God's human flock. Parley's weak mind is the entry point through which sin can destroy mankind. None stands with Parley, and his master (God) 'was more afraid of him . . . than of the rest'.[52] He is, as the full title of the tract suggests, a traitor, a wilful actor in his ignorance rather than an uncomprehending dolt.

In More's view, the weak mind was no longer the God-given misfortune under which the idiotic must labour as best they can, with a promise of leniency and redemption if they did their best. It was a degenerate threat at the heart of the moral universe, a conduit through which sin, destruction and blasphemy could undermine the Christian faith. In the moral world that More and her fellow evangelists were framing for the dull and the poor, 'the most dim-sighted might see,'[53] and there were consequences for them, and others, if they failed to do so.[54]

More and her fellow evangelists attached a moral imperative and religious duty to the art of reading, and regarded the dull-witted as morally culpable should they fail to master it. This presaged the exclusion of those who lacked the capacity to read and learn from the hope of salvation, which in turn framed the idiot type as one outside the human sphere, lacking the will or capacity to determine their own fate. Without the knowledge and the moral sense provided by literacy, and in particular the reading of the Bible, the will could not operate. All of this amounted to a vituperative indictment of the ignorant that left no room for pleas of incapacity. If the ignorant failed to respond to instruction, they were either damned for their wilfulness or, through their incapacity, outside the sphere of salvation altogether.

This framing of the moral responsibilities of the ignorant, the culpability of the unlearned and the equation of moral virtue with literacy were deeply influential in nineteenth-century bourgeois thinking. It can be seen in the poetic homilies of Martin Tupper, who from 1837 began to publish regular editions of his *Proverbial Philosophy: A Book of Thoughts and Arguments*, which enjoyed 25 years of 'phenomenal popular success'.[55] *Proverbial Philosophy* reflected back to its hundreds of thousands of bourgeois readers, in a rapidly expanding literate public, the 'moral commonplaces' in which they believed, and Tupper was worshipped in return by his mass audience as a sage throughout the 1840s and '50s.[56] Tupper both reflected, and formed, bourgeois opinion in his newly literate readership. Like More he saw the weak, infirm mind as bearing a threat of moral degradation.[57] He speculated whether there was a great 'common hall of intellect' that brought together the universal learning that all humanity had achieved. Modern people, he argued, no doubt to the delight of his newly affluent and literate readership, did not live in 'isolated worlds' but rather as 'converging radiations, part of one majestic whole', brought together by memory and knowledge. Only two groups of people were excluded from this interconnected globe of wisdom: 'A brutish man knoweth not this, neither can a fool comprehend it.'[58] Like More, Tupper preached that the inability to read was a direct moral failing that cut a human being off from God, with incapacity no excuse:

> To be without books, or the capacity to read is:
> To be thrust from the feet of Him who spake as never Man spake,
> To have no avenue to heaven but the dim aisle of superstition.[59]

The intellectually incapacitated, with their traitorous 'infirmity', were a dangerous threat to morality: they belonged outside the common store of human memory and knowledge and were impervious to redemption or salvation. Framed in this way, their excommunication from society, the removal of their link from the chain of community, was almost total.

The moralists preached that survival in modern society, and the ability to achieve salvation, required active engagement and the will for self-improvement. Their secular radical opponents preached a similar doctrine, with different aims. Both social conservatives and left-wing radicals made demands on the minds of the common people they so desperately wished to improve. An exasperated Augustus Hare, minister of a rural parish in Wiltshire, preached to his dullard rural congregation in the 1820s:

> To profit by a sermon, a man must attend to it; he must hear it thoroughly; he must understand it; he must think it over with himself, when he gets home. How few in the congregation will go to all this trouble. You come, and sit, and hear, and I hope you are able in some degree to follow the meaning of what I say to you from the pulpit;

yet how far is this from the understanding and knowledge by which grace and peace are to be multiplied.[60]

To sit passively, and hear uncomprehendingly, was no longer enough. The path to salvation was knowledge and learning. Political salvation, for the radicals, lay in improving the minds and affecting the consciousness of the mentally dull. For the religious conservatives, it was to cultivate the mind of each person to know their place, and the word of God. Each offered future happiness, either worldly or heavenly, as a reward. Yet for those who could not participate in these processes of improvement there was no way forward, only an exit from the stage of human community. The idiot began slowly to disappear from communal consciousness, cast adrift in a sea of progress they did not know how to navigate.

This path was reflected in the fate of Simple Simon, the much-loved dimwit of the eighteenth century. He survived into the nineteenth, but in a very different form. Mostly he mutated into a silly child – as he is still known today – from the bawdy, boozy knucklehead of the previous century. He did, however, also have one early nineteenth-century reincarnation as an adult in John Wallace's play *Simple Simon* (1805). In this play Simon the country fool, in common with many of his real-life compatriots, has urbanized, but he is not coping well. Living in London, an ex-chimney sweep, he is assailed on all sides by designing 'friends' and exploitative characters with names such as Moneytrap and Lovegold. Despite committing a crime, Simon survives to be imposed upon another day – not by any intervention from family, friends or community but by luck. He avoids the hangman's rope, yet we are left in no doubt that his simplicity will place him in danger again: it will only be a matter of time. Simon's concern is more with his hungry stomach than his life: 'Be hanged – without getting my dinner?'[61] This was a very different Simon, cut adrift from the more secure rural communities his predecessors had known, alone in the city, surrounded only by exploitation and hostility, and dangerously unaware of the peril he was in. Beneath the loveable foolery lay a man heading for oblivion.

Utilitarianism

Both radicals and the second wave of evangelists were influenced by, and wrote within the wider context of, the doctrine of utilitarianism, first hypothesized by Jeremy Bentham and later expanded and developed by J. S. Mill. The doctrine of the 'greatest happiness of the greatest number' had been posited by Bentham in his *Introduction to the Principles of Morals and Legislation* (1789). When Mill developed Bentham's ideas around the mid-nineteenth century, he paid much attention to the link between faculty, or capacity, and happiness. It was faculty of mind that created a hierarchy of happiness (or what he preferred to call 'contentment') within a society. Those with higher faculties struggled more to attain happiness than those with lower faculties, because of their greater awareness and sensitivity:

> A being of higher faculties requires more to make him happy, is capable probably of more acute suffering and is certainly accessible to it at more points than one of an inferior type; but in spite of these liabilities, he can never really wish to sink into what he feels to be a lower grade of existence.[62]

'No intelligent human being', explained Mill, 'would consent to be a fool, no instructed person would be an ignoramus . . . even though they should be persuaded that the fool, the dunce, or the rascal is better satisfied with his lot than they are with theirs.'[63] Why was this? In Mill's explanation it was because those endowed with higher mental faculties were possessed of a greater sense of dignity than those with undeveloped minds, and therefore had a greater awareness of their own imperfections. This greater mental endowment did not make them happier than the fool, who was easily pleased with very little, not knowing any better. It did, however, make them content.[64] Mill summarized it famously:

> It is better to be a human being satisfied than a pig satisfied; better to be Socrates dissatisfied than a fool satisfied. And if the fool, or the pig, is of a different opinion, it is because they only know their own side of the question. The other party to the comparison knows both sides.[65]

It was the person who could know both sides, who had the facility of mental curiosity and enquiry, whose judgement must prevail. The principal requirement for satisfaction, or content, was the capacity for 'mental cultivation'. The cultivated mind was not, according to Mill, only the province of the elite philosopher or theorist. It was 'any mind to which the fountains of knowledge have been opened, and which has been taught, in any tolerable

Engraving of 'Imbecility', in Alexander Morison's *Outlines of Lectures on Mental Diseases* (1826). Over the 19th century, utilitarian philosophy saw the imbecile as a detached person incapable of true happiness.

degree, to exercise its faculties'.[66] Such a degree of 'mental culture'
was possible for 'every one born in a civilized country . . . who
has this moderate amount of moral and intellectual requisites'.[67]

Mill conceded that this did not quite mean everyone:

> It is, perhaps, hardly necessary to say that this doctrine is
> meant to apply only to human beings in the maturity of
> their faculties . . . those who are still in a state to require
> being taken care of by others must be protected against
> their own actions as well as against external injury.[68]

The person without sufficient capacity was, for Mill, only an
object of charity. There was no point in attempting to improve
the unimprovable mind; its owner only needed looking after.
The satisfied fools and pigs of Mill's imagination could simply
be farmed out, to a place where they could wallow in their own
stupefied and undemanding satisfaction. Society, with its cultivated minds, was not for them. Mill even suggested, despite
his aversion to unnecessary state interference in the liberty of
the subject, public examinations of all children, beginning at an
early stage, to ascertain 'if he (or she) is able to read. If a child
proves unable, the father, unless he has some sufficient ground
of excuse, might be subjected to a moderate fine.'[69] As in More's
eyes the inability to learn to read had become a sin, for Mill it
was now a crime.

This was all a far cry from pre-Benthamite eighteenth-century
thinking, which saw the idiot, the half-idiot, the imbecile, the
soft, the weak and the easy all fitting neatly into impercepti-
ble gradations of the human mind that formed the great chain
of being, placed there by God and therefore rightfully there.
Imperfection was acknowledged to be a universal characteristic: idiots, and the dull, just happened to be somewhere lower
down the chain than the rest. Utilitarianism, which demanded
more from its citizens than simply being born to be understood
as human, placed this fatalistic creed, and its easy tolerance of
community, under threat. Nineteenth-century thought had little

room for the terminally dull. The intellectual and philosophical drive was towards the perfectibility of Man, either as a religious or a social being, and the position of the chronically imperfect, particularly those with imperfections of the mind, was quickly destabilized. Both the revolutionary and counter-revolutionary movements that sprang from the turmoil of 1789 framed a world in which idiocy had no place. They had more in common than they thought. Each demanded self-improvement, the shedding of the embarrassment of mass dullness, to create a new world, either here on earth or in a future kingdom. Both these new worlds had strict admission criteria, primary among them the possession of what Mill called a 'cultivated mind'.

As Mill wrote his words, in 1859 and 1861, an exodus of the idiot population from society into institutions was in progress. The climates of religious, political, medical and social opinion that had been in train since the 1789 revolutionary events in France allowed them to begin to slip almost unnoticed from mainstream society, assailed from all sides. They could not meet the moral improvement demands of the new evangelists, the quest for human perfection of the radicals, or the prerequisites for private and public happiness of the utilitarians.

The Drift to the Asylum

The easing of the path towards the institution for the idiot, and the ending of inclusion in Britain's communities, had begun quietly in 1808 when Parliament passed the County Asylums Act, which gave optional powers to counties to build asylums. Its main purpose was to remove 'lunatics', and other people seen as mentally 'diseased' or incurable, from jails and private madhouses to buildings where they would be easier to manage and separated from society. Its effect was to establish the first network of state hospital provision for those seen as mentally different, previous asylums and madhouses having been either charitable or private and collectively housing only a few hundred people. More importantly, the creation of these institutions established the principle that there was a state duty to intervene in the identification, treatment and control of such people.

The legislation allowed magistrates and parochial authorities to send 'dangerous idiots and lunatics' for special treatment and care at a weekly charge.[70] This would provide both convenience and safety in dealing with the unwanted and dangerous, whereas, as the Act put it, 'the practice of confining such lunatics and other insane persons [that is, idiots] as are chargeable to their respective parishes in Gaols, Poor Houses and Houses of Industry, is highly dangerous and inconvenient.'[71] Between 1808 and 1834, twelve county asylums were established under this system.[72] Some idiots drifted into these institutions, although they were primarily established for the reception and cure of lunatics, as gaols, workhouses and parish Poor Law guardians sought to move them out of their sphere of responsibility.

The drift into institutions was significantly accelerated by the 1834 Poor Law Amendment Act, which saw a sharp policy shift towards 'indoor' (meaning institutional) relief and away from 'outdoor' (meaning community) relief. The destitute, indolent, unemployed and feeble would no longer be supported to live in their own homes but would be forced to move to workhouses. These new workhouses, which were established across the country at an exponential rate following the 1834 legislation, were deliberately designed to be punitive, uncomfortable and forbidding. This reflected wider harshening public and political attitudes towards those who appeared unable or unwilling to accept their social, moral or religious responsibilities to belong and contribute to society.

The system was deliberately harsh, with minimum comfort (chairs were made backless to avoid ease of sitting), basic diet and separation of the sexes. Husbands and wives would live apart, as would parents and children. The theory was to punish the workshy so that only the truly destitute or incapable would accept relief. In the five years after the passing of the Act, some 350 new workhouses were constructed. A further two hundred were built before the end of the century. Designs, based on standard model plans, excluded any sort of extravagance, were sited on the edges of towns to avoid offence to the citizens, and aimed for a standard below the average labourer's cottage, so as not to be too attractive to the destitute. Segregation was strict, diet meagre, work punitive. Gruel, bread and cheese formed the diet, with soup or meat and potatoes once a week. Water was the only drink (with tea a privilege for the elderly). Women made sacks or worked in the kitchen and laundry. Men chopped wood or ground corn.[73] The consequence was that soon many work-houses were housing not the able-bodied poor but the old, the sick, the mentally ill and those with physical or mental impair-ments deemed unable to work. In 1835 the Birmingham workhouse established purpose-built wards for 'insane' residents. The Leicester workhouse segregated 'idiots and lunatics', pro-viding specialized nursing attendants. By 1837, parish officials had 6,368 idiots in their care. They had become an important

In the 1830s and 1840s, many idiots drifted into the harsh workhouse system, as seen in this illustration of a workhouse dinner by Hablot K. Browne (Phiz) from James Grant's *Sketches in London* (1838).

object of official attention, care and control, and part of the nation's burgeoning institutionalized population.[74]

In 1845 a new County Asylums Act was passed under the government of Sir Robert Peel which, in contrast to the permissive legislation of 1808 that merely allowed counties to build asylums if they wished, now required every county to build an asylum to provide treatment for its pauper lunatics and idiots.[75] As a result of this legislative drive, by the end of the century there would be around 120 state-run asylums in England and Wales housing more than 100,000 people. An accompanying Lunacy Act defined three categories of insanity, based on John Haslam's medicalized definition of 1823, which were 'lunatics, idiots or persons of unsound mind'.[76] With this legislation the idiot population had become specifically defined as the responsibility of the state, from a position of profound state disinterest just fifty years earlier.

However, in the early days of the new asylums, admission rates of idiots remained low, estimated at just 1,000, or 6 per cent of the asylum population, by 1850.[77] Although the asylums were theoretically open for anyone deemed lunatic, idiotic or of unsound mind, there was a focus on admitting either those who were curable, and could therefore be treated and subsequently discharged, or those who were deemed dangerous and needed to be behind institutional walls for the protection of society. Harmless, incurable idiots fell into neither category. They continued therefore to flow into workhouses, up to 10,000 of them by 1850. Workhouses found themselves having to adapt to these inflows by creating special idiot and imbecile wards. In 1856 the Lunacy Commission commented that the huge wards in some workhouses were asylums 'in everything but the attendance and appliances which insure . . . proper treatment'.[78]

In an age of institutionalization for those considered unable to cope with, or unfit for, life in society, the idiot population started therefore to be drawn into institutional life, mostly to workhouses but in smaller numbers to lunatic asylums. If there was such a thing as an appropriate institutional environment for idiots, neither of these fitted the bill. Incurable, unchanging people did not fit into the projected site of curability that the early lunatic asylums promised. Indeed, asylums actively sought to exclude them, as they risked 'silting-up' a dynamic system of treatment and discharge.[79] Nor did they fit into the workhouse system, whose aim was to wean people off economic dependence on the state through a harshly punitive environment. Idiots were therefore subsumed, incidentally rather than with any purposeful intent, under the general category of 'insane persons' and became just part of a growing general confinement and clinical management of the pauper deviant. The idiot became a problem within the new state institutional system, deemed unfit for the community but in practice also unfit for the lunatic asylum.

Rather than questioning whether the idiot population should be confined to institutions at all, or considering how they might live their lives within communities, reformers and philanthropists concluded that they were in the wrong sort of institutions and that they needed something more customized and specialist. A succession of British asylum superintendents with an interest in idiocy visited the Bicêtre asylum in Paris to observe the work of Édouard Séguin, who was pioneering moral treatment of idiots, a method that sought to inculcate self-restraint, conformity and obedience through an educative regime without recourse to physical restraint or physically punitive sanctions. Among them was John Conolly from the Hanwell asylum, himself a pioneer of moral restraint for lunatics in British asylums.[80] Conolly had noted the uneasy plight of the handful of young idiots among Hanwell's lunatic population. In 1845 he started a programme for this group, based on Séguin's Bicêtre work.[81] Pressure to establish a separate asylum for idiots in England was exerted by Conolly and other like-minded physicians inspired by Séguin.[82] Conolly joined forces with a group of wealthy charitable donors and, in 1848, working closely with the prominent Nonconformist reformer and philanthropist Andrew Reed, opened a small asylum for idiots at Park House in Highgate, north London. (Park House was visited by Charles Dickens in 1853, after which he wrote his article 'Idiots' for *Household Words*.) The small asylum opened initially to just eight inmates but within two years had a waiting list of 170 people. To meet demand, the board of governors leased a larger site, Essex Hall in Colchester, aided by a £1,000 loan from the Baptist philanthropist and railway magnate Samuel Morton Peto. Idiot inmates began to be moved in from 1850 and by 1853 Essex Hall was full, with 123 patients.

Since demand for specialist idiot asylum places seemed to be growing exponentially, Reed decided on the need for a national asylum. After sufficient funds had been raised, Reed, Conolly and their fellow benefactors settled on some land on Earlswood Common, near Redhill in Surrey, and the foundation stone was laid in 1853, the ceremony of turning the first sod performed by Albert, the Prince Consort.[83] In 1855, with the building only partially complete, the first transfer of patients from Park House and Essex Hall took place.

The world's first purpose-built specialist idiot asylum was eventually fully completed in 1863, with five hundred beds. In 1858 the unheralded young physician John Langdon Down, protégé of John Conolly, was appointed as Earlswood's superintendent.[84] In his first report, Down preached 'the advantages of separate institutional care and education of idiot children'.[85] He practised the enlightened doctrine of moral treatment and, after the obligatory pilgrimage to the Bicêtre in 1860, devoted himself to the study of the idiots in his care. In 1866 he announced his 'discovery' of 'Mongolian imbecility', discussed in the previous chapter, and his findings were published in the *Journal of Mental Science* the following year.[86] In 1868 Down left Earlswood to establish a new private asylum for idiots, the Normansfield Training Institution for Imbeciles in Teddington, Middlesex.

Essex Hall remained and became the Eastern Counties Asylum for Idiots from 1859. In 1864 the Western Counties Idiot Asylum was built near Exeter, Devon, and in 1870 the Royal Albert Hospital for Idiots and Imbeciles of the Seven Northern Counties opened its doors, just outside Lancaster.[87] A much smaller Midlands Counties Idiot Asylum was established in

Knowle, near Birmingham, in 1872. Thus in just 24 years from the opening of Park House in Highgate, a network of specialist idiot asylums was established that covered all parts of England. All of these were charitable institutions, built and funded through subscription, and largely aimed at the idiot children of the middle classes. As institutionalization continued to proliferate, pressure mounted to house 'pauper' idiots. In 1870 the Metropolitan Asylums Board (established by the Metropolitan Poor Act of 1867) opened the Caterham Imbeciles Asylum in Surrey and the Leavesden Imbeciles Asylum in Hertfordshire, each with 1,560 beds to accommodate the idiot and imbecile poor of London.

The transformation was now complete. From accepted, if odd, members of the community in the eighteenth century, the idiot and the imbecile were now creatures of the institution. Medicine had gained ascendancy over them and the power to identify, control and treat them. Society had turned its back on them. A constellation of factors brought about this radical transformation in the social status of the intellectually challenged which enabled them to be quietly ushered from the social stage to spend their lives behind the walls of the asylum. New modes of thought could find no space for them. Radical

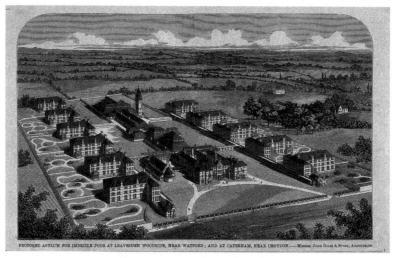

Bird's-eye view of the Leavesden Imbeciles Asylum, which opened in Hertfordshire in 1870, illustrated in *The Builder*, 25 July 1868.

politicians of the left wanted active, contributing citizens whose minds could be transformed towards a state of social perfection and harmony. Reactionary evangelists wanted a quiescent but Bible-reading, devout and morally strong population of the poor. Anthropologists found dark reminders of our savage and uncivilized past in the undeveloped idiot mind. Novelists and poets could see only the husk of a human, an object of pity or exoticized prurience. The medical profession saw a new opportunity to exert its authority, in courtroom and institution. Society as a whole saw a group of people they would rather not see, who no longer amused them but who brought a whiff of dangerous unease to their communities, and who should best live their lives safely removed to institutional medical care. They pitied them, sometimes they loathed or feared them, and either way they did not want to be near them. As the nineteenth century neared its end, the idiot population found themselves not only behind the brick walls of the new asylums but surrounded by a high metaphorical wall of social condemnation and exclusion.

PART THREE

From Eugenics to Care in the Community, 1870 to the Present Day

8

After Darwin:
Mental Deficiency, Eugenics
and Psychology, 1870–1939

Any observer contemplating the idiot and imbecile population in the 1870s saw a very different picture to what would have been observed a century, or even half a century, earlier. While by no means all people labelled idiotic or imbecilic were institutionalized, the idiotic person had come to be perceived as a creature of the institution, a fit object for medical care, treatment and control. This medical ascendancy was entirely new – the idiot and imbecile had not come under the medical gaze in the preceding centuries. However, their place was no longer within society but locked away from it, in the new medical terrain of the asylum. Their institutionalization was justified either as ostensibly benevolent protection from their own vulnerability or as in the interests of public protection against their dangerousness. There were even new terms to describe them and to proclaim their newly medicalized framing. Idiocy was still in use as a general term but idiots were now 'mental defectives' or the 'feeble-minded' as far as doctors were concerned. The locus of care had switched decisively from the family to the institution, from charitable initiatives to the state.

The process of institutionalization was unremitting. An 1886 Idiots Act, the first piece of legislation addressed exclusively to the 'problem' of idiocy, had enabled the certification of idiots separately from lunatics, and allowed local rates to be used for building specialist idiot or mental deficiency facilities.[1] By 1905 there would be just under 2,000 mental defectives housed in the five charitable idiot institutions at Earlswood, Lancaster, Colchester, Devon and Birmingham. There would be more than 3,000 lower-class idiots and imbeciles in the Leavesden, Caterham and Darenth Park imbecile asylums encircling London.[2] Many more were subsumed into larger general asylums across the country, such as Colney Hatch in north London and the West Riding Pauper Lunatic Asylum in Yorkshire, both of which had a sizeable idiot population. Concentration of the mental defective population into institutions made them an object of study, experiment, reflection and theorization by medical men, scientists, psychologists and anthropologists. They were gazed at as something mysterious, exotic, a different species from which we could learn just as surely as zoologists and botanists could learn from the study of animal and plant species.

Wider political developments had been a catalyst in the separation of mental defectives from society. The introduction of universal elementary education in 1870 brought into focus a hitherto unidentified, and statistically significant, cohort of school-age children deemed in need of specialist training and intervention.[3] The pressing desire to identify, control and contain the mentally different was reflected in the 1871 census, which was the first to ask how many people in each household were blind, deaf and dumb, imbecile or idiot, or lunatic. The stipulation to collect this information had been made in the Census (England) Act of the previous year. Rising voter participation through the Reform Acts of 1867 and 1884–5 provoked fears in the middle and upper classes about the aptitude of the so-called feeble-minded, who seemed so prevalent among the newly enfranchised lower classes, to be the active and engaged participants that citizen suffrage demanded of them. This reflected the long-running fears of both radicals and reactionaries, set in train by the events of the French Revolution almost a century earlier, about the capacity of the dull-witted to be contributing members of society. In 1899 the reported poor physical and mental condition of working-class recruits to the British Army for the Boer War further heightened this class anxiety, as did the extension of the franchise to almost universal suffrage in 1918.[4]

Two new modes of thought would reflect these heightened anxieties and serve to ostracize the mentally deficient in public consciousness as dangerous or threatening outsiders, or as un-developed not-quite-human people. The first was the 'science' of eugenics; the second was the emergence of evolutionary psy-chology, sometimes known as comparative or animal psychology. These two modes of thinking overlapped at times but were also quite distinct. Eugenics preached the need for intervention to improve the racial stock in the face of human degeneration. Evolu-tionary psychology tried to demonstrate that humankind was the product of an evolutionary process by identifying a progressive link between non-human animal and human consciousness, using the idiot mind as a signifier of the narrow consciousness gap between humans and other species. Both owed their origins to Darwin's theory of natural selection posited in his *On the Origin of Species* (1859), although neither were theories explicitly developed by Darwin himself.

Eugenic Theory

The theory of eugenics was developed by Francis Galton, a half-cousin of Darwin who, motivated by Darwin's work on evolution and by fears of persistent poverty and its impact on English society, became fascinated by individual differences and hered-ity and their consequences for society.[5] In his *Hereditary Genius: An Inquiry into Its Laws and Consequences* (1869) he argued that heredity rather than environment was largely responsible for human differences. Galton speculated that if by careful selection farmers and botanists could breed strong animals and plants, 'could not the race of men be similarly improved? Could not the undesirables be got rid of and the desirables multiplied?'[6] In his later work, *Inquiries into Human Faculty and Its Development* (1883), he introduced the term 'eugenics'. This advocated a national policy of social engineering that would increase the number of people with the necessary mental intelligence to meet the challenges of a complex, newly industrialized and economically globalized society. It involved promoting differential birth rates for groups with differing hereditary characteristics. People of good stock, especially the intellectually gifted young of the middle and upper class, should be encouraged to marry and have as many children as possible, while the feckless lower classes should be discouraged, or indeed prevented, from breeding at high rates.[7] This would be a reversal of the current trend where the intelligent middle classes produced only small families while the lumpenproletariat masses of the new industrial cities seemed to produce limitless offspring. There were deep middle-class social and racial anxieties that civilized society would eventually be overwhelmed by the sheer numbers of ignorant, criminal, morally depraved and intellectually blighted members of the lower orders.

Eugenic thought, with the mentally deficient at the bottom of its hierarchy of the low, began to become part of a public mindset, on both sides of the Atlantic. In the United States the sociologist Richard Dugdale published in 1877 his study of the anonymized 'Juke' family, *The Jukes: A Study in Crime, Pauperism, Disease and Heredity*. This traced the ancestry of a family comprising criminals, prostitutes, the mentally ill and, of course, the mentally deficient through seven generations. Dugdale's veneer of scientific analysis underpinned eugenic theories that identified the feeble-minded person not just with low intelligence and poor bodily and mental health but also with crime, poverty and disorder. Although Dugdale made some concessions to environment as a cause of degradation, alongside heredity, he concluded that 'hereditary pauperism rests chiefly upon disease in some form, tends to terminate in extinction, and may be called the sociological aspect of physical degeneration.'[8] An example of such disease was the 'arrest of development' of congenital idiocy. He described, in the cold, authoritative, scientized form that the study took,

'Case 8, Line 24, generation 4'. This was a young woman who was a congenital idiot, the arrested development of her brain and nervous system proceeding from insufficient nutrition during ante-natal life and . . . scrofulous or syphilitic disease in the parents.[9]

She was, by the time of publication, Dugdale surmised, 'probably dead'. In this presentation the idiot was a struggling, dying organism unable to survive the degradation heaped upon it by heredity, unequal to the task of evolutionary survival, best isolated and allowed to be put out of its misery.

Dugdale's study would become a template for a whole genre of family studies that claimed to identify the spread of deficiency through the unrestrained breeding habits of large, poverty-stricken, dysfunctional and feckless families, seen as a sort of poison eating away at society from within. These publications sowed alarm by detailing how one feckless couple could produce within a few generations hundreds of degenerate, deficient offspring, a sort of knotweed strangling and undermining the social fabric. The Reverend Oscar McCulloch initiated in 1877, the year in which the Jukes study was published, over a decade of research into the poor white upland southerners of Indiana, whom he associated with a particularly dysfunctional family known as the Ishmaels. When his research was published (by the Charity Organization Society) as *The Tribe of Ishmael: A Study in Social Degradation* in 1891, it was revealed that in McCulloch's original pre-publication talk he had presented a diagram 1 metre (3 ft) wide and almost 3.75 metres (12 ft) high containing 1,720 names of the Ishmael tribe, which it had been impossible to reproduce in the book. Particularly keen, or worried, readers could, however, obtain by post a reduced 74-by-168 centimetre (29 by 66 in.) version for 50 cents. The family were presented in terms of an evolutionary struggle, where the higher class 'becomes degraded in form and function . . . because some remote ancestor left its independent, semi-helpful life, and began a parasitic, or pauper life'.[10] There was an almost pornographic, voyeuristic fascination with the lives of the most degraded idiot humans, their lives luridly described before the ritualistic calls for their incarceration, sterilization and eventual extinction. Welfare and misguided philanthropic handouts, McCulloch argued, served only to perpetuate unworthy lives and foolish brains.

There were no such specific published family studies in Britain, but in the 1880s social reformers and investigators fretted in similar ways about the 'residuum' in Britain's cities. This comprised the feckless poor, characterized by degeneration, crime, prostitution, alcoholism, hereditary disease and uncontrolled procreation. The residuum were distinguished from the hardworking 'respectable' working classes and were also known as the 'hopeless classes', 'the unfit', 'the abyss', the 'quagmire', the 'pauper Frankenstein' and the 'submerged tenth'. The social investigator Charles Booth proposed segregating them into industrial labour colonies, to separate them from, and liberate, the respectable poor.[11] Such a strategy was already under way for their imbecile and idiot offspring, who were packed off in increasing numbers to the imbecile asylums sprouting rapidly in the hinterlands of the growing urban conglomerations across Britain.

The urban poor became an object of investigation in wholly new ways. The fourth volume of Henry Mayhew's *London Labour and the London Poor*, with its focus on prostitutes, beggars, thieves, swindlers and other outcasts, appeared in 1861, while Charles Booth's *Life and Labour of the People in London* appeared in nine volumes in the 1890s. As far as the majority of the poor were concerned they became perceived not as the authors of their own misfortune, as the 1834 Poor Law Amendment Act had implied, but as the victims of social and economic circumstances beyond their control, who were deserving of assistance and support to rise from their condition. However, not all poor people were deserving: less optimism was extended to those among them seen as wilfully feckless or irredeemably degenerate. Mayhew described his encounters with clusters of imbeciles as he wandered through the lodging houses of the deeply impoverished rookery of St Giles:

many of them were middle-aged men . . . very shabbily
dressed, and some half naked. There was little manliness
left in the poor wretches . . . the inspector told us they
were chiefly vagrants, and were sunk in profound ignorance, from which they were utterly unable to rise.[12]

On the streets he noted a specific type of 'cripple' beggar: 'the
idiotic-looking youth who "stands pad with a fakement" shaking
in every limb as if he were under the influence of Galvanism'. He
expressed surprise that there was 'no home or institution for cripples from this class. They are certainly deserving of sympathy and
aid for they are utterly incapacitated from any kind of labour.'
The institution was the solution for the imbecile and idiotic
population: reformers could see no way in which they could rise
up from their condition and become part of the respectable working masses. Indeed, they were a drag on the aspirations of the
deserving poor, an obstacle to progress that needed to be removed
in some way, preferably through institutionalization.

Anxieties about the impact of low intelligence on social progress were reflected in wider culture, particularly in H. G. Wells's
widely read science fiction novels *The Time Machine* (1895) and
The War of the Worlds (1898). In *The Time Machine* the unnamed
Time Traveller moves forward to the year 802,701 to find that
Earth seems to be populated by small communities of Eloi, happy,
carefree, almost childlike adults who live in a garden paradise.
He then discovers that beneath the surface of the earth live larger
communities of brutal ape-like Morlocks, who surface only at
night and who operate the machinery and carry out the heavy
industrial tasks that make the leisured life of the Eloi possible.
The world of the future is a degenerationist's nightmare: 'Man
had not remained one species, but had differentiated into two
distinct animals.'[13] The mentally challenged, brutal Morlocks,
'bleached, obscene nocturnal things', are far more numerous, and
physically strong, than the delicate Eloi. They only remain cowed,
at least momentarily, by some half-remembered notion of service
to their betters. However, worse than this, the elegant, playful,

giggling upper-class Eloi are themselves degenerating, decayed though a life of luxury and ease over generations: 'were these creatures fools?' the Time Traveller asks himself.[14] Intelligence is being lost to the human race through the proliferation of the imbecile-minded, and the blindness of the intelligent classes to the demise with which they are threatened. Three years later, in *The War of the Worlds*, Wells imagined Martian invaders who appear to have moved beyond the bodily organism to become creatures of pure intelligence and who, without emotion or feelings, destroy humans like ants. Intelligence, the book suggests, is the key to domination and survival, although in the book's ironic finale the Martians are stopped by an unforeseen physical vulnerability. Wells professed himself a progressive socialist but, like many on the left, enthusiastically embraced eugenic theory and its fears about the deficient. For Wells it was the duty, and right, of the state to intervene to ensure a healthier and more intelligent working class: 'the children people bring into the world can be no more their private concern entirely, than the disease germs they disseminate or the noises a man makes in a thin-floored flat.'[15] His fellow progressive intellectual Havelock Ellis argued that social improvement was impossible if society allowed 'entry into life . . . more freely to the weak, the incompetent, and the defective than to the strong, the efficient, and the sane'.[16]

Evolutionary Psychology

While the theories of eugenics seeped into public consciousness, Darwin's evolutionary theory spawned another field of thought that reframed thinking about the mentally deficient. This was comparative or animal psychology, which sought to explain mental evolution through comparative studies of the minds of humans, non-human animals and infant humans. Darwin had been reticent about the evolution of humans in his *On the Origin of Species*, concentrating on plant and animal species, but the implication was clear. If the theory of evolution and adaptation through natural selection was correct, then humans had evolved from lower life forms. Moreover, they had not only evolved physically but must also have evolved mentally. At some point, consciousness must have emerged from nothingness. How did this happen, and at what point had humans developed a level of consciousness bestowing the self-awareness and self-knowledge that seemed to distinguish them from all other animal species?

The job for evolutionists was therefore to show continuity between species, to demonstrate that humans could have evolved from animal ancestors, but to prove also that there was some sort of developmental process applicable to the mind as well as to the physical organism. Darwin did eventually attempt to offer an explanation of human mental development in two books written more than a decade after *Origin*, *The Descent of Man* (1871) and *The Expression of the Emotions in Man and Animals* (1872). His main object in both these works was to narrow the consciousness gap between humans and animals, to show that basic emotions, instincts and reflexes were shared across species and were the basis of human conscious thought. Such a shared mental heritage made the concept of an evolutionary process of mind through adaptation feasible and would place the human species within his overarching theory.

A perfect explanatory mechanism for bridging the consciousness gap between the higher animals and fully developed humans was, for Darwin, idiot minds. He referred to them in both books. In *Descent* he drew on the anthropologist Karl Vogt's 1867 *Mémoire sur les microcéphales* to link microcephalic idiots upwards to 'lower types of mankind' (by which he meant 'savages') and downwards to lower animals. Darwin described their smaller skulls, less complex convolutions of the brain, projecting foreheads and strongly prognathous jaws.[17] The link to animals was made explicit when he described idiots as 'Strong and remarkably active, continually gamboling and jumping about, and making grimaces. They often ascend stairs on all fours, and are curiously fond of climbing up furniture or trees.'[18] All of this reminded Darwin of 'how lambs and kids, originally Alpine

Pl.3

Darwin considered joy an instinctive reaction that was easily aroused
in idiots, as in this heliotype of a smiling girl and man from his *The Expression
of the Emotions in Man and Animals* (1872).

animals, delight to frisk on any hillock, however small'. He went on to describe a number of other ways in which, he claimed, idiot behaviour resembled animal behaviour: smelling every mouthful of food before eating it; the ape-like use of the mouth to aid the hands while hunting for lice; filthy habits; lack of decency; and remarkably hairy bodies.[19]

This construction of animal-like behaviour and appearance in idiots, often based on the scantiest of 'evidence' from second-hand sources and far from the rigour and scientific elegance of Darwin's powerful direct observations and deductions in *Origin*, aimed to demonstrate a theory of 'reversion'. Reversionary theory argued that arrested structures in members of higher species gave a snapshot of that species in earlier stages of its evolution. Thus in idiots one could observe an earlier stage of the development of humankind: in behaviour like primates and in language like parrots (because imitative and without meaning).[20]

From this grew the new 'science' of animal psychology, led by Darwin's young protégé George Romanes, to whom Darwin passed on his unpublished notes on instinct before his death. Romanes devoted himself to proving the evolution of mind through comparative studies of the mental processes of Man and lower animals. Like Darwin he used the idiot comparison to build a useful bridge between the human and non-human species. In three books, *Animal Intelligence* (1882), *Mental Evolution in Animals* (1883) and *Mental Evolution in Man: Origin of Human Faculty* (1888), Romanes developed a theory that mental evolution was a progression from reflex (the purely unconscious reaction of the nervous system to external stimuli), through instinct (learned adaptive behaviour to specific stimuli, passed on through whole species and containing a limited amount of consciousness), to, in the highest species, conscious, intentional actions in response to previously unencountered stimuli.[21] Idiots, he argued, were a largely reflexive and instinctive type of human rather than consciously intentional, and they were therefore closer in many ways to non-human animals than to their human confreres. He claimed to have observed instinctive mannerisms at work in

Charles H. Bennett, 'Monkey Trick', 1863, wood engraving representing
Darwin's evolutionary theory – within the rational, civilized, evolved person
lurked the hidden beast of the deep past.

idiot asylums, such as 'to and fro' rhythmical movements and
habitual movements of the hands, limbs and features.[22] He saw
these as atavistic remnants of instinctive behaviours in early
humankind, behaviours that had outlived their purpose but survived, a snapshot of the ancient past, in these unevolved humans.
He compared them to the actions of what he called an 'idiotic
dog' circling twenty times before lying down – a remnant, he
claimed, from its ancestors who had to form a bed in long grass.

The idea of the idiot as presented in evolutionary psychology was of a reflexive and instinctive being, arrested in their

development before the stage of fully developed consciousness, offering a snapshot of man's evolutionary past and forming a bridge, or the missing link, between the human animal and the non-human animal. This idea contrasted with the central tenet of eugenics, which was that humanity was at risk of degenerating backwards from its evolved state through poor breeding, heredity, and interference with selection by allowing the weak to thrive. Evolutionary psychology saw the deficient person as the product of a failure to evolve in the first place, and as a throwback to the pre- or early human stage in the evolutionary process. The two ideas coexisted, and both necessitated the removal of the idiot and imbecile population from society as irredeemably unfit to exist as a social being.

For the evolutionists, idiocy showed the closeness of the human to the animal self. Within the rational, civilized, evolved person lurked the hidden beast of the deep past, demonstrated by the idiot brain unable to conceal its primeval origins. Darwin had proved that humans were closer to non-humans than they cared to acknowledge, and deficient humans came to be seen as an uncomfortable and unwelcome reminder of this. H. G. Wells again, in *The Island of Dr Moreau* (1896), tapped into public anxieties with his portrayal of a remote island where human–animal hybrids are bred though vivisection. Disturbing and dangerous creatures, 'little better than an idiot' and with 'dwarfed brains', roam the island loaded with 'cravings, instincts, desires that harm humanity, a strange hidden reservoir to burst forth suddenly'. Leading a 'mockery of a rational life', these semi-humans, with basic language and some increased intelligence from their original animal state, are driven by instinct and subject to the same reversionary drives as psychologists had attributed to deficient humans. They combine, in the end, 'the distinctive silliness of man with the natural folly of a monkey'.[23] For Wells, Moreau's island was only in part an exotic fantasy: it was also an unsubtle metaphor for the threat that the semi-evolved, bestial idiot human mind posed to the security and progress of civilization in its fatal fusion of human form and animal instinct.

Moral Imbecility

The theories of evolutionary psychology also influenced practitioners of mental science. In 1883 the eminent medico-
psychological specialist Henry Maudsley outlined in *Body and
Will* what would become the concept of the 'moral imbecile'.
Maudsley accepted the idea put forth by animal psychologists
such as Romanes that conscious intelligence evolved in all living
beings from reflex and instinct through to conscious action. He
then argued that in humans it went through two further stages
– first the development of rationality, and then the acquisition
of a sense of morality. Idiots never developed far beyond the
semi-conscious state of instinct and could therefore develop neither reason nor morality. Maudsley described them as a '*reductio
ad absurdum*' of humanity. Imbeciles, however, might acquire
some form of rational intelligence and conscious intentionality
– but they could never move on to the further stage of moral
intelligence. Though this gave them the appearance of intelligence, they would be dangerously unbounded by any moral
sense. Such an amoral human would show acute cunning 'to
gratify its evil inclinations . . . a moral idiot without being an
idiot in self-seeking and self-serving intelligence'.[24] This was
therefore a dangerous person, one possessed of a certain amount
of cunning 'nous' but with no moral framework to guide their
actions. The idea of a form of idiot who appeared intelligent but
was morally depraved had figured in medicine since the classifications of Fodéré and Georget, in the wake of the French
Revolution, with their morally deviant 'charlatans et fripons'
(charlatans and rascals). However, Maudsley had met the challenge of evolutionary theory by incorporating the semi-evolved
moral idiot into its explanatory system, a mind that had evolved
so far as to know right from wrong, but not so far as to care anything about it. This new class of imbecile subsequently became
a target not only of public concern but of state policy.

In this way the mentally deficient came under a two-
pronged attack, demonized by eugenic theory as the lowest of

Ellen Sutcliffe, 'imbecility' patient at West Riding Lunatic Asylum in Wakefield, Yorkshire, photographed by Sir James Crichton-Browne, *c.* 1869.

the degenerate hordes eating away at human evolutionary progress, and relegated by the early psychologists to a precarious position somewhere between the human and the animal. Already firmly under the medical gaze since the growth of the asylum system, they became an important explanatory factor in mental science's theorization of the development of mind, and a signifier of the arrests and diseases that could afflict it. From a position of obscurity and an absence of intellectual curiosity a hundred years earlier, they were, by the 1890s, fully scientized and pathologized, an important object of both social scientific and medical study.

The Birth of IQ

This process intensified as the concept of IQ (intelligence quotient) was introduced in France by Alfred Binet in the early 1900s. Binet was the director of the psychology laboratory at the Sorbonne in Paris and had an interest in the measurement of intelligence. He began, as psychologists and anthropologists of his generation were wont to do, by measuring skulls, and wrote optimistically in 1898 that 'the relationship between the intelligence of subjects and the volume of their head . . . is very real and had been confirmed by all methodical investigators, without exception . . . [and] must be considered as incontestable.'[25] By 1900 he was questioning the merits of this craniometry, his own research finding that if skull measurements were rigorously rather than wishfully applied, there were

Alfred Binet,
the 'father' of IQ,
c. 1898.

no discernible or consistent differences between the skull sizes of the intelligent and the non-intelligent, including, apart from microcephalics, the idiotic.[26]

Abandoning craniometry and seeking new methods, Binet was commissioned in 1904 by the French minister of public education to develop techniques for identifying children who were struggling in classrooms – a growing phenomenon with the advent of mass education – and who appeared to need some form of specialist education. Binet brought together a series of everyday problem-solving tasks, such as counting coins, which he hoped were diverse enough in range and content to be able to assess a child's general potential. His first published set of tests in 1905 showed a series of tasks in ascending order of difficulty, but by 1908 Binet was assigning an age level to each task, the basis for assessing so-called intelligence quotient ever since. The last tasks a child could perform signified their 'mental age'; the gap between this mental age and the child's true chronological age indicated their general intellectual level. In 1912 the German psychologist William Stern began dividing mental age by chronological age, giving the modern intelligence quotient, or IQ level.[27]

The notion of IQ sealed the scientific colonization of mental deficiency. In an age of anxiety, fear and concern about the effect of feeble-mindedness on society, it appeared to offer an indisputable, precise and scientific method of measuring a thing called intelligence, that was reliable across all people and cultures. It made, in its precision and measurability, the threat of mental deficiency more identifiable, less mysterious and more solvable. The power attached to the notion of IQ went far beyond the general indication of intellectual potential that Binet had envisaged. As it was taken up enthusiastically in Europe and the United States, intelligence somehow became 'a thing' that the power of psychology and its practitioners could extract from people's minds in perfectly measured form. The deficient could now be identified and exposed, even those duplicitous menaces the morally imbecile – there was no hiding from science. The enthusiasm with which IQ was peddled reflected the desperation of psychologists to be seen as practitioners of an exact science, like physics, rather than, as some derided the field, a mixture of philosophy and wishful thinking. The cultural biases of IQ testing, its failure to acknowledge that there could be multiple types of intellectual faculty, the arbitrariness of its methodology – all went unnoticed as a grateful educational, social scientific and medical establishment embraced its certainties and its functional utility. Its cultural biases, which ensured that the educated middle and upper classes scored well in IQ testing, while the poor and uneducated scored badly, seemed to confirm the heredity of intellectual capacity. Even when the first experiment in mass IQ testing, led by the psychologist Robert M. Yerkes and carried out on 1.75 million U.S. Army recruits during the First World War, came up with the unlikely results that the average mental age of white American adults was 13 (or 'semi-moron' level) while the average mental age of 'negro' Americans was 10.4 (or 'moron' level), the scientific validity of IQ as a measure was not doubted. Instead a mass middle-class panic ensued.[28]

A Royal Commission

If, as psychology and eugenic science seemed to suggest, feeble-mindedness was largely hereditary and resistant to improvement, and constituted a threat to social stability and progress, then it was the duty of the state to intervene and isolate this part of the population in some way. Amid constant public anxiety from the 'respectable' classes, it was clear that some form of state action needed to be taken against such threats. Joseph Conrad's novel *The Secret Agent* (1907) featured Stevie, the mentally deficient brother-in-law of secret agent Adolf Verloc, who is manipulated by anarchist revolutionaries into agreeing to plant a bomb at the Greenwich Observatory designed to murder and maim members of the public (the bomb explodes prematurely and kills him). The threat of feeble-mindedness was presented not as some abstract concern but as a palpable, material risk to society and its citizens.

The response of Arthur Balfour's Conservative government to these concerns in Great Britain was to establish in 1904 a Royal Commission on the Care and Control of the Feeble-minded. Its membership included politicians, lawyers, charity representatives and civil servants. Among them were W. H. Dickinson, a Liberal Party MP and chairman of the National Association for the Promotion of the Welfare of the Feeble-Minded, and Charles Loch of the Charity Organisation Society, a voluntary organization that preached radical eugenic solutions to the problems of poverty, crime and perceived mental decline of the racial stock. Doctors were co-opted to assist with questions of the definition and explanation of feeble-mindedness.[29]

The commission's 1908 report recommended a system of specialized institutional care for three broad categories: idiots, imbeciles and the feeble-minded. The imbecility category also included 'moral imbeciles' of the sort identified by Maudsley in the 1880s. Other groups such as epileptics, inebriates, the deaf and dumb and the blind would be included provided they were also mentally deficient. It identified large numbers of the mentally deficient inappropriately placed in prisons and lunatic asylums. While not a full-scale eugenicist document, the report identified heredity as the primary cause of mental deficiency and downplayed the significance of environment, training or education. This led to some inter-departmental rivalries between the Home Office and Board of Education, whose aim of expanding the special school system was undermined by the report's findings. Such rivalries were a contributory factor to the delay of five years – until 1913 – in enacting legislation.[30]

Similar developments, although not legislative, were taking place in the United States, led by the crusading psychologist and director of research at the Vineland Training School for Feeble-minded Girls and Boys in New Jersey, Henry H. Goddard. Goddard had visited first London and then Paris in 1908 to tour institutions for the feeble-minded. In Paris he was introduced to what was now known as the Binet–Simon intelligence scale, a collaboration between Alfred Binet and Théodore Simon to produce a more precise intelligence test than Binet's earlier model.[31] It was Goddard who would popularize Binet and Simon's work in America, translating Binet's publications into English, agitating for them to be applied across the population and spreading the idea that scores from these tests constituted some form of single innate entity that could be identified as intelligence. He saw the tests as an opportunity to implement eugenic theory by identifying and isolating the feeble-minded to prevent inferior breeding. Although this deviated sharply from Binet's original purpose in establishing the tests, and while Binet continued to deny that intelligence could be reified in this way, Goddard was in agreement with Binet that the tests worked most effectively in identifying people just below the 'normal' range.[32] In 1910 Goddard proposed at the annual meeting of the American Association for the Study of the Feeble-minded a new system for classifying the mentally deficient using IQ. Above idiots, whom he placed in an IQ range of 0–25, and imbeciles, in a range from 26–50, he placed a new category, invented and coined by himself, of 'moron', in a range from 51–70. He coined the term from the Greek word for foolish. The moron in the United States occupied a similar position to the moral imbecile in Britain – deceptively 'normal' and with some intelligence, but dangerously amoral, criminally inclined and unrestrained. Goddard advocated their incarceration or sterilization alongside idiots and imbeciles.

In 1912 Goddard published his infamous eugenic study of a single family, *The Kallikak Family: A Study in the Heredity of Feeble-mindedness*. This was inspired by Richard Dugdale's *The Jukes* of 1877 and contained similarly lurid narratives about the proliferation of defectiveness that can arise from a single act of bad breeding. In this case it was the impregnation of a feeble-minded woman in a tavern by an otherwise eugenically sound hero of the Revolutionary War, named as Martin Kallikak. Goddard gave the family the pseudonym Kallikak, a fusion of the Greek words for 'good' and 'bad', to illustrate how the offspring of the act of folly in the tavern were both numerous and irredeemably feeble-minded, while the descendants of Kallikak's original 'respectable' marriage remained eugenically healthy. He wrote:

> The surprise and horror of it all was that no matter where we traced them, whether in the prosperous rural district, in the city slums to which some had drifted, or in the more remote mountain regions, or whether it was a question of the second or sixth generation, an appalling amount of defectiveness was everywhere found.[33]

Despite its methods, assumptions and conclusions all being later deeply discredited (even allegations of tampering with photographs were made), Goddard's work, once published, quickly became 'a primal myth of the eugenics movement'.[34] Two similar studies emerged in the same year: Florence Danielson and Charles Davenport's *The Hill Folk: A Report on a Rural Community of Hereditary Defectives*, and Arthur H. Estabrook and Davenport's study of *The Nan Family*. Estabrook, who worked for the U.S. Eugenics Record office, also wrote a deeply pessimistic follow-up to Dugdale's original study, *The Jukes in 1915*. These works, with their panic-inducing stories of uncontrollable hordes of defectives relentlessly spreading across the plains, mountains, towns and cities of America, fed into and stoked existing anxieties about racial decline.

The Move to Legislation

The eugenic scare was therefore at its height on both sides of the Atlantic in the years after the report of Britain's Royal Commission on Feeble-mindedness in 1908. In Britain, therefore, proponents of action against mental deficiency were frustrated by the delay in moving to legislation. They began to take matters into their own hands. The Eugenics Education Society (later the Eugenics Society) and the National Association for the Care of the Feeble-minded drafted a bill proposing detention and long-term incarceration of the mentally deficient. In 1911 the two organizations, supported by sympathetic MPs, held a meeting at Westminster to promote the bill and urge action on the government. The meeting was attended by, among others, Dr Reginald Langdon Down (son of John Langdon Down), who argued that the bill's demands were only the minimum possible given the threat of mental deficiency.[35] The main speaker at the event was Alfred F. Tredgold, one of the country's leading medical 'experts' on mental deficiency. He divided humanity into just two categories: 'Human beings are divisible into two great groups – the *normal* and the *defective*. The normal range from great brilliance to dullness. The defective group . . . is divided into three degrees, namely *idiocy, imbecility* and *feeble-mindedness*.'[36] Although, he acknowledged, there were some grey areas in diagnosis at the intersection between the feeble-minded – who were 'the least mentally deficient' – and the simply dull, if left to competent doctors such issues would not be an insurmountable problem. It was imperative that both diagnosis and the incarceration of those diagnosed should proceed swiftly, because: 'All that we desire to do is secure control over those persons whose condition or surroundings are such that their liberty is a source of injury or misery to themselves or a menace to the welfare of the community.'[37] The evening ended with a clarion call to do something towards 'stemming the increasing tide of degeneracy'. This was such an urgent task that this bill had been drafted in haste to ensure that there was at least some action, although it was far from a 'complete solution'.[38]

In the face of this pressure, within two years the Liberal government introduced an Act to Parliament that was overwhelmingly passed. It provided 'an apparatus for the compulsory and permanent segregation of the feeble-minded'.[39] The Mental Deficiency Act 1913 introduced a new government department, the Board of Control, to administer all mental health care, centralizing as a state function both the detention and surveillance of the mentally deficient population. There were two central planks to the legislation: the establishment of a network of 'colonies' to house the mentally deficient, and the creation of a system of community control and surveillance for those who were not institutionalized. Resistance to the Act in Parliament was feeble amid a strong cross-party consensus. For the Liberal government and the 42 socialist Labour MPs, it represented a step in an advancing programme of welfare reform that placed in the hands of the state that which had previously been left to charitable groups. For the Conservative opposition, eugenic anxiety trumped any concerns about state interference. All three parties were united in their belief that the degenerate population had to be 'dealt with' in some way. Only Josiah Wedgwood, a Liberal MP and self-styled 'last of the radicals', held out against it. His opposition was based not on a specific commitment to, or even interest in, those labelled mentally deficient, but on his fierce commitment to the ideas of liberty and democratic accountability. In Wedgwood's view, all citizens had rights, whoever they were and whatever label was attached to them. They could not simply be summarily dismissed from society or closely controlled within it just because they did not meet with approval. He saw the Act as a tool for giving power to illiberal groups such as the Eugenics Society and as a threat to democracy. He tabled 120 amendments and made 150 speeches, but all to no avail. Resistance was futile: 358 MPs voted for the legislation, just fifteen against.[40]

A great irony was that implementation of the Act was delayed by the First World War, which broke out in the year after it was passed. Many thousands of mentally deficient people, deemed dangerous, unproductive and parasitical in 1913, took up valuable and skilled work roles to fill labour shortages caused by men departing for the front. The problem, as the end of the war loomed, was that they would now have to give up those roles as soldiers returned. In 1917 the Central Association for the Care of the Mentally Defective expressed anxiety that 'Large numbers of low-grade, even imbecile defectives, now in remunerative work ... will assuredly leave their work when there is any displacement of labour and we are anxious to make plans for their protection and assistance.'[41] 'Protection and assistance' meant detention or supervision, as the Act would now be fully implemented: there was no pause to consider that those deemed mentally deficient had shown themselves competent to work and posed no threat during the war years.[42]

The Act provided for three forms of what it called 'care, supervision and control'. These were institutional care, guardianship and community supervision. Institutional care would be the preserve of the colonies. Guardianship would allow a defective to be placed in the care of a guardian with parental powers over them. Community supervision took the form of a network of statutory health visitors, school nurses and social workers, alongside volunteer home visitors from local mental welfare associations, mainly the Central Association for Mental Welfare.[43] All of this came under the organizational gaze of the new Board of Control. The system of community monitoring, surveillance and control was at least as important as the institutional provision, if not more so. By 1939 there were almost 44,000 defectives under statutory supervision or guardianship, with 46,000 in institutions.[44] The numbers illustrate the lengths to which state authorities were prepared to go, and the public support, or at least acquiescence, they enjoyed, in their aim of controlling the defective population.[45]

The passing of the 1913 Act was a defining moment for those who found themselves drawn into the net that the label of mental deficiency cast over society. It marked the culmination of more than a century of transition from being accepted members of society, whatever difficulties that might entail, to state-defined outcasts and objects of fear, loathing and pity. It also marked the culmination of the triumph of psychiatric medicine and the new 'scientific' endeavour of psychology in their claim to identify, control and treat this group. The legislation was so all-embracing, covering childhood to old age and ranging from the profoundly disabled to dubiously constructed moral imbeciles, that hardly any further legislation related to deficiency was enacted over the next 45 years. In 1914 an Elementary Education (Defective and Epileptic Children) Act came into force, compelling all local authorities to provide special schools. A 1925 Mental Deficiency Amendment Act allowed greater use of guardianship as an alternative to institutionalization. The minor 1927 Mental Deficiency Act expanded institutional provision and placed a duty on local authorities to provide some form of training and occupation. Apart from these few, and in the case of the 1925 and 1927 legislation minor, exceptions, the 1913 Act remained the enduring legislative framework within which mental deficiency was governed and understood in Britain until the Mental Health Act of 1959. It was almost as if in their dispatch to lifelong institutions or subjection to control in their family homes, those deemed to have inadequate minds could be forgotten about.

Implementation of the Act

Existing asylums and workhouses adapted to specialist use for the mentally deficient, such as the Sandlebridge Colony in Cheshire, became repositories for the implementation of the Act's institutional aims in the interwar years. Added to this institutional mix was the new 'colony system', and new buildings were leased or constructed across the country. Their construction spanned the entire interwar period. Meanwood Park Colony in Leeds was leased by Leeds Corporation from 1919; Cell Barnes in Hertfordshire was established in 1933; and Botleys Park Colony for Mental Defectives was built in Surrey as late as 1939. The drive to incarcerate the deficient was relentless.

The Hedley Report by the Departmental Committee on Colonies for Mental Defectives of 1931 described this institutional innovation, based on a very different design to the asylum system. Each so-called colony was a small, usually rural, self-contained world. Between 900 and 1,500 people would live in a typical colony setting, housed in detached 'villas' for up to sixty people, grouped around a central administrative block. This block always formed a barrier between male and female villas, as separation of the sexes to prevent 'breeding' was deemed essential, with the exception of the lowest grade idiots, who were judged incapable of sexual congress. Children and adults lived separately and there would also be a special villa for 'difficult cases' – those whose behaviours were regarded as needing control. The villas for 'low grade idiots' and for 'difficult cases' would be as far from the hospital approaches as possible, to avoid offence to visitors. Villas housing the 'better class of working patients' were allowed to be furthest from the administrative block, with their own cooking and heating facilities. Patients slept in multiple rows, closely packed together in large dormitories with little or no space for privacy or the storage of personal possessions.

In abstract terms the colonies were almost idyllically conceived. As well as the villas there would be a children's school, workshops for the adults, kitchens, bakery, laundry, recreation hall (seating up to 750 patients and doubling as a chapel), staff quarters, playing fields (particularly for the males) and a small mortuary and cemetery. Many colonies had their own farms with market gardens, stables, poultry, pigs, herds of cows and greenhouses. As well as nurses they employed farm bailiffs, firemen, engineers and, of course, gatekeepers.[46] Most patients worked unpaid in the laundries and workshops or on the farm. In reality the colonies were harsh, joyless environments, with

A group of mentally deficient Girl Guides at the Royal Eastern Counties Institution, 1929.

punitive disciplinary regimes, no concession to individuality and rapidly spreading contagious disease in the closely packed wards, as oral histories looking back on the period have revealed.[47] The presence of the school, mortuary and cemetery was deeply symbolic as well as practical: the fate of the defective was to enter a colony as a child and to remain there for their whole life, not in the world they had been born into but in a different world that had been built for them.

Outside the colonies, systems of guardianship and statutory or voluntary supervision were in place. Under guardianship, defectives living in their own homes were subject to the control of a suitable guardian, who could be a parent, other relative or employer. Under the supervision system, defectives were overseen though visits to their homes by salaried officials, health visitors, school nurses, social workers or local mental welfare associations, usually affiliated to the Central Association for Mental Welfare. Visitors, uniformly middle class, would make reports to local mental deficiency committees, and where it was reported that control was not being properly exercised institutionalization or guardianship would be likely to ensue. There was therefore a system of surveillance, regulation and control in place both inside and outside the institution. This could be construed as having welfare and protectionist aims as well as constraint and suppression – financial assistance, clothing and other support could be provided to those not receiving poor relief.[48] The overriding aim, however, of both the institutional and community systems was to control behaviour and prevent breeding. Public anxiety and concern were not helped by the 1929 report of the Joint Committee on Mental Deficiency, which after a five-year survey pronounced that there were at least 300,000 mental defectives in England and Wales, double the number estimated in the Royal Commission's 1908 report. They were described by the report as a 'social problem group' comprising around 10 per cent of the English and Welsh population.[49] Given that by 1926 there were still only about 36,000 defectives either institutionalized or under some form of guardianship or supervision,[50] anxieties that hordes of defective humans were roaming the land unrestrained, committing depredations and polluting the racial stock, continued to haunt the minds of the eugenicist cult.

General Social Attitudes

There was a widespread consensus across the British ideological spectrum in the first half of the twentieth century that mental deficiency was in some way a problem that needed to be 'fixed'. It came not just from eugenic theory about threats to the racial stock and the degeneration of civilized society, although this of course played a significant part. There was also a feeling that in heavily industrialized, newly technological and highly urbanized Western societies, people without sufficient brain power would be simply unable to cope with the demands of modernity. Welfare only perpetuated their misery and prevented them from withering away as the laws of natural selection suggested they should. The eugenic publicist Albert E. Wiggam addressed a gathering at the American Museum of Natural History in 1930 with the words: 'Civilization is making the world safe for stupidity.'[51] Protective shielding of people seen as essentially unproductive carried a social cost. The 1931 Hedley Report was in part initiated by governmental panic about the costs of the colony system, and this was often alluded to in dialogue on deficiency. In 1930 Julian Huxley, the zoologist, biologist, humanist and eugenicist, wrote:

> What are we going to do? Every defective man, woman and child is a burden. Every defective is an extra body for the nation to feed and clothe, but produces little or nothing in return. Every defective needs care, and immobilises a certain quantum of energy and goodwill which could otherwise be put to good use.[52]

His brother, the novelist and commentator Aldous Huxley, satirized the social engineering dreams of eugenicists in his dystopian

Wall panel showing 'The Relation of Eugenics to Other Sciences', based
on a paper by Dr Harry H. Laughlin, at the Third International Eugenics
Congress, New York, 21–3 August 1932. Eugenic theory formed part
of a national consensus about mental deficiency in the first half of the
20th century.

novel *Brave New World* (1932). In this world humans are factory-
bred in test tubes to produce specified numbers at different grades
of intelligence and ability, in order to fulfil different social functions. Menial tasks such as lift-operator are carried out by grinning
'Epsilon-Minus Semi-Morons'.[53] It was satire, but it demonstrated how ideas about deficiency were deeply embedded in

national consciousness, and unconsciously adopted. The great and good of 'progressive' politics, such as the socialists and founders of Fabianism Sidney and Beatrice Webb, H. G. Wells, the birth control pioneer Marie Stopes and members of all the major political parties, signed up to the repression, isolation and eventual eradication of mental deficiency.[54] It was not so much an ideological standpoint as a shared cultural assumption.[55]

The idea that intelligence quotient testing could identify a person's capacity with extreme precision, and that a quantifiable thing called intelligence was the sole driver of human worth and capacity, was perpetuated in British psychology's laboratories and experiments. In 1911 Karl Pearson, the social Darwinist and statistician, had become the first Galton Chair of Eugenics at University College London, a position endowed from Francis Galton's estate. Pearson shaped psychology's study of intelligence in Britain and introduced statistical expertise as an indicator of psychology's scientific authority. He introduced, building on the work of Galton, the normal distribution (or bell-shaped) curve, which isolated both the genius and the defective mind and created a normative intellectual range that indicated social belonging.[56] His lecture, at the age of 73, to the staff of the Board of Control in 1930 'On the Inheritance of Mental Disease' was an unapologetic doubling down on the case for heredity, backed up by an intimidating array of statistical charts and diagrams. Echoing Dugdale's Jukes and Goddard's Kallikaks, he presented a 'scientific' statistical analysis of a series of family case histories and gave grim warnings of the consequences of poor breeding:

Case ix. A feeble-minded woman married a man who was afterwards legally separated on account of cruelty. He had two brothers paralysed imbeciles, both of whom died in idiot asylums. He himself became insane and was certified. The insane man and the feeble-minded woman had two sons, the first an imbecile in an asylum, the second sound in health, but morally a high-grade defective.[57]

As psychologists gained increasing public authority they became seen as arbiters of what constituted human ability and, with that, human belonging. They described human life in terms that placed intelligence as the cause of ability, its level an indicator of a person's capacity to cope as a human being. They presented themselves as the people who knew how to measure this elixir of the human condition, and therefore the people able to police the boundaries of human belonging. Those boundaries were marked by the high walls of the colony, and the invisible walls surrounding the supervised and surveilled defective in their community.

So things stood as the Western world moved towards war in the late 1930s. The Act that had been passed on the eve of the last war appeared now to a large extent fulfilled. Some 90,000 defectives found themselves under the controlling gaze of the British state, either in their community or in an institution. The advocates of eugenic science might look upon their work in progress with some satisfaction. Yet, unforeseen, in Germany the murderous ideology of Nazism began to lock itself into a fatal embrace with the 'science' of eugenics. A catastrophic new chapter in the story of mental deficit was about to begin. Stupidity was indeed fatally at large in the world. It was not, however, to be found where it might be expected to be found, in the minds of those labelled as deficient.

9

Back to the Community?
From 1939 to the Present

E ven at the height of eugenic thinking, the organized mass
killing of people with intellectual disabilities had never
seemed a feasible scenario. While eugenic theory held sway
across Britain, the United States and much of Europe in the
interwar period, it had not remained unchallenged and was held
in check to some extent by democratic safeguards, which meant
for example that proposals for euthanasia or even sterilization of
the deficient never gained serious traction in Britain. The British
Eugenics Society presented itself as moderate and opposed
to coercion, in contrast to the United States and particularly
Germany. They advocated only voluntary sterilization. Total
institutionalization of those deemed deficient was rejected on
both moral and financial grounds across the West. There were
protests and legal challenges against sterilization, not least from
the Catholic Church. These were not always successful, and in
the United States there were legal sterilization programmes, but
the protests were enough, certainly in Britain, to arrest wholesale state medical intervention to prevent 'deficient' breeding.

Furthermore, the move towards universal suffrage in this
period meant that there was a need to accommodate the working
classes and their offspring within shared ideological aspirations
rather than ostracizing them as the products of faulty heredity.
Freedom of expression also meant that eugenic views in extreme
form were challenged and sometimes ridiculed. In the United

States the social worker Stanley P. Davies's *Social Control of the Feebleminded* (1923), despite its alarming title, advocated welfare and social support strategies and denounced the 'alarmist period' of eugenic scare, which he located in the first twenty years of the twentieth century.[1] The journalist Albert Deutsch's huge *The Mentally Ill in America* (1937) devoted two chapters to mental deficiency, condemned the so-called eugenic 'alarmist period' and, while not fully rejecting eugenic science, called for a return to the optimism of Séguin's 'moral treatment' and reorientation regimes, arguing: 'there are a great many . . . mentally deficient children who . . . require only temporary institutional care and training with the intention of eventually returning them to the community.'[2]

Nobody in this age of eugenic science – which, however vicious and demeaning its language, was to some extent socially policed and therefore restrained – foresaw the catastrophe that was looming in Germany. The National Socialist Party came to power in 1933 with an ideology built on the most extreme form of eugenic science at its heart. A Nazified faction of the German eugenics movement replaced the original 'eugenics' (*Eugenik*) label for their movement with the name 'race hygiene' (*Rassenhygiene*), expressing their total commitment to genocidal purification of the human stock through purging those deemed mentally, physically or racially degenerate. Inspired by the work of the legal scholar Karl Binding and the psychiatrist Alfred Hoche,[3] euthanasia was redefined to encompass not only easing the final days of people suffering painful terminal illness but bringing about the death of people 'unworthy of life'.[4] Action was immediate after Adolf Hitler came to power in 1933, with a sterilization law 'For the Prevention of Offspring with Hereditary Diseases' passed in the same year. This listed ten categories of person suitable for sterilization, ranging from schizophrenics to alcoholics, but at the top of the list sat those with congenital feeble-mindedness. It is generally agreed that around 400,000 people were sterilized during the Nazi period (1933–45).[5] The specific targeting of the feeble-minded is reflected in the figures

Healthy parents with healthy children, representing benefits of the National Socialist policy on the struggle against inherited diseases, 1936, colour lithograph after F. Würbel. Nazi ideology combined with eugenic science to wage war on 'mental disease'.

for 1934, when 53 per cent of all those sterilized belonged to that category. From this point on the genocidal war against the disabled intensified, and extermination began under cover of war from 1939. A decree of October 1939 allowed the mercy killing of 'garbage children' (*Ausschusskinder*). Under the programme, children with supposedly hereditary disabilities such as mental deficiency were dispatched by German doctors, nurses, health officials and midwives to paediatric killing wards where doctors administered lethal injections or left them to starve in specialist 'hunger houses'. Somewhere between 5,000 and 25,000 children were killed under this programme.[6]

In the same year, a larger operation was launched against disabled adults, also by decree. This killing programme became known as Aktion T4, derived from the address at Tiergartenstrasse 4 in Berlin where it was housed. Six killing centres were established by the T4 programme, at Brandenburg, Grafeneck, Hartheim (in Austria), Sonnenstein, Bernburg and Hadamar. After experiments with killing methods, mass gassing became the preferred technique, and all six centres were equipped with a gas chamber and crematorium. The use of gas on disabled people presaged, and laid the ground for, the Holocaust against the Jewish people and other minority populations that would soon follow. Recruitment of physicians, nurses, scientists, police officers and other workers to administer and carry out the killing programme proved to be remarkably unproblematic, with virtually no one turning down the opportunity to work voluntarily in the T4 programme. By 1941, when Hitler brought the gassing programme to an end after news of it leaked out to the public and rare protests against the Nazi regime were made by religious figures and families, around 80,000 disabled people had been gassed to death.[7] The proportion of those that were labelled feeble-minded is not known, although the 1934 sterilization statistics suggest that it may have been over half. The killing did not end with the cessation of the gassing programme. After 1941, killings were decentralized to various institutions across the expanding territory of the Reich and disabled people's lives were ended using deadly medication, starvation and, outside the Reich, mass shootings, in a process known as 'wild euthanasia'. Killings even continued in hospitals and elsewhere in the months after the defeat of Nazism.[8]

The effect of these atrocities on thinking about mental deficiency once the war was over was significant, although information about the killings emerged slowly and was often dwarfed by the sheer scale of other Nazi atrocities. The so-called Doctors' trial that took place in Nuremberg in 1946–7 was the first time the details of the killings came to wide public attention. Part of the shock was the revelation that the mass exterminations had been carried out by medical professionals – doctors in white coats and nurses in uniforms, who carried out their work in an orderly, planned bureaucratic fashion. It had been, for them, an act of reason, and justifications were made at the Doctors' trial that it was right to shorten 'the painful lives of these miserable creatures'. T4 was not the work of crazed SS ideologues but the result of collaboration across the medical system, from those who actually carried out the killings to those in institutions and social work offices who filled out the forms that dispatched people to their deaths. Eugenic science was itself built on reason, as far as its advocates were concerned: the application of the principles of heredity and natural selection to human populations in a quest to achieve better humans and better societies for them to live in. This was one reason why eugenics appealed to so many intellectuals. In its fatal collision with Nazi ideology, eugenics was simply taken to its logical conclusion.

In Britain the war had a significant impact on the lives of the mentally deficient, although in very different ways to the horrors that were unfolding in the Reich. Increased use of mental testing had been made from 1942 by the armed forces. Despite concern that soldiers with the lowest intelligence were more likely to become maladjusted or delinquent, there were fears that if the mentally weak were exempted from service, resentment would ensue among enlisted troops. Those regarded as dull or defective were therefore often recruited to the Pioneer Corps, whose tasks included construction of airfields, bridges and roads in theatres of war as well as stretcher-bearing and handling of stores.[9] Once again, as in the First World War, those deemed incapable of work or any form of social usefulness in peacetime suddenly became perceived as capable and competent in a time of war. In a parallel development, the mentally deficient were discharged from the colony system, crowded into reduced spaces or placed into temporary annexes to make way for the anticipated deluge of military casualties. Staffing was affected by nurses leaving to support the war effort in the Emergency Hospital Service and other fields. Across Britain, 25,000 were evacuated from all mental hospitals, including mental deficiency colonies, to make space for military casualties.[10]

Once the war was over, eugenic thinking became largely discredited through its association with fascist excess and atrocity, and the drive to remove the deficient from society altogether diminished in intellectual and medical prominence. The social and political acceptability of eugenic ideas in Britain reduced sharply. The Eugenics Society, which as early as 1933 had publicly dissociated itself from Nazi 'race hygiene', never recovered its peak membership figures from the 1930s and lost the support of public intellectuals it had enjoyed before the war. In 1963 it became a charity and ceased its propaganda activities, surviving today as the insignificant Galton Institute, supporting the scientific study of human heredity and its social implications.

In Britain this rush to disown eugenics did not, however, lead to immediate improvements in the quality of life for those labelled deficient, or bring about significant alterations in practice. Institutionalization did not cease: it remained the default position of state and local government authorities whenever faced with a decision about a mentally deficient child or adult. In fact, 1946 saw the highest ever notification of defectives, at over 35,000. Staff shortages continued and there were post-war shortages of labour, materials and finances.[11] All of this served to usher in a period of neglect and invisibility. With a large proportion of the known deficient population in institutions as a result of the Mental Deficiency Act, and intensive referrals to the institutions continuing, the people themselves became quietly forgotten, a hidden group within the wider population. There was no countervailing thrust of advocacy and new ideas within medicine to replace the collapse of the vociferous pre-war eugenic advocacy of control and prevention, and the newly discovered public reticence of its most determined supporters.

When the National Health Service (NHS) was launched in 1948 as a key building block of the new cradle-to-grave welfare state under construction by the post-war Labour government, it was widely celebrated. The mental deficiency colonies and local authority, charity and privately run hospitals were transferred to the NHS, creating a monolithic state system for the mentally deficient. This embedded a universal medical model for mental deficiency – an institutional system run by doctors and staffed by nurses and nursing auxiliaries. Mental deficiency hospitals were starved of resources, and many struggled to recruit staff, as general hospitals were prioritized. What worked well for the lives and health of the majority population served only to worsen the lives of its lowest out-group. The modern medical profession was faced with a strikingly similar dilemma that had caused doctors in the eighteenth century to shun any involvement with the 'idiot' population. What role could medicine play in the lives of these people who were simply who they were, who happened to have a lower level of mental faculty than others but for whom there was no form of medical intervention that could treat, change or cure? The difference after 1948 was that while in the eighteenth century doctors could choose to ignore the idiot population and leave them to be absorbed into their communities, their twentieth-century counterparts found themselves working in locked institutions controlling the lives of and 'treating' tens of thousands of people labelled (by their own profession) as defective.

A process of degradation ensued, with people trapped in a medical system that had little interest in or understanding of them as people. The statist bureaucracy of the NHS supplied all food and resources, so that the farms and workshops of the colony institutions, which had at least provided occupation and purpose, even if unpaid and often involuntary, fell into disuse.

The NHS priority was the general population and their medical needs, from cradle to grave, but not those who failed to meet some pre-agreed but vague definition of mental faculty. There was no move to community care amid the renewed optimism and clamour for greater justice and equality that imbued society once the war was over. The institutionalized defective population rose from 46,000 in 1939 to 60,000 in 1955. There were also 79,000 defectives under community supervision or guardianship.[12] They could truly lay claim to the title of out-group of all out-groups, the most surveilled, controlled and incarcerated population in the land.

Life in the NHS hospitals and colonies was almost unremittingly grim. In interviews in the 1980s, former patients recalled their daily lives, characterized by dull routine and minute regulation. As one ex-patient from the north of England put it: 'You'd all have to be up for half-past six or seven. We couldn't wear us own clothes. We weren't allowed to talk to any boys, Staff used to be in 'bathroom with you. When we went anywhere we had to have staff.'[13] For the convenience of staff, and to tie in with changing shifts, patients would sometimes be woken up at 5 a.m. Hygiene routine was governed by a written rule book posted in every bathroom, and patients were bathed in alphabetical order once a week:

> You never got bathed on your own, you'd got staff with us and you had to wait in queues. You weren't allowed to touch the baths yourself. Taps were took off 'cos they were like taps you had to screw on and when you'd had your bath they took 'em away. Or else some people would kill themselves, drown themselves.[14]

An oppressive disciplinary regime was in operation, with prison-like rules in force to control and regulate behaviour. Leave to visit home, if patients still had contact with their families, was seen as a privilege that could be granted in return for obedience or withheld as a punishment for disobedience. Former patients

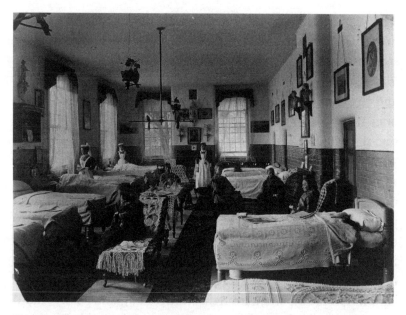

Photograph of a ward for women, with nurses and parrots on a perch, in an unidentified mental hospital in Britain. Regimentation and isolation in mental handicap hospitals continued after the Second World War.

recalled litanies of cruelty and abuse. A refusal to scrub floors could elicit a bucket of cold water over the head; minor 'infringements' entailed incarceration in a locked side room; 'offenders' were forced to scrub floors wearing pyjamas, underwear or stripped naked for the purpose of humiliation. More serious 'crimes', such as absconding or attempting to have sexual contact, warranted dispatch to the punishment villa, straitjacketing or injection with tranquilizers, and locking up in a dark room with a mattress but no bed for as long as a month.[15] The pervasive regulation and the ferocity of the punishments and treatment reflected not only the suffocating institutional moral corruption, and the dehumanization of the deficient patients, but a form of rage against a group who had come to be seen as inadequate humans and who needed to be somehow kept for their whole lives in a form of netherworld, leading useless, purposeless existences. Even the leisure and social activities that bring pleasure and variety to most were sucked dry by regulation, discipline and strange subversions of normative social conventions. At dances and parties, men and women were not allowed to mix, even if in the same venue, such was the fear that defectives would breed. On Fridays there would be 'outside' days for organized physical activity. There were Scout and Guide groups, but for grown men and women, not boys and girls, and in their uniforms they would parade with flags and drums.[16]

The birth of a mentally deficient child was seen as an unfortunate aberration by medical professionals, and parents were invariably advised to have the child institutionalized, forget about them and try for a more successful outcome. As one parent described: 'I had my son in 1955. I was just told that he was a "Mongol", as they called them in those days, and there would be no future for him, and that he'd probably not live longer than five. They said the best thing for us to do was put him in an institution.'[17] Parents recalled the incessant pressure from medical professionals, an authority that was so elevated and unquestionable in the 1950s that it was difficult to resist, even when parents were desperate to keep their child. One mother suffered what she described as a total breakdown after first resisting and finally succumbing to the blandishments of doctors to institutionalize her son: '"Put him away and forget all about him" – that used to be the advice – "put him away and have a another child."'[18] If parents did choose to keep their children at home they faced a significant challenge. The 1944 Education Act stipulated the testing of children for mental deficiency, now relabelled as 'educationally subnormal' or 'maladjusted', from the age of two. Children found to score less than 50 on IQ tests were designated 'ineducable' and parents either had to fund private education for them or keep them at home.[19] The diagnosis of ineducability would be conveyed by letter: 'I received a letter from the education authorities telling me he was "ineducable" and should be excluded from school. I still have that very hurtful letter. Ineducable. It's a terrible blow. I tried to fight it but I knew I didn't have a leg to stand on.'[20]

Medical opinion about mental deficiency therefore changed little after the war, and the care and treatment of the deficient was consigned to a quiet professional backwater. However, in the face of this professional and still deeply eugenics-influenced (if disguised) assault there were changes in attitude and response from groups of parents, who began to stand up to the soulless arrogance of the doctors who dismissed their offspring as less than human. Correspondence in a new publication, *Nursery World*, between parents of 'backward' children, led to the establishment of the National Association for the Parents of Backward Children in 1946, led by a young mother, Judy Fryd. This became the National Society for Mentally Handicapped Children in 1956, with adults added to the title in 1981, and is known today as Mencap. It was a radical step for parent power to be asserted against powerful doctors in this way, but they had been effectively put into a position of advocating for the lives, and the human status, of their children. As one activist recalled:

[We] were trying to get support and recognition as much as anything to try and get people to treat our people as though there was at least a certain amount of normality. They were all human beings . . . And also to try and get the children, although they weren't children all of them, recognised as people.[21]

Parents fought for a new community-based system of support to challenge the hegemony of the institutionalized hospital behemoth. They agitated for, and set up through their own efforts, nurseries, occupational centres, youth clubs, respite and even residential homes. They also lobbied nationally for every child to have the right to schooling.[22] Most of all they provided a site of opposition to medical authority.

In wider society, new libertarian attitudes began to emerge that dismissed pre-war eugenic, social and moral fears about degenerates. A libertarian campaign began in 1947, led by the National Council for Civil Liberties (NCCL; now Liberty) against the exploitation and undue restriction of liberty of patients in mental deficiency colonies. The campaign objected to the perpetual extension of licences to detain defectives in colonies: failure of the Board of Control to respond to complaints; and exploitation of patients in paid work. In 1951 the NCCL published a book called *50,000 outside the Law: An Examination of Those Certified as Mentally Defective*, which catalogued cases of abuse. This produced banner headlines in the press about 'slave labour' and led to a Royal Commission on the Law Relating to Mental Illness and Mental Deficiency in 1954. The medical profession conspicuously failed to back the campaign or the cause of reform, and while some minor modifications ensued, these were limited in scope and the central injustices of the Mental Deficiency Act and its colony and guardian systems remained. It was significant, however, that in a changing climate of opinion the forgotten population of defectives had been brought to public attention as people in need of justice rather than a menacing subgroup requiring isolation.

Both the parental and NCCL campaigns were indicators of the first stirrings of a revolt against the social indictment and abuse of the so-called defective population. A similar process began to occur in the United States, where, as in Britain, after the war eugenics had lost its most vociferous public proponents but eugenic assumptions remained in place. Tens of thousands of 'morons' and other 'retarded' people continued to wither away in large state-run institutions. Physicians and psychologists still recommended to parents that their retarded child should be institutionalized and forgotten about.[23] However, small numbers of parents opted to shun this advice and keep their child within the family, their cause popularized by celebrities who spoke out about their own children and started to bring about a shift in public attitudes. Prominent among these were the actress, singer and songwriter Dale Evans and her 'singing cowboy' husband Roy Rogers, famous for the *Roy Rogers Show* (1951–7) on television in which he appeared with his horse Trigger and dog Bullet. Their daughter Robin was born with Down syndrome and lived until she was two years old. The couple opted, against medical advice, to keep her at home, and Evans's book about Robin, *Angel*

Unaware, became a best-seller on publication in 1953. The deeply Christian Evans and Rogers offered a countervailing standpoint to the 'menace of the feebleminded' eugenic indictment that had stood firm for half a century.[24] Reviving the centuries-old notion of the holy innocent, Evans described her child as an angel sent to bring the family closer to God: 'I believe with all my heart that God sent her on a two-year mission to our household, to strengthen us spiritually and to draw us closer together in the knowledge and love and fellowship of God.'[25] Although this may sound, to twenty-first-century ears, sentimental, evangelical and, as the theorist Wolf Wolfensberger would describe it, consigning the disabled child into the role of 'living saint',[26] it was a courageous and important riposte to the prevailing viciousness of eugenics discourse. It was lent weight by the celebrity status of the parents, who could reach out to the general population in ways that were beyond more earnest campaigners, and both Dale Evans and Roy Rogers risked the public goodwill on which their careers depended by taking a principled stand against current professional opinion.

Helped by this sort of positive publicity, activist parent groups began to spring up across the United States in the 1940s and '50s. In 1950 the National Association of Parents and Friends of Mentally Retarded Children was formed, which became in 1952 the National Association for Retarded Children. Invariably denied access to mainstream schooling for their children, and always with the threat of institutionalization looming, these parent groups formed alternative education systems, set up summer camps and recreational facilities, and campaigned for special educational provision under slogans such as 'for every child a fair chance'.[27] All this presented a potent threat to eugenic libels of both the defective population and the families into which they were born, particularly as it was underpinned by the strong 1950s moral authority of respectable parenthood, the movements being almost exclusively middle class.

Meritocratic Anxieties

Democratization, rising affluence and increasing technological sophistication in industry and farming after the war led to a general anxiety about whether society could still retain any place at all for the so-called dull and unintelligent. In Britain this anxiety concerned not only those specifically diagnosed as defective or imbecile but all those who were in some way 'dull' in their mental faculties. It seemed that modern society was becoming so sophisticated that only the mentally agile and gifted could find a meaningful role within it. In a 1957 book called *The Foreseeable Future* the Nobel Prize-winning physicist Sir George Thomson expressed fears about what he described as 'the future of the stupid' in the face of growing mechanization and the looming threat of cybernetics. In the 'most civilized communities', the disappearance of routine work, the emergence of supermarkets where customers collected their own groceries, and machines taking over any job that didn't require 'full human faculties' forced the question, he suggested: 'what is to happen to the really definitely stupid man, or even the man of barely average intelligence?'[28] Thomson could suggest little to avert the looming catastrophe, which he estimated could affect the 80 per cent of the population not intelligent enough to go to grammar school. Tending the aged, supported by state subsidy, was one option, but otherwise he foresaw the ongoing stratification of society and allocation of resources according to intelligence as nothing less than a headache for future politicians. H. G. Wells's late nineteenth-century vision in *The Time Machine* of a species split into a small community of luxuriating Eloi menaced by a tribe of resentful unskilled Morlocks seemed to be coming to pass.

Michael Young, the sociologist and founder of the Open University, foresaw a similar problem. In a 1958 satirical book he coined the phrase 'meritocracy' to denote a society in which intellectual merit, and nothing else, determines social position and privilege. *The Rise of the Meritocracy* was written from the viewpoint of 2034 (at that point 76 years away) in a United

Kingdom where unrest is stirring among the unintelligent classes (in the form of the Populist Party) against the elite intellectually gifted class. Young was trying to elucidate two problems that arose from the meritocratic ideal, however alluring it might sound. First, a system based on intellectual merit alone simply creates a new class system to replace old caste systems, equally unjust, and equally exclusive and oppressive of the lower orders, who in this system are the intellectually dull. Second, the new meritocratic system will contain within it the shadow of the old caste system, with those who gained privileged positions in the old system able to find ways to attain prominence in the new order. This indeed will be worse than the old system, because those who occupy positions of power in a meritocracy will consider themselves to have achieved their status solely through merit, while many of them will have in fact attained them through long-standing but concealed systems of inherited wealth and status by birth. This will attach an overweening sense of entitlement and self-worth to the elite.[29]

The book was interpreted by many – particularly, as Young quipped, those who had not read it – as an endorsement of the meritocratic system, on the grounds that the achievement of privilege through individual intellectual merit had to be much fairer than achieving a dominant position through the simple fact of birth into a privileged caste, regardless of talent or intellect. Meritocracy was still privilege through birth, however, and operated on a belief that those with inferior brains somehow deserved less than did a select minority born with high intellects. As Young commented:

Even if it can be demonstrated that ordinary people had less native ability than those selected for high position, that would not mean that they deserved to get less. Being a member of the 'lucky sperm club' confers no moral right to advantage. What one is born with, or without, is not of one's own making.[30]

The dilemma with which both Thomson and Young wrestled was in truth an important consequence of the demonization and isolation of the defective over the past seventy years. It was becoming evident that once a society begins to apportion privilege, status and position on the basis of intellectual faculty alone, the process of isolation of the mentally dull begins to reach out further and further across the population. The philosophy of meritocracy is bolstered by its ability to convey a language of fairness, merit and even equality, while in practice it embeds deeply stratified new layers of inequality. Those diagnosed as mentally defective or imbecile were largely either entirely removed from society into institutions, or at least deprived of any meaningful participation in society through surveillance and guardianship, under the Mental Deficiency Act. This dispatch of the most obvious outgroup into a forgotten and largely unseen existence precipitated the creation of a new out-group – the dullest of those left behind. This led Thomson to ask the question 'of what our descendants will do with the stupider people in their new world'.[31] By this he did not mean the defective who had been dealt with by the Mental Deficiency Act; he meant the dull-witted who had moved into the vacancy created by their departure. Young talked about 'how sad, and fragile, a meritocratic society could be' and warned how in a society where the rich and powerful come to believe that they fully deserved all that they had, 'how arrogant they could become, and, if they believed it was for the common good, how ruthless in pursuing their own advantage'.[32] Young and Thomson both reflected a growing unease, at least in some parts, about the assumed hegemony of those blessed with inherited intellectual gifts, which signalled a questioning of the vitriolic indictment of the mentally dull that had prevailed since the late nineteenth century.

Parental campaigns, concerns of civil liberty groups and general unease about the eugenics legacy led to demand for changes in both policy and law. There was no fundamental shift in professional attitudes, particularly among the majority of medical practitioners. Many advocates of eugenic science from the interwar period remained in influential posts in mental health and mental deficiency in the 1950s, their views largely unchanged if less vociferously expressed. Eugenic mistrust of the deficient remained very much alive but appeared in new forms. Its shadow could be clearly discerned in optimistic talk about meritocracy and opportunities for 'gifted' working-class children. Language changed and explicit eugenic anxieties transcended into a softer language of sociological concern about 'problem families' and 'social problem groups'.[33]

Reform

A Royal Commission on the Law Relating to Mental Illness and Mental Deficiency was established in 1954 and became known as the Percy Commission. Its remit was to review the existing legislative framework governing the detention and care of people with mental illness and mental deficiency. The two groups, the mentally deficient and the mentally ill, were united again under the same policy umbrella, as they had been for most of the nineteenth century, after the separation that had occurred under the 1913 Mental Deficiency Act. Reporting in 1957, the commission concluded that 'the law should be altered so that whenever possible suitable care may be provided for mentally disordered patients with no more restriction of legal formality than is applied to people who need care because of other types of illness, disability or social difficulty.'[34] It also recommended treatment in the community rather than large-scale hospitals wherever possible, greater absorption of treatment for mental conditions into the NHS and more local authority provision of accommodation. The Mental Health Act of 1959,[35] which covered both mental illness and mental deficiency, broadly followed its recommendations and repealed not only the Mental Deficiency Act but the previous Lunacy and Mental Treatment Acts. It sought to create a legal framework for hospital treatment of mental disorder approximate to that of physical illness. Local authorities became responsible for the social care of people who did not need inpatient medical treatment. Voluntary treatment rather than legal certification became the norm for treatment, in line with the open access of the rest of the NHS.

As is often the case when mental illness and mental disability are brought together, the concerns of the more numerous and more curable mentally ill dominated the legislation. A gap opened between what Matthew Thomson has called 'high priority and well-resourced services for the curable, and a continuing decay and neglect of services for the incurable and chronic'.[36] Under the Mental Health Act, the first major piece of legislation concerning this group since 1913, the mentally deficient acquired a new name, becoming the 'mentally subnormal', a term rooted decisively in the fetishization of IQ. 'Feeble-minded', 'idiot' and 'imbecile' were also dropped, at least from the official lexicon, and it was stipulated that a person may no longer be identified as suffering from a mental disorder 'by reason only of promiscuity

George Edward Shuttleworth, 'Mongolian imbeciles – highest grade', 1902, photograph. The idea of the moral imbecile only came to an end in 1959.

or other immoral conduct'. This was an attempt to bring to an end the incarceration of the 'moral imbecile' on the grounds of amoral or immoral behaviour alone. The term 'community care' replaced 'supervision', but there was no significant move to empty the mental deficiency hospitals and colonies, where the mentally subnormal continued to languish, newly named but otherwise their lives unchanged, still excluded from the concept of citizenship and the rights that it brought with it. Nothing had been solved, and lives continued to be wasted. Stagnation, indifference and neglect, combined with scarce resources, continued to characterize what were now known as subnormality or mental handicap hospitals.

A series of scandals, including one at Normansfield Hospital, originally founded by John Langdon Down, erupted into public awareness, usually through press exposure, to shine light into the dark corners of these forgotten islands of misery. In 1967 the *News*

A patient at Normansfield Hospital, Teddington, Middlesex, 12 February 1979. Founded by John Langdon Down in 1868, the hospital was the focus of an abuse and neglect scandal in the 1970s.

of the World newspaper exposed a litany of abuses in Ely Hospital, Cardiff. This included cruel ill-treatment of four particular patients by six named members of staff, inhumane and threatening behaviour towards patients, and theft of patients' food, clothing and other items. This led to a committee of inquiry that reported in 1969, recounting countless acts of cruelty, verbal abuse, beatings of patients and a lack of medical care. The report, written by Geoffrey Howe, later to become a senior Conservative politician, went beyond Ely itself to examine the systemic abuse of people with mental handicap under the NHS.[37] A subsequent government White Paper in 1971, called 'Better Services for Mentally Handicapped People', proposed a shift from hospitals towards non-medical services in the community, with targets for places in hostels, schools and training centres.[38] The previous year, bowing to years of parental pressure to reject the exclusion of children classed as 'ineducable' from the education system, the government had passed the 1970 Education Act, which transferred responsibility for education of severely mentally handicapped children from health authorities to local authorities, enshrining in law the principle of entitlement of all children to an education.

The exclusionary thrust and the isolating foundations of the mental deficiency era were therefore beginning to crumble, but slowly. For the newly born and their parents there was now a route, an emerging system, that offered an alternative to the institution. In 1978 the Warnock Report on 'special educational needs' recommended integration for some (but not all) children with disabilities. However, many young people and adults were still locked inside the institutional system, and as attention shifted even further away from the institutions to what would replace them, they became lethal places to live. In 1981 a documentary film, *Silent Minority*,[39] highlighted the conditions of patients at two English mental handicap hospitals, St Lawrence's in Caterham, Surrey (formerly the Metropolitan Asylum for Chronic Imbeciles) and Borocourt in Berkshire. The film, whose makers had been invited by the managers of the hospitals in the belief that it would show the effect of their funding difficulties and the need for hospital investment, showed highly disturbing scenes. These included a 'troublesome' young patient tied to a pillar, a person locked in an isolation room and forgotten about, and, in one extraordinary segment, a group of patients trying to tunnel their way out from an open-air pen (which was surrounded by high wire and had been donated by the friends of the hospital) after being left there with no food, water or shelter on a hot day. It was indicative of the isolation of the hospitals, and the normalization of this sort of treatment of the people within them, that the managers had thought that filming daily life there would simply result in a desire to make better hospitals.

This seemed to be a tipping point in the public's response to the accumulation of instances of cruelty, neglect and dehumanization that had been regularly forcing its way to their attention from the netherworld of mental handicap institutions since the 1960s. Two years earlier, the Report of the Committee of Enquiry into Mental Handicap Nursing Care (the Jay Report) had made radical proposals for the adoption of a social model of community care, rather than a medical model of long-term hospital 'care', however severe a person's handicap.[40] It stated:

> Mentally handicapped people have a right to enjoy normal patterns of life within the community [but] too often . . . the concept of 'as normal a life as possible' has tended to stop short of those with severe problems. It is still unfortunately assumed that if a mentally handicapped person has additional physical handicaps or severe behaviour disorder he must live in hospital.

The Jay Report was a clear signal that the day of the idiot asylum, the mental deficiency colony, the mental handicap hospital, was over. In 1980 the King's Fund, a health think tank, published *An Ordinary Life*, which made the case that people with mental handicaps should not lead separate lives isolated from their communities but should live in the same streets, in the same sort of housing, using the same health, transport and other social facilities, as the rest of the community. That the argument even had to be made in such a way, making the case that people were entitled to a simple ordinary life, indicated the depth of the chasm that had opened up between the citizens of society and the denizens of the parallel world of the mental handicap institution.

In 1981, two years after the Jay Report was published, and as the horrors of *Silent Minority* flickered across the prime-time screens of an aghast and squirming public, a Green Paper called 'Care in the Community' was published by the government, proposing the transfer of money and care from the NHS to local councils and voluntary organizations.[41] This meant the wholesale closure of the hospitals, to be replaced by a new system of community care and involving the resettlement of tens of thousands of hospital patients to new lives outside the institution. The unlikely liberator of those who had entered hospital as mental defectives and would now leave as the mentally handicapped was Prime Minister Margaret Thatcher, not renowned for her support of oppressed minorities but convinced by the logic of the arguments that had built up over the past thirty years. In fact, the devastation that the state had wrought in the lives of people it had first labelled as mentally deficient, then as mentally handicapped, and whom it would soon call people with learning disabilities, was grist to the mill of her creed of economic liberalism and her belief that the state should stay out of the lives of individuals as much as possible.

Over the 1980s and '90s, tens of thousands of people moved out of the mental handicap hospitals into new lives in their communities. The old hospitals, such familiar features of the British landscape for the past 140 years, breathed their last as institutions. Many were converted into (often luxury) housing or demolished to make way for housing developments. Sometimes a small rump of the old hospital endured, newly formed or occasionally even rebuilt as 'specialist' health facilities for people deemed to have the most complex needs. The former patients moved into smaller residential or group housing provided by local authorities or voluntary organizations, supported by a community infrastructure of day centres, community mental handicap teams, special education in schools and colleges, and social clubs.

The medical model was over, it was proclaimed; the social model would now prevail. Such a transformation in living arrangements required a change in public perception, and therefore, as always, another change in name. From the 1990s, 'mentally handicapped' came to be seen as a bogus term. A handicap was defined not as something intrinsic to the person but as the series of obstacles that society placed across their everyday existence to prevent them from living an ordinary life – institutions, inaccessible environments, social hostility. A disability was what lay within and caused difficulties in the person's capacity to learn, adapt and develop. The right support in the community could minimize these difficulties and enable the disabled person to overcome the restrictive handicaps of the everyday world. Also, people with disabilities should be seen as people first and foremost – as individuals with rights. The person came first, not the disability. And so, in the new era of community, they were no longer mentally handicapped people: they were people with learning disabilities.

As ever, policy and practice in Britain and the United States moved closely in parallel. After a series of similar institutional scandals and attendant revelations of profound systemic failures, deinstitutionalization and the creation of community services began. This process in the U.S. was optimistically called 'a total reorientation of society to the care and treatment of mentally retarded persons'.[42] The movement towards community resettlement was led by family advocacy campaigns, given a huge boost by the active involvement of the Kennedy family. Rosemary Kennedy, whose older brother John would become president of the United States in 1961, was born in 1918 and was assessed as 'mentally deficient' at the age of seven. The wealthy Kennedy family were able to keep her at home rather than institutionalize her. A disastrous prefrontal lobotomy in 1941, when she was

A competitor in the Special Olympics, 2019.

aged 23, left her much more significantly disabled and she was institutionalized from 1949. Her younger sister Eunice Kennedy (later Shriver) became a driving force in the advocacy movement and pressured John, once he became president, to take action and bring the retarded population, and the institutions that housed them, to public attention. He made several visits to overcrowded institutions, with press and photographers present, to expose the cruel neglect and abuse that was occurring.[43] Shriver would go on to launch and lead the Special Olympics movement, which held its first Special Olympic Games in 1968.

The Kennedy family's openness about Rosemary Kennedy emboldened advocacy movements and reduced social stigma. In this new atmosphere, civil rights campaigners launched a series of legislative actions to bring people with mental retardation under the equal protection of the law as American citizens. In *Wyatt v. Stickney* (1972) it was determined that people should be served in the least restrictive environment, including the community. *Halderman v. Pennhurst State School and Hospital* (1977) disallowed the condition of mental retardation as sole justification for institutionalization and established the community as the central site of services.[44] The move from institutions began, the journey back to the communities for which people had been deemed unfit a century earlier.

Theorization

The gradual re-emergence of people to some sort of social visibility attracted the attention of social theorists, who sought to explain what it was that had caused this segment of humanity to be dehumanized and banished from society in a toxic atmosphere of social indictment. The German American scholar Wolf Wolfensberger argued in 1968, as a critical light fell on institutions, that perceptions of the retarded person by the non-retarded determined the dehumanizing abusiveness of the institutional setting, from its conception through its design to its daily operations. He identified three obvious ways in which the retarded person was dehumanized: through being perceived as sick, as a subhuman organism or as a menace. He then, however, identified three more subtle and concealed ways in which dehumanization occurred: by being seen as an object of pity, a burden of charity or as a holy innocent. These of course were long-standing popular beliefs about the 'idiot', discernible from at least the medieval period. Such ostensibly benevolent conceptions of retardation were, for Wolfensberger, in some ways more dangerous than the overtly hostile perceptions. Pity infantilized those on whom it was bestowed and had synergies with the subhuman model, in that it perceived the retarded person as a form of human being not taken seriously or assigned importance. The idea of holy innocence conceived the retarded person as incapable of committing evil and therefore as harmless and childlike, and in this way lacking full human status in the eyes of others. The 'burden of charity' perception was merely a cold, often contemptuous objectification of the retarded person through reluctant support bestowed to enable them to live with their misfortune, which was often seen as providential. The importance of Wolfensberger's theoretical approach, apart from its insights into the cruelties of institutional systems, was its argument that the retarded person (or whatever label was attached to them across time and space) was constructed in the minds of others rather than representing some universal, unchanging, knowable human type. It was these perceptions that led to their institutionalization and abuse, rather than any innate incapacity to live as accepted members of human society.[45]

In 1967 the anthropologist Robert B. Edgerton published *The Cloak of Competence*, which, based on one-to-one interviews, described the lives of one hundred individuals labelled as retarded who had left a Californian institution in 1961. He described them as mentally imprisoned by the stigma of intellectual incompetence:

That the incompetence of these retarded persons is most important in these 'intellectual areas' leads to the conclusion that their deficit is truly a partial and limited one – a lack of intellectual competence, not a lack of social competence. In fact, however, for the ex-patient in this study, any distinction between 'intellectual' and 'social' competence is factitious. In the course of these ex-patients' everyday lives the two competencies – intellectual and social – cannot be separated.[46]

He saw the group as locked into a constant battle for their self-esteem and the esteem of others, in which they attempted, usually unsuccessfully, to 'pass' as normal, clothing themselves in a transparent and tattered 'cloak of competence'. Once identi-fied as 'deviant' they struggled to maintain their place in society, only surviving by being 'given a niche . . . in which they are permitted to live incompetently as long as in the course of this living they do not cause the wrong persons too much trouble'.[47] The argument was that even with a return to the community the stigma of retardation was such that membership of society was conditional, not an entitlement, and dependent on the goodwill of the majority community. Edgerton's work reflected the work of the sociologist Erving Goffman, whose books *Asylums* (1961) and *Stigma* (1963) explored the perverse impact of the institu-tion on individual identity, and how classes labelled deviant shored up their social identity by passing as 'normal' as best they could. Edgerton's study was as important for its method, in that it saw its retarded subjects as human individuals whose thoughts and feelings were valid and worthy of consideration, as for its conclusions.

Wolfensberger also developed the concept of 'death-making' as a function of services for and professional attitudes to retar-dation. Medical services fail such people because their lives are perceived to have low quality and value: 'Handicapped people are given massive doses of psychoactive drugs, so that they die from drug effects – even though the death certificate will list only the complications, such as cardiac arrest, pneumonia.'[48] The British psychoanalyst Valerie Sinason took this idea further and wrote how 'the widespread wish for medical science to eradicate intellectual disability means that those born and living "with it" are not emotionally welcomed nor included,' living in a world where, if their defects had been detected in utero, they would have been prevented from living, and where at a primitive level mothers are blamed for producing defective children.[49] It is in this gap between the expectation of what comprises a full human being and the appearance of the 'deficient' human that death-making can lie.

In 1969 the Swedish theorist Bengt Nirje produced a theory of 'normalization', which emphasized that people defined as intellectually disabled (or whatever particular nomenclature was used) had the right to the same quality of life of life as non--disabled people, and the right to participate fully in society. A normal life course should occur within normal environments rather than within large institutions. Wolfensberger developed this theory and named it 'social role valorization'. His argument was that only a change in perception about the value of the lives of intellectually disabled people could improve their social standing and drain the lethal toxicity within which they were usually framed. This devaluation could be combatted by equipping them with 'social valorization' through teaching positive personal skills, training for highly valued work and encouraging association with non-disabled individuals.[50] The American advocate John O'Brien built on the idea of social role valorization to propose a set of competencies and rights to enable social integration: the right to community inclusion, to have valued relationships with non-disabled people and to make choices, while being supported to develop the competencies to do these things, and the right to full respect as a person within communities. While this integrationist approach represented a welcome rejection of the isolationist and medical models that had been prevalent throughout the century, its ideas have more recently been critiqued for their closeness to the concept of 'conditional acceptance', the requirement for intellectually disabled people to attempt to be like others in order to be able to participate fully in community life. Proponents of inclusion have since argued that it is the job of society to demonstrate sufficient flexibility and adaptation to include all its members, rather than insist on an adherence to a prescribed set of norms.[51]

The Great Return

This sudden glut of attention by theorists signalled the impending return to communities of a group whose exclusion and isolation from society had begun in the 1840s, accelerated in the 1860s and continued into the 1970s. The move back to the communities from which their predecessors had first been ousted over 130 years previously was accompanied by a renewed focus of concern from academics, policymakers and the public. This was generally far more positive than the collective indictment they had faced from eugenicists, psychologists, intellectuals and politicians in the post-Darwin era of eugenics and evolutionary psychology. It also represented an end to the collective forgetting to which they had been subjected after the Second World War, lingering in abusive and neglected hospitals while affluence and health improved outside the walls behind which they were hidden. When the 'great return' began in the 1980s and continued into the 1990s it was surprisingly successful. People moved back in their tens of thousands to the communities in which they had been born, many of them re-encountering their birthplaces for the first time in decades, or even coming 'home' for the first time. Their moves were largely successful, and a new network of community services grew around them. There was a decisive move from the medical model to the social model. Many lived successful new lives doing things that had been denied to them previously: simple things like sleeping in their own bedrooms, having their own clothes and making their own choices about what they wanted to eat or watch on television. They were also able to make larger choices about how they wanted to live their lives, reunite with families, work, and have personal relationships.

No such large social transformation is perfect, and 130 years of institutionalization and denigration does not disappear overnight. There have been concerns that forms of invisible institutionalization can occur, even within small community-based services – that people can be 'in' their communities but not 'of' them. Whether most people feel fully part of their communities or not remains open to question. Revealing language is sometimes used by service organizations, which talk about 'accessing community-based opportunities', living in a 'community-based learning disabilities context' or 'resettling into community provision' and 'acculturation'. When community is talked about in this way, 'it refers to a space in which "we", the non-intellectually disabled, belong, and which "they", the intellectually disabled, are given support to "access", a process managed and negotiated through a series of quality of life assessments, risk profiles, funding decisions and personalised plans.'[52]

This can be seen as a 'gift' model of inclusion, where people are only allowed to be part of their communities subject to certain conditions. Truly integrated people do not have to 'access' their communities, they are simply part of them. The 'idiots' of the eighteenth century, popularly imagined as a far more brutal and cruel time, were included in their communities in ways that the highly technological, controlling, risk-averse and bureaucratized societies of the twenty-first century find hard to contemplate. In the 2000s a worrying new trend has emerged: the return of the institution in a new form, private and NHS 'assessment and treatment units' (ATUs). In these medicalized facilities, thousands of people with learning disabilities have been detained indefinitely under the Mental Health Act because of 'challenging behaviour'. From them a catalogue of abusive incidents and horror stories of neglect and restraint, some ending in death, has emerged. Is the murderous beast of the institution on the march again?

Despite such lingering or re-emerging threats, the changes that occurred in the last quarter of the twentieth century and the death of the old hospital system should be celebrated. There have

The world has moved on, and thousands have taken control of their own lives.

been numerous success stories, and many thousands of people have been able to live the 'ordinary lives' that, remarkably, in the 1980s appeared an impossible and utopian dream. A personalization movement has enabled thousands of people to take control of their own lives and of the funding they need for their support. Actors with learning disabilities appear on prime-time television and in films; self-advocates speak in parliaments and at the United Nations. Self-advocacy movements have grown across the world.

Whatever the problems that persist, whatever new dangers need to be guarded against, the world has moved on from the words spoken in 1904 by Martin W. Barr, superintendent of the Pennsylvania Training School for Feeble-minded Children and president of the American Association for the Study of Feeble-mindedness: 'the idiot intelligently sees nothing, feels nothing, hears nothing, does nothing.'[53] Whatever terms society has chosen to label them with – idiots, imbeciles, defectives, morons, mentally handicapped, subnormal, learning disabled or intellectually disabled – these people have, even in the darkest hours, consistently shown what they can see, what they feel and hear, and most of all what they do. Society's task today, the duty of communities, is to adapt to all its human members and never allow the darkness of the institution, or the horrors of the T4 programme, to shame humanity again.

References

All italics in quoted material are original unless otherwise stated.

Introduction

1 Anne Digby, 'Contexts and Perspectives', in *From Idiocy to Mental Deficiency: Historical Perspectives on People with Learning Disabilities*, ed. Anne Digby and David Wright (London, 1996), p. 1.
2 Roy Porter, 'Mother Says It Done Me Good', *London Review of Books* (16 April 1997), p. 6.
3 Martin W. Barr, *Mental Defectives: Their History, Treatment and Training* (Philadelphia, PA, 1904). Leo Kanner, *A History of the Care and Study of the Mentally Retarded* (Springfield, IL, 1964); Kathleen Jones, *A History of the Mental Health Services* (London, 1972); O. Conor Ward, *John Langdon Down, 1828–1896: A Caring Pioneer* (London, 1998).
4 Jones, *History of the Mental Health Services*, pp. xi–xii.
5 James W. Trent, Jr, *Inventing the Feeble Mind: A History of Mental Retardation in the United States* (Berkeley, CA, 1994). Richard Neugebauer, 'Mental Handicap in Medieval and Early Modern England: Criteria, Measurement and Care', pp. 22–43; Peter Rushton, 'Idiocy, the Family and the Community in Early Modern North-east England', pp. 44–64; and Jonathan Andrews, 'Identifying and Providing for the Mentally Disabled in Early Modern London', pp. 65–92, all in *From Idiocy to Mental Deficiency*, ed. Digby and Wright; Irina Mezler, *Fools and Idiots? Intellectual Disability in the Middle Ages* (Manchester, 2016). S. Noll and J. W. Trent, Jr, eds, *Mental Retardation in America: A Historical Reader* (New York, 2004), p. 8.
6 D. Atkinson, M. Jackson and J. Walmsley, *Forgotten Lives: Exploring the History of Learning Disability* (Kidderminster, 1997); D. Atkinson et al., *Good Times, Bad Times: Women with Learning Difficulties Tell Their Stories* (Kidderminster, 2000); S. Rolph et al., *Witnesses to Change: Families, Learning Difficulties and History* (Kidderminster, 2005); Jan Walmsley, Dorothy Atkinson and Sheena Rolph, 'Community Care and Mental Deficiency, 1913–1945', in *Outside the Walls of the Asylum: The History of Care in the Community, 1750–2000*, ed. Peter Bartlett and David Wright (London, 1999), pp. 181–203; M. Potts and R. Fido, *A Fit Person to Be Removed: Personal Accounts of Life in a Mental Deficiency Institution* (Plymouth, 1991); Mark Jackson, *The Borderland of Imbecility:*

Medicine, Society and the Fabrication of the Feeble Mind in Late-Victorian and Edwardian England (Manchester, 2000); Mathew Thomson, *The Problem of Mental Deficiency: Eugenics, Democracy and Social Policy in Britain, c. 1870–1959* (Oxford, 1998); David Wright, *Mental Disability in Victorian England: The Earlswood Asylum, 1847–1901* (Oxford, 2001); David Wright, *Downs: The History of a Disability* (Oxford, 2011).

7 C. F. Goodey, 'What Is Developmental Disability? The Origin and Nature of Our Conceptual Models', *Journal on Developmental Disabilities*, VIII/2 (2001), pp. 1–18. C. F. Goodey, *A History of Intelligence and Intellectual Disability: The Shaping of Psychology in Early Modern Europe* (Farnham, 2011); Patrick McDonagh, *Idiocy: A Cultural History* (Liverpool, 2008); Patrick McDonagh, C. F. Goodey, T. Stainton, eds, *Intellectual Disability: A Conceptual History, 1200–1900* (Manchester, 2018).

8 For a more global perspective see Jan Walmsley and Simon Jarrett, eds, *Intellectual Disability in the Twentieth Century: Transnational Perspectives on People, Policy and Practice* (Bristol, 2019).

1 Poor Foolish Lads and Weak Easy Girls: Legal Ideas of Idiocy

1 John Cowell, *A Law Dictionary; or, The Interpreter of Words and Terms Used Either in the Common or Statute Laws of Great Britain and in Tenures and Jocular Customs* [1607] (London, 1727).

2 C. F. Goodey, *A History of Intelligence and Intellectual Disability: The Shaping of Psychology in Early Modern Europe* (Farnham, 2011), p. 141.

3 Margaret McGlynn, 'Idiots, Lunatics and the Royal Prerogative in Early Tudor England', *Journal of Legal History*, XXVI/1 (2005), pp. 5–6.

4 Richard Neugebauer, 'Mental Handicap in Medieval and Early Modern England: Criteria, Measurement and Care', in *From Idiocy to Mental Deficiency: Historical Perspectives on People with Learning Disabilities*, ed. Anne Digby and David Wright (London, 1996), pp. 25–6.

5 Anthony Fitzherbert, *The New Natura Brevium* (London, 1652), pp. 580–83.

6 John Rastell, *Les Termes de la Ley; or, Certaine Difficult and Obscure Words and Termes . . .* [1527] (London, 1636), pp. 201–2.

7 Cowell, *Law Dictionary*.

8 *Court of King's Wards*, 32 Henry VIII; c. 46, 33 Henry VIII, c. 22.

9 H. E. Bell, *An Introduction to the History and Records of the Court of Wards and Liveries* (Cambridge, 1953), pp. 85–6.

10 Ibid.

11 Ibid., p. 163.

12 Richard Neugebauer, 'Treatment of the Mentally Ill in Medieval and Early Modern England: A Reappraisal', *Journal of the History of the Behavioural Sciences*, XIV/2 (1978), pp. 164–6.

13 Sir Edward Coke, *Institutes of the Laws of England* [1628], cited in George Dale Collinson, *A Treatise on the Law concerning Idiots, Lunatics, and Other Persons Non Compotes Mentis* (London, 1812), pp. 57–8.

14 Collinson, *Treatise*, p. 59.

15 John Brydall, *Non Compos Mentis; or, The Law Relating to Natural Fools, Mad Folks and Lunatick Persons Inquisited and Explained for the Common Benefit* (London, 1700).

16 Ibid., pp. 8, 10, 12–16, preface A2.

17 Ibid., pp. 5, 8, 10, 38.

18 Ibid., p. 38.

19 Ibid., pp. 3, 6, 8–9.

20 Ibid., p. 6.

21 Ibid., pp. 35–6.

22 William Hicks, *Oxford Jests* [1671], in *A Nest of Ninnies and Other English Jestbooks of the Seventeenth Century*, ed. P. M. Zall (Lincoln, NE, 1970).

23 Brydall, *Non Compos Mentis*, pp. 36–8.

24 Tobias Smollett, *The Adventures of Roderick Random* [1748] (London, 1975), p. 253.

25 Old Bailey Proceedings (hereafter OBP), online, at www.oldbaileyonline. org, July 1723, trial of Thomas Allen (t17230710-39); and OBP, July 1775, trial of Joseph Muggleton, William Jackling, James Lewis (t17750712-49).

26 In B. E., Gent., *A New Dictionary of the Terms Ancient and Modern of the Canting Crew in its Several Tribes, of Gypsies, Beggars, Thieves, Cheats &c.* (London, 1699); Francis Grose, *A Classical Dictionary of the Vulgar Tongue* (London, 1788).

27 Johann Wilhelm von Archenholz, *A Picture of England: Containing a Description of the Laws, Customs, and Manners of England* (London, 1789), vol. I, p. 31.

28 The National Archives (hereafter TNA), *Bennet v. Vade*, 1742, TNA PROB 18/54/18.

29 *Bennet v. Vade*, 1739, TNA PROB 18/51/5.

30 Ibid.

31 Ibid.

32 *Bennet v. Vade*, Deposition, 1740, TNA PROB 18/52/11.

33 *Bennet v. Vade*, 1739, TNA PROB 18/51/5.

34 Ibid.

35 Collinson, *Treatise*, pp. 60–61.

36 Brydall, *Non Compos Mentis*, p. 6.

37 *Bennet v. Vade*, 1739, TNA PROB 18/51/5.

38 Anon., *The Case of Henry Roberts, Esq., a Gentleman Who by Unparalleled Cruelty Was Deprived of His Estate under the Pretence of Idiocy* (London, 1767).

39 Ibid., pp. 4–12.

40 Richard Sharp, 'Lynch, John (1697–1760)', *Oxford Dictionary of National Biography*, www.oxforddnb.com, May 2009.

41 Anon., *The Case of Henry Roberts*, p. 12.

42 TNA C211/22/R34.

43 Anon., *The Case of Henry Roberts*, pp. 13–14.

44 *Birkbeck v. Birkbeck*, 1750/51, TNA E 134/24/GEO2/MICH 9.

45 *Bowerman v. Fust*, 1789, TNA DEL 1/644.

46 Ibid., pp. 132–9.

47 Ibid., pp. 369, 147–81, 259–69.

48 Ibid., pp. 195–214, 295–329, 311, 333–5, 348–9, 365.
49 'Westminster Hall', *The Times*, 22 April 1790, p. 3, *The Times* Digital Archive, accessed 18 June 2014.
50 *Bowerman v. Fust*, 1789, TNA DEL 1/644, pp. 67, 164, 203, 212.
51 OBP, December 1710, trial of Mary Bradshaw alias Seymour (t17012o6-22).
52 OBP, September 1719, trial of Mary Tame (t17190903-33).
53 OBP, February 1748, trial of Robert Left (t17480224-48).
54 OBP, October 1804, trial of Charles Viton (t18041024-20).
55 OBP, February 1804, trial of John Smith (t18040215-50); and OBP, July 1804, trial of Charles Witholme (t18040704-23).
56 Allyson N. May, *The Bar and the Old Bailey, 1750–1850* (Chapel Hill, NC, and London, 2003), pp. 15, 17.
57 Ibid., p. 7.
58 Brass weight: OBP, February 1748, trial of Robert Left (t17480224-48); coat: OBP, February 1759, trial of Peter Cunniford (t17590228-10); ribbon: OBP, January 1762, trial of Ann Wildman (t17620114-11); breeches: OBP, February 1804, trial of John Smith (t18040215-50); saw: OBP, December 1807, trial of Conrad Frederic (t18071202-46); frock: OBP, July 1819, trial of Charlotte Lawrence (t18190707-154).
59 May, *The Bar and the Old Bailey*, p. 13.
60 OBP, July 1723, trial of Thomas Allen (t17230710-39).
61 B. E., *New Dictionary*; Grose, *Classical Dictionary of the Vulgar Tongue*.
62 OBP, September 1716, trial of Richard Price (t17160906-2); OBP, May 1740, trial of Arthur Bethell (t17400522-9); OBP, July 1775, trial of William Jackling (t17750712-49).
63 OBP, May 1732, trial of John Longmore (t17320525-6).
64 OBP, February 1759, trial of Peter Cunniford (t17590228-10); OBP, December 1807, trial of Conrad Frederic (t18071202-46).
65 OBP, February 1743, trial of Elizabeth Camell (t17430223-8).
66 OBP, May 1732, trial of John Longmore (t17320525-6).
67 OBP, February 1759, trial of Peter Cunniford (t17590228-10).
68 OBP, June 1780, trial of Thomas Baggott (t17800628-113).
69 George Rudé, *The Crowd in History* [1964] (London, 2005), pp. 57–9.
70 OBP, January 1762, trial of Ann Wildman (t17620114-11).
71 OBP, September 1716, trial of John Love, Thomas Bean, George Purchase, Richard Price, William Price (t17160906-2).
72 OBP, January 1723, trial of Mary Radford (t17230116-38).
73 OBP, May 1732, trial of John Longmore (t17320525-6); OBP, January 1734, trial of James Belford (t17340116-25).
74 S. Deveraux, 'The City and the Sessions Paper: "Public Justice" in London, 1770–1800', *Journal of British Studies*, XXXV/4 (1996), p. 480.
75 James Beattie, 'Scales of Justice: Defence Counsel and the English Criminal Trial in the 18th and 19th Centuries', *Law and History Review*, IX/2 (1991), p. 221.
76 May, *The Bar and the Old Bailey*, p. 21.
77 Beattie, 'Scales of Justice', p. 223.
78 May, *The Bar and the Old Bailey*, p. 3.

79 John H. Langbein, *The Origins of Adversary Criminal Trial* (Oxford, 2003), p. 36.
80 Quoted in John H. Langbein, 'The Criminal Trial before the Lawyers', *University of Chicago Law Review*, XLV/2 (1978), p. 311.
81 Nicola Lacey, 'Historicising Criminalisation: Conceptual and Empirical Issues', *Modern Law Review*, LXXII/6 (2009), p. 955.
82 A. Highmore, *A Treatise on the Law of Idiocy and Lunacy* (London, 1807).
83 Collinson, *Treatise.*
84 Ibid., p. 58; italics in original.
85 Ibid., p. 65.
86 Ibid., p. 100.
87 Ibid., p. 65.
88 Ibid., pp. 43–6.
89 Highmore, *Treatise,* pp. vi, xii.

2 Billy-noodles and Bird-wits: Cultural Ideas of Idiocy

1 Jonathan Andrews, 'Begging the Question of Idiocy: The Definition and Socio-cultural Meaning of Idiocy in Early Modern Britain', Part 1, *History of Psychiatry*, IX/33 (1998), pp. 65–95; and Part 2, IX/34 (1998), pp. 179–200.
2 Johann Wilhelm von Archenholz, *A Picture of England: Containing a Description of the Laws, Customs, and Manners of England* (London, 1789), vol. I.
3 Simon Dickie, *Cruelty and Laughter: Forgotten Comic Literature and the Unsentimental Eighteenth Century* (Chicago, IL, 2011).
4 Ibid., pp. 21, 30.
5 Ibid., pp. 32–3.
6 Julie Coleman, *A History of Cant and Slang Dictionaries*, vol. I: *1567–1784* (Oxford, 2004), p. 4.
7 Lee Beier, 'Anti-language or Jargon? Canting in the English Underworld in the Sixteenth and Seventeenth Centuries', in *Languages and Jargons: Contributions to a Social History of Language*, ed. P. Burke and R. Porter (Cambridge, 1995), p. 81.
8 Piers Egan, *Grose's Classical Dictionary of the Vulgar Tongue, Revised and Corrected* (London, 1823), pp. xxxvi–xxxvii.
9 Julie Coleman, *A History of Cant and Slang Dictionaries*, vol. II: *1785–1858* (Oxford, 2004), p. 1.
10 Beier, 'Anti-language or Jargon?', p. 81.
11 John Taylor, *Wit and Mirth* (London, 1630), jest 256.
12 Anon., *England's Merry Jester* (London, 1694), p. 31, jest 36.
13 Anon., *Pinkethman's Jests; or, Wit Refined* (London, 1721), p. 24.
14 Anon., *The Merry Medley; or, A Christmas-box, for Gay Gallants and Good Companions* (London 1750), p. 57; Anthony Copley, *Wits, Fits and Fancies* (London, 1607), jest 852.
15 Simon Jarrett, '"A Welshman Coming to London and Seeing a Jackanapes . . .": How Jokes and Slang Differentiated Eighteenth-century Londoners from the Rest of Britain', *London Journal*, XLIII/2 (2018), pp. 120–36.

16 These and subsequent slang references are taken, unless otherwise indicated, from the following slang dictionaries: B. E., Gent., *A New Dictionary of the Terms Ancient and Modern of the Canting Crew in Its Several Tribes, of Gypsies, Beggars, Thieves, Cheats &c.* (London, 1699); *A New Canting Dictionary* (London, 1725); *An Apology for the Life of Mr Bampfylde-Moore Carew* (London, 1750); John Shirley, *The Scoundrel's Dictionary* (London, 1754); Humphry Tristram Potter, *A New Dictionary of All the Cant and Flash Languages* (London, 1787); Francis Grose, *A Classical Dictionary of the Vulgar Tongue*, 2nd edn (London, 1788); James Caulfield, *Blackguardiana; or, A Dictionary of Rogues, Bawds, Pimps, Whores... &.* (London 1795).

17 Jarrett, '"A Welshman"', pp. 127–9.

18 Thomas Doggett, *Hob; or, The Country Wake: A Farce* (London 1715), pp. 26–7.

19 Fanny Burney, *Camilla; or, A Picture of Youth* [1796] (Oxford, 1972), pp. 184, 534.

20 Ibid., pp. 212, 225, 500, 505.

21 Isaac Cruikshank, *Paddy Whack's First Ride in a Sedan*, 1800, based on Ferdinando Foot's *The Nut-cracker* (London, 1751), p. 61; Isaac Cruikshank, *The Buck and the Goose*, 1801, based on Joe Miller, *Joe Miller's Jests* (London, 1740), p. 28, joke 124.

22 Patrick McDonagh, *Idiocy: A Cultural History* (Liverpool, 2008), p. 15.

23 Old Bailey Proceedings (hereafter OBP), April 1690, trial of Edward Munden (t16900430-28).

24 C. F. Goodey, *A History of Intelligence and 'Intellectual Disability': The Shaping of Psychology in Early Modern Europe* (Farnham, 2011).

25 This following argument is rehearsed and developed more fully in S. Jarrett and C. F. Goodey, 'Learning Difficulties: Intellectual Disability in the Long Eighteenth Century', in *A Cultural History of Disability in the Long Eighteenth Century*, ed. D. Christopher Gabbard and Susannah B. Mintz (London, 2020), especially pp. 125–33.

26 *The Jests of Beau Nash* (London, 1763), pp. 40–42.

27 'Tom Fool', *The History of Tom Fool* (London, 1760), p. 72.

28 Hurlo Thrumbo, *The Merry Thought; or, The Glass-window and Bog-house Miscellany* (London, 1731), p. 69.

29 Daniel Defoe, *Mere Nature Delineated; or, A Body without a Soul* (London, 1726), p. 37.

30 Anon., *The Complete London Jester* (London, 1781), Epigrams, p. 139.

31 Anon., *Pinkethman's Jests*, p. 91.

32 Ibid., pp. 74–5, joke 100.

33 Burney, *Camilla*, p. 39.

34 Robert Darnton, 'Peasants Tell Tales', in *The Great Cat Massacre and Other Episodes in French Cultural History* (Philadelphia, PA, 1984), p. 43.

35 Grose, *Classical Dictionary*.

36 Ibid., see entry for 'cripple'.

37 Iona and Peter Opie, eds, *The Oxford Dictionary of Nursery Rhymes* (Oxford, 1987), p. 459.

38 Anon., *A Pleasant Song, of Many More Sad Misfortunes of Poor Simon: With an Account of His Drinking a Bottle of Sack to Poison Himself, Being Weary of His Life* (London, 1775), pp. 21–4.

39 Ibid., pp. 21–2.

40 Ibid., p. 24.

41 Anon., *Simple Simon's Misfortunes and His Wife Margery's Cruelty, Which Began the Very Next Morning after Their Marriage* (London, 1775), pp. 4–6.

42 Ibid., pp. 6, 8, 15, 19.

43 Ibid., p. 17.

44 Darnton, 'Peasants Tell Tales', p. 43.

45 'The History of Joseph Jollyboy', in Anon., *Entertaining Memoirs of Little Personages; or, Moral Amusements for Young Gentlemen* (London, 1790), p. 14.

46 'Simple Simon's History', in Anon., *Entertaining Memoirs*, p. 68.

47 Ibid., pp. 75, 83.

48 Grose, *Classical Dictionary* (asterisks in original).

49 Anon., *Coffee House Jests* (London, 1686), p. 130, joke 220.

50 'Simple Simon', in Anon., *The Muse in Good Humour* (London, 1745), comic tale xii, pp. 86–7.

51 John Cleland, *Fanny Hill; or, Memoirs of a Woman of Pleasure* [1748–9] (London, 1994), pp. 91–3.

52 Ibid., p. 94.

53 Ibid., p. 192.

54 Ibid., pp. 191–2.

55 Grose, *Classical Dictionary*.

56 'Tom Fool', p. 3.

57 Ibid., p. 26.

58 Cleland, *Fanny Hill*, p. 190.

59 Ibid., p. 192.

60 Julia V. Douthwaite, *The Wild Girl, Natural Man, and the Monster: Dangerous Experiments in the Age of Enlightenment* (Chicago, IL, 2002), p. 21.

61 Ibid., p. 68.

62 Keith Thomas, 'The Place of Laughter in Tudor and Stuart England', *Times Literary Supplement*, 21 January 1977, p. 80.

63 Jean-Baptiste de La Salle, *Les Règles de la bienséance et de la civilité chrétienne* (Rouen, 1729), p. 44, cited in Norbert Elias, *The Civilizing Process* [1939] (Oxford, 2000), pp. 112–13.

64 Anon., *Coffee House Jests, Being a Merry Companion* (London, 1760), pp. 109–10, joke 203.

65 La Salle, *Les Règles*, p. 24, cited in Elias, *The Civilizing Process*, p. 113.

66 Elias, *The Civilizing Process*, pp. 50, 57.

67 Anon., *Coffee House Jests* (1760), p. 65, joke 119.

68 Dickie, *Cruelty and Laughter*, pp. 3, 6.

69 John Brewer, *The Pleasures of the Imagination: English Culture in the Eighteenth Century* (London, 1997), p. 102.

70 Anon., *An Essay on Polite Behaviour* (London, 1740), cited in Brewer, *Pleasures of the Imagination*, p. 110.

71 Cited in Brewer, *Pleasures of the Imagination*, p. 110.

72 *A New Canting Dictionary*.

73 John Bee, *Sportsman's Slang* (London, 1825).

74 'J. S.', *England's Merry Jester* (London, 1694), p. 31, joke 36.

75 Ibid., pp. 84–5, joke 112.

76 Ibid., pp. 74–5, joke 100.

77 'Robert Nixon', in *A True Copy of Nixon's Cheshire Prophecy* (London, 1715), pp. 3, 5.

78 Ibid., p. 3.

79 Ibid., pp. 14–15.

80 Burney, *Camilla*, pp. 306, 308.

81 Ibid., p. 309.

82 Ibid., p. 311.

83 'The Handsome Idiot', in 'Luke Lively', *The Merry Fellow; or, Jovial Companion* (Dublin, 1757), p. 29.

84 La Salle, *Les Règles*, p. 35, cited in Elias, *The Civilizing Process*, p. 131.

85 Mary Cowling, *The Artist as Anthropologist: The Representation of Type and Character in Victorian Art* (Cambridge, 1989), p. 9.

86 Ibid., pp. xvii–xix, 1.

87 Joanna Bourke, *What It Means to Be Human: Reflections from 1791 to the Present* (London, 2013), p. 208.

88 Cowling, *The Artist as Anthropologist*, p. 19.

89 L. P. Curtis, *Apes and Angels: The Irishman in Victorian Caricature* (Washington, DC, 1997), p. xxx.

90 James Gillray, *Doublures of Caricature* (London, 1798).

91 Curtis, *Apes and Angels*, pp. 2, 7.

92 Cowling, *The Artist as Anthropologist*, p. 42.

93 Ibid., pp. 79–80.

94 François E. Fodéré, *Traité de médecine légale et d'hygiène publique, ou de police de santé: tome premier* [1792], 2nd edn (Paris, 1813), p. 203; Étienne-Jean Georget, *De la folie: considérations sur cette maladie* (Paris, 1820), pp. 103–5.

95 Cowling, *The Artist as Anthropologist*, p. 124.

96 Georget, *De la folie*, p. 131.

97 OBP, November 1762, trial of Ann Wildman (t17620114-11); OBP, January 1723, trial of Mary Radford (t17230116-38).

98 Innes Herdan and Gustav Herdan, trans., *Lichtenberg's Commentaries on Hogarth's Engravings* [1784–96] (London, 1966), pp. 143–5.

99 N.A.M. Roger, *The Wooden World: An Anatomy of the Georgian Navy* (London, 1988), p. 214.

100 Roger Lund, 'Laughing at Cripples: Ridicule, Deformity, and the Argument from Design', *Eighteenth Century Studies*, XXXIX/1 (2005), p. 111.

101 Dickie, *Cruelty and Laughter*, p. 18.

102 Burney, *Camilla*, p. 780.

103 OBP, February 1723, trial of John Thomas (t17230227); OBP, May 1723, trial of John Smith (t17230530-44).

104 OBP, May 1798, trial of Sarah Holloway (t17980523-23).

105 OBP, January 1723, trial of Mary Radford (t17230116-38).

106 OBP, May 1744, trial of Ann Terry (t17440510-8).

107 John Thomas Smith, *Vagabondiana; or, Anecdotes of Mendicant Wanderers through the Streets of London* (London, 1818).

108 OBP, May 1748, trial of Robert Miller (t17480526-15).

109 OBP, February 1759, trial of Peter Cunniford (t17590228-10).

110 OBP, July 1737, trial of John Bullock (t17370706-4).

111 OBP, December 1732, trial of Richard Albridge (t17321206-5); OBP, June 1825, trial of John Battle (t18250630-67); OBP, January 1828, trial of Caleb Brookes (t18280110-71).

112 B. Williams, *The Whig Supremacy, 1714–1760*, 2nd edn (Oxford 1960), p. 95.

113 Ibid., p. 36.

114 Samuel Price, 'Sermon IV: The Moral Perfection of God', in Isaac Watts, *Sermons on the Principal Heads of the Christian Religion Preached at Bury Street* (London, 1733), p. 62.

115 Isaac Watts, 'Sermon VIII: A Hopeful Youth Falling Short of Heaven', part 2, in Watts, *The Works of the Reverend and Learned Isaac Watts* [1753] (London, 1810), vol. II, pp. 85–96.

116 Watts, 'The Strength and Weakness of Human Reason', ibid., p. 391.

117 Watts, 'Sermon VII: A Hopeful Youth', part 1, ibid., p. 79.

118 John Wesley, 'The First Fruits of the Spirit', in Wesley, *Complete Sermons* ebook (2016).

119 Wesley, 'Awake Thou That Sleepest, April 4 1742', ibid.

120 Wesley, 'First Fruits of the Spirit', ibid.

121 Wesley, 'Christian Perfection', ibid.

3 Idiots Abroad: Racial Ideas of Idiocy

1 Richard Hough, *Captain James Cook: A Biography* (London, 1994), p. 139.

2 Ibid., pp. 139–40.

3 Joseph Banks, *The Endeavour Journal of Joseph Banks, 1768–1771*, ed. J. C. Beaglehole, vol. II (Sydney, 1962), p. 54.

4 Ibid.

5 Gilbert White, *The Natural History of Selborne* [1789], ed. Ann Secord (Oxford, 2013), Letter 27, 12 December 1775, p. 161.

6 Ibid.

7 Ibid.

8 Tobias Menely, 'Traveling in Place: Gilbert White's Cosmopolitan Parochialism', *Eighteenth-century Life*, XXVIII/3 (2004), p. 53.

9 Ann Secord, 'Introduction', in White, *Natural History of Selborne*, p. xiii.

10 Menely, 'Traveling in Place', p. 53.

11 N.J.B. Plomley, *The Baudin Expedition and the Tasmanian Aborigines, 1802* (Hobart, 1983), p. 6.

12 Menely, 'Traveling in Place', p. 55.

13 Ibid.

14 Francis Place, *The Autobiography of Francis Place (1771–1854)*, ed. Mary Thrale (Cambridge, 1972), p. 90.

15 F. E. Fodéré, *Traité du goitre et du crétinisme* (Paris, 1799 [Germinal viii]), p. 121 (author's translation).

16 Phillipe Pinel, *Medico-philosophical Treatise on Mental Alienation* (Paris, 1800), trans. G. Hickish, D. Healy and L. Charland (Chichester, 2008).

17 William Dampier, *A New Voyage around the World: The Journal of an English Buccaneer* [1697] (London, 1998), p. 221.

18 Louis Hennepin, *A New Discovery of a Vast Country in America* [1698] (Toronto, 1974), p. 552.

19 Jemima Kindersley, *Letters from the Island of Tenerife, Brazil, the Cape of Good Hope and the East Indies* (London, 1777), p. 181.

20 Watkin Tench, *Sydney's First Four Years* [1793], ed. L. F. Fitzhardinge (Sydney, 1979), pp. 52–3.

21 Charles Grant, *Observations on the State of Society among the Asiatic Subjects of Great Britain* (London, 1797), p. 50.

22 Banks, *Endeavour Journal*, vol. II, p. 70.

23 Plomley, *The Baudin Expedition*, p. 19.

24 John Lawson, *A New Voyage to Carolina* [1709], ed. Hugh T. Lafler (Chapel Hill, NC, 1967), p. 27.

25 Edward Bancroft, *An Essay on the Natural History of Guiana in South America* (London, 1769), p. 328.

26 Sydney Parkinson, *A Journal of a Voyage to the South Seas in His Majesty's Ship the Endeavour* (London, 1773), p. 14.

27 Dampier, *New Voyage*, p. 427.

28 Parkinson, *Journal of a Voyage*, p. 7.

29 Plomley, *The Baudin Expedition*, p. 83.

30 James Lackington, *Memoirs of the First Forty-five Years of the Life of James Lackington, the Present Bookseller in Chiswell-Street, Moorfields, London* (London, 1794), pp. 57–8.

31 Dampier, *New Voyage*, p. 219.

32 James Isham, *James Isham's Observations on Hudsons Bay* [1743] (London, 1949), p. 101.

33 The National Archives (hereafter TNA), *Ingram v. Wyatt*, 1/725, 1828, pp. 486 and 495.

34 James Bruce, 'Travels between the Years 1768 and 1773, through Parts of Africa, Syria, Egypt and Arabia into Abyssinia, to Discover the Source of the Nile' [1790], in *Travel Writing, 1700–1830: An Anthology*, ed. Elizabeth Bohls and Ian Duncan (Oxford, 2005), pp. 222–3, 233.

35 Hennepin, *New Discovery*, p. 469.

36 Peter Kolben, *The Present State of the Cape of Good Hope* (London, 1731), p. 201.

37 Isham, *Observations on Hudsons Bay*, p. 77.

38 Edward Long, *The History of Jamaica* (London, 1774), p. 383.

39 TNA, *Ingram v. Wyatt*, 1/725, 1828, p. 506.

40 Ibid., pp. 477, 486.

41 TNA, *Bowerman v. Fust*, DEL 1/644, p. 141.

42 Plomley, *The Baudin Expedition*, pp. 19, 124.

43 Ibid., p. 125.

44 Lackington, *Memoirs*, pp. 412–13, 420.

45 Elizabeth Bohls and Ian Duncan, 'Introduction', in *Travel Writing*,
   p. xviii.
46 John Harris, *Navigantium atque itinerantium biblioteca; or, A Compleat
   Collection of Voyages and Travels* (London, 1744), Preface.
47 Frances Trollope, *Domestic Manners of the Americans* [1832], ed. Elsie B.
   Michell (Oxford, 2014), p. 14.
48 The copy of Harris's *Navigantium* in the British Library was originally
   owned by Banks (BL C.115.i.5. [1-2]).
49 James Burney, *A Chronological History of the Discoveries in the South Sea
   or Pacific Ocean* (London, 1803), p. 178.
50 Menely, 'Traveling in Place', p. 53.
51 Secord, 'Introduction', in White, *Natural History of Selborne*, p. xxvii.
52 David Hall, 'Introduction', in Hugo Grotius, *The Rights of War and Peace*
   [1625], ed. A. C. Campbell (London, 1901), p. 2.
53 Grotius, *Rights of War and Peace*, pp. 18–19.
54 Ibid., p. 18.
55 Ibid., p. 135.
56 Ibid., p. 269.
57 Ibid.
58 Ibid.
59 Samuel von Pufendorf, *The Whole Duty of Man According to the Law of
   Nations* [1673], 2nd edn (London, 1698), p. 2.
60 Ibid., p. 118.
61 Ibid., p. 150.
62 John Locke, *Two Treatises of Government* [1690], ed. P. Laslett
   (Cambridge, 2014), pp. 280, 289.
63 Ibid., p. 291.
64 Ibid., pp. 296–7.
65 Ibid., p. 306.
66 Dampier, *New Voyage*, pp. 13, 219, 227.
67 Hennepin, *New Discovery*, pp. 455, 462.
68 Ibid., p. 462.
69 John Brydall, *Non Compos Mentis; or, The Law Relating to Natural Fools,
   Mad Folks and Lunatic Persons Inquisited and Explained for the Common
   Benefit* (London, 1700), p. 2.
70 Ibid., p. 3.
71 Alexander Hamilton, *British Sea Captain Alexander Hamilton's 'A New
   Account of the East Indies' from the Year 1723*, ed. J. Corfield and I. Merson
   (Lampeter, 2002), p. 19.
72 Kolben, *Present State of the Cape*, vol. I, pp. 46–7.
73 Isham, *Observations on Hudsons Bay*, p. 112; Harris, *Navigantium*, p. 310.
74 Dampier, *New Voyage*, p. 148; Lawson, *New Voyage to Carolina*, p. 38;
   Isham, *Observations on Hudsons Bay*, p. 80.
75 F. E. Fodéré, *Traité de médecine légale*, 2nd edn (Paris, 1813), p. 203
   (author's translation).
76 Emer de Vattel, *The Law of Nations; or, Principles of the Law of Nature,
   Applied to the Conduct and Affairs of Nations and Sovereigns* [1758]
   (Indianapolis, IN, 2008), p. xii.

77 Ibid., p. 71.
78 Ibid., p. 73.
79 Ibid., p. 213.
80 Ibid., p. 129.
81 Ibid., p. 216.
82 Thomas Munck, *The Enlightenment: A Comparative Social History, 1721–1724* (London, 2000), p. 14.
83 Ibid.
84 Hough, *Captain James Cook*, p. 193.
85 Johann Reinhold Forster, *Observations Made during a Voyage around the World on Physical Geography, Natural History and Ethic Philosophy* (London, 1778), Preface, p. ii.
86 Antoine-Nicholas de Condorcet, *Sketch for a Historical Picture of the Progress of the Human Mind* [1795], trans. Jane Barraclough (London, 1955), p. 8.
87 Charles de Secondat, Baron de Montesquieu, *The Spirit of Laws* [1748], 7th edn, trans. Thomas Nugent (Edinburgh, 1778), p. 345.
88 Ibid., p. 281.
89 Ibid., p. 333.
90 George W. Stocking Jr, *Victorian Anthropology* (New York, 1991), p. 14.
91 Anne Robert Jacques Turgot, 'A Philosophical Review of the Successive Stages of the Human Mind' [1750], in *Turgot on Progress, Sociology and Economics*, trans. Ronald L. Meek (Cambridge, 1973), p. 41.
92 Ibid., p. 42.
93 Ibid.
94 Fodéré, *Traité de médecine légale*, p. 186 (author's translation).
95 Ibid., p. 203.
96 Dampier, *New Voyage*, p. 219.
97 Hennepin, *New Discovery*, p. 462.
98 Turgot, 'Philosophical Review', p. 42.
99 Ibid.
100 Dampier, *New Voyage*, p. 218.
101 Kolben, *Present State of the Cape*, p. 37.
102 Forster, *Observations*, p. 251.
103 Ibid., pp. 231, 286.
104 Ibid., p. 287.
105 John Adams, *Curious Thoughts on the History of Man, Chiefly Abridged from the Celebrated Works of Lord Kaimes, Lord Monboddo, Dr Dunbar, and the Immortal Montesquieu* [1789] (Bristol, 1995), p. 30.
106 Ibid., p. 4.
107 Forster, *Observations*, pp. 303–4.
108 Ibid., p. 304.
109 Ibid., pp. 303–4.
110 Ibid., p. 304.
111 Ibid.
112 Fodéré, *Traité du goitre at du crétinisme*, p. 20 (author's translation).

4 Medical Challenge: New Ideas in the Courtroom

1 David Wright, *Mental Disability in Victorian England: The Earlswood Asylum, 1847–1901* (Oxford 2001), p. 19.

2 F.-E. Fodéré, *Traité de médecine légale et d'hygiène publique, ou de police de santé: tome premier* [1792], 2nd edn (Paris, 1813), Preface, p. xii.

3 Deborah B. Weiner, 'Foreword', in Philipe Pinel, *Medico-philosophical Treatise on Mental Alienation* [1800], trans. Gordon Hickish, David Henly and Louis C. Charland (Chichester, 2008).

4 Pinel, *Treatise*, p. 72.

5 Ibid.

6 Fodéré, *Traité de médecine*, pp. v, ix.

7 Ibid., p. xxxiv.

8 Ibid.

9 Ibid., pp. 192–3 (author's translation).

10 Ibid., p. 186.

11 Ibid. (author's translation).

12 Ibid., p. 202.

13 Ibid., p. 203.

14 Ibid.

15 Ibid., p. 184.

16 Hurlo Thrumbo, *The Merry Thought; or, The Glass-window and Boghouse Miscellany* (London, 1731), pp. 43–4.

17 Fodéré, *Traité de médecine*, p. 202.

18 Jan Goldstein, *Console and Classify: The French Psychiatric Profession in the Nineteenth Century* (Chicago, IL, 2001), p. 78.

19 Fodéré, *Traité de médecine*, p. 285.

20 Ibid., p. 203.

21 Étienne-Jean Georget, *De la folie: considérations sur cette maladie* (Paris, 1820); Étienne-Jean Georget, *Discussion médico-légale sur la folie, ou aliénation mentale* (Paris, 1826).

22 Georget, *De la folie*, pp. 103–4.

23 Ibid., pp. 104–5.

24 Georget, *Discussion médico-légale*, p. 1.

25 Ibid., p. 132.

26 Ibid., p. 134.

27 Ibid., pp. 132, 139.

28 Ibid., pp. 135–6.

29 Ibid., p. 136.

30 Ibid., pp. 136–7 (author's translation).

31 Ibid., p. 138.

32 Ibid. 'Niaiserie' would acquire the meaning of 'moronism' by the early twentieth century.

33 Ibid., p. 141.

34 Ibid., p. 140.

35 Ibid., pp. 175–6.

36 John Haslam, *Medical Jurisprudence as It Relates to Insanity According to the Law of England* (London, 1817).

37 Ibid., pp. ii–iii.
38 Andrew Scull, Charlotte Mackenzie and Nicholas Harvey, *Masters of Bedlam: The Transformation of the Mad-doctoring Trade* (Princeton, NJ, 1996), pp. 31–7.
39 Haslam, *Medical Jurisprudence*, pp. 3, 97–8.
40 Ibid., p. 98.
41 Ibid.
42 Ibid.
43 Ibid., pp. 8–9.
44 Ibid., pp. 4, 8.
45 Ibid., p. 3.
46 Ibid., pp. 94–6.
47 Ibid., p. 103.
48 Ibid., pp. 10, 42.
49 Thomas S. Legg, 'Amos, Andrew (1791–1860)', *Oxford Dictionary of National Biography* (Oxford, 2004), www.oxforddnb.com.
50 Professor Amos, 'Lectures in Medical Jurisprudence Delivered in the University of London: On Insanity', *London Medical Gazette*, 8 (1831), pp. 418–20.
51 Leonard Shelford, *A Practical Treatise on the Law concerning Lunatics, Idiots and Persons of Unsound Mind* (London, 1833). On Shelford see E. I. Carlyle, 'Shelford, Leonard (1795–1864)', revd Jonathan Harris, *Oxford Dictionary of National Biography* (Oxford, 2004), www.oxforddnb.com.
52 Shelford, *Practical Treatise*, pp. 45–6.
53 Ibid.
54 Ibid., p. 4.
55 Ibid., p. 5.
56 Ibid.
57 Ibid.
58 J. Chitty, *A Practical Treatise on Medical Jurisprudence* (London, 1834), p. 344.
59 Ibid., p. 345.
60 Ibid., pp. 341–2, 344.
61 Theodric Beck, *Elements of Medical Jurisprudence* (London, 1836), p. 402.
62 Isaac Ray, *A Treatise on the Medical Jurisprudence of Insanity* (London, 1839).
63 Ibid., p. xxviii.
64 Ibid., pp. 24, 49.
65 Ibid., pp. 54–5.
66 Ibid., p. 71.
67 Ibid., pp. 115–17.
68 John Peter Eigen, *Witnessing Insanity: Madness and Mad Doctors in the English Court* (New Haven, CT, 1995), p. 112.
69 Sabine Arnaud, *On Hysteria: The Invention of a Medical Category between 1670 and 1820* (Chicago, IL, 2015), pp. 207–25.
70 See for example William Guy, *Principles of Forensic Medicine*, 2nd edn (London, 1861).

71 James Beattie, 'Scales of Justice: Defence Counsel and the English Criminal Trial in the Eighteenth and Nineteenth Centuries', *Law and History Review*, IX/2 (1991), p. 229.

72 Allyson N. May, *The Bar and the Old Bailey, 1750–1850* (Chapel Hill, NC, 2003), p. 1.

73 Ibid., p. 77.

74 Old Bailey Proceedings (hereafter OBP), June 1789, trial of John Glover (t17890603-90).

75 OBP, July 1800, trial of John Leck (t18000709-21).

76 Ibid.

77 OBP, December 1807, trial of Conrad Frederic (t18071202-46).

78 OBP, July 1819, trial of Charlotte Lawrence (t18190707-154).

79 OBP, June 1825, trial of John Battle (t18250630-67).

80 For a full trial account see Mark Jackson, '"It Begins with the Goose and Ends with the Goose": Medical, Legal and Lay Understandings of Imbecility in *Ingram v. Wyatt*, 1824–1832', *Social History of Medicine*, XI/3 (1998), pp. 361–80.

81 Ibid., pp. 361–7.

82 Ibid., pp. 375–7.

83 Ibid., p. 377.

84 Ibid., p. 378.

85 The National Archives (hereafter TNA), *Ingram v. Wyatt*, 1828, DEL 1/725, p. 441.

86 Ibid., pp. 478, 488, 490, 502.

87 Ibid., p. 484.

88 Ibid., p. 502.

89 Ibid., pp. 512–13.

90 Ibid., pp. 478, 509.

91 Ibid., p. 484.

92 Ibid., p. 487.

93 Ibid., p. 513.

94 Jackson, '"It Begins with the Goose"', pp. 370–71.

95 Ibid., pp. 373–4.

96 Shelford, *Practical Treatise*, p. 5.

97 Jackson, '"It Begins with the Goose"', p. 377.

98 'Commission of Lunacy, Bagster v. Newton', *London Medical Gazette*, 10 (21 July 1832), pp. 520–22.

99 Ibid., pp. 519–28.

100 Scull, Mackenzie and Harvey, *Masters of Bedlam*, p. 149.

101 Ibid. (also sometimes referred to as Munro or Munroe).

102 Ibid., pp. 123, 143, 149.

103 'Commission of Lunacy, Bagster v. Newton', pp. 520, 522.

104 Ibid., p. 525.

105 Ibid., p. 523.

106 Scull, Mackenzie and Harvey, *Masters of Bedlam*, pp. 36–7.

107 'Commission of Lunacy, Bagster v. Newton', pp. 526–7.

108 Ibid., pp. 520–22.

109 Ibid.

110 'Editorial', *London Medical Gazette*, 10 (28 July 1832), pp. 556–7.
111 Ibid., p. 527.
112 Ibid., p. 528.
113 Ibid., p. 554.
114 Ibid., p. 556.
115 Ibid., pp. 553, 558.
116 Ibid., p. 554.
117 'Vice Chancellor's Courts, Dec 4', *The Times*, 5 December 1861, p. 8, The Times Digital Archive (hereafter TDA).
118 TNA, *Windham v. Windham*, J77/60/W 128/1; J77/60/W 128/2; J77/60/W 128/11; J77/60/W 128/12; J77/60/W 128/25; J77/60/W 128/29.
119 An Eastern Counties Traveller, 'Amateur Railway Drivers', *The Times*, 14 December 1861, p. 8, TDA.
120 'The Case of Mr W. F. Windham', *The Times*, 17 December 1861, p. 3, TDA.
121 The death of Prince Albert received 132,902 words of coverage between 15 December 1861 and 31 January 1862, while the case of William Windham received 148,606 words of coverage over the same period. (Source: TDA.)
122 'The Jury Have at Last Found That Mr WINDHAM', *The Times*, 31 January 1862, p. 6, TDA.
123 Ibid.
124 'The Late Mr W. F. Windham, – On Saturday', *The Times*, 5 February 1866, p. 11, TDA.
125 John Langdon Down, *On Some of the Mental Afflictions of Childhood and Youth, Being the Lettsomian Lectures Delivered before the Medical Society of London in 1887* (London, 1887), pp. 28–9.
126 John Langdon Down, 'On the Condition of the Mouth in Idiocy', *The Lancet*, 1 (1862), pp. 65–8.
127 Down, *Mental Afflictions*, p. 29.
128 Down, 'Condition of the Mouth', pp. 65–8.
129 Down, *Mental Afflictions*, p. 29.
130 Ibid.
131 Ibid.
132 'Commission of Lunacy, Bagster v. Newton', p. 520.
133 VIATOR, 'The Great Eastern Railway', *The Times*, 6 December 1862, p. 12, TDA.

5 Pity and Loathing: New Cultural Thinking

1 William Wordsworth, 'The Idiot Boy' [1798], *Selected Poetry* (Oxford, 1998), pp. 36–49.
2 Ibid., p. 48, ll. 407–8.
3 Ibid., p. 40, l. 122.
4 William Wordsworth, 'Preface', *Lyrical Ballads* [1800], cited in Patrick McDonagh, *Idiocy: A Cultural History* (Liverpool, 2008), p. 27.

5 Samuel Taylor Coleridge, *Biographia Literaria* [1817] (London, 1827), p. 166.
6 Ibid.
7 Cited in McDonagh, *Idiocy*, pp. 25–6.
8 S. Jarrett and C. F. Goodey, 'Learning Difficulties: Intellectual Disability in the Long Eighteenth Century', in *A Cultural History of Disability in the Long Eighteenth Century*, ed. D. Christopher Gabbard and Susannah B. Mintz (London, 2020), p. 134.
9 Frances Burney, *Camilla; or, A Picture of Youth* [1786] (Oxford, 1999), p. 309.
10 Julie Colman, *A History of Cant and Slang Dictionaries*, vol. II: *1785–1858* (Oxford, 2004), p. 259.
11 Ibid., p. 260.
12 Piers Egan, *Grose's Classical Dictionary of the Vulgar Tongue, Revised and Corrected* (London, 1823).
13 Piers Egan, *Life in London* (London, 1821).
14 Egan, *Grose's Classical Dictionary*, p. xi.
15 Colman, *Slang Dictionaries*, vol. II, pp. 171–2.
16 Egan, *Grose's Classical Dictionary*.
17 John Bee, *Sportsman's Slang* (London, 1825).
18 Ibid.
19 A dictionary of university slang, much of it classically inspired, was published in 1803: *Gradus ad Cantabrigium; or, A Dictionary of Terms, Academical and Colloquial, or Cant, Which Are Used at the University of Cambridge* (London, 1803).
20 James Hardy Vaux, *A New and Comprehensive Dictionary of the Flash Language* (Newcastle, NSW, 1812); *The Flash Dictionary* (London, 1821); Bee, *Sportsman's Slang*; George Kent, *The Modern Flash Dictionary* (London, 1835).
21 Anon., *The Sailor's Jester; or, Merry Lad's Companion* (London, 1790), p. 3; 'Joe Miller', *Joe Miller's Complete Jest Book* (London, 1832), joke 583, p. 178.
22 'Christopher Grin', *The New Loyal and Patriotic Jester; or, Complete Library of Fun*, 2nd edn (London, 1800), p. 17.
23 Anon., *The Lively Jester; or, Complete Museum of Fun* (London, 1800), p. 33.
24 Anon., *Pinkethman's Jests; or, Wit Refined* (London, 1721), p. 91; 'Miller', *Joe Miller's Complete Jest Book*, p. 35.
25 'Mark Lemon', *The Jest Book: The Choicest Anecdotes and Sayings Selected and Arranged by Mark Lemon* (London, 1865).
26 Anon., *Lively Jester*, p. 62; 'Grin', *Loyal and Patriotic Jester*, pp. 49–50.
27 'Grin', *Loyal and Patriotic Jester*, p. 47.
28 'Miller', *Complete Jest Book*, p. 471.
29 Vic Gatrell, *City of Laughter: Sex and Satire in Eighteenth-century London* (London, 2006), p. 547.
30 Ibid., p. 425.
31 Ibid., pp. 419–21.
32 Ibid., p. 432.

33 The substitution of lithography for etching around 1830, with its softened images, 'admirably suited the general turning away from satirical savagery' by the new lithographic caricaturists. John Wardroper, *The Caricatures of George Cruikshank* (London, 1977), p. 23.

34 William Thackeray, 'Review', *Westminster Review* (June 1840), p. 6.

35 Ronald Paulson, *Popular and Polite Art in the Age of Hogarth and Fielding* (Notre Dame, IN, 1979), p. 102.

36 Simon Dickie, *Cruelty and Laughter: Forgotten Comic Literature and the Unsentimental Eighteenth Century* (Chicago, IL, 2014), p. 22.

37 'Miller', *Complete Jest Book*, Preface.

38 William Wordsworth, *Lyrical Ballads* [1800], cited in Ian Watt, *The Rise of the Novel: Studies in Defoe, Richardson and Fielding* [1957] (London, 1974), p. 342.

39 'Lemon', *Jest Book*.

40 Stuart M. Tave, *The Amiable Humorist: A Study in the Comic Theory and Criticism of the Eighteenth and Early Nineteenth Centuries* (Chicago, IL, 1960), p. viii.

41 Ibid.

42 'The Comic Blackstone', *Punch*, 13 January 1844, p. 25.

43 'Punch's Essence of Parliament', *Punch*, 24 February 1866, p. 78.

44 'The Temperate Temperance League', *Punch*, 11 May 1867, p. 190.

45 David Wright, '"Mongols in Our Midst": John Langdon Down and the Ethnic Classification of Idiocy, 1858–1924', in *Mental Retardation in America: A Historical Reader*, ed. Steven Noll and James W. Trent, Jr (New York, 2004), p. 96.

46 'Mitchell at Home', *Punch* [1847?], p. 110; 'A Palpable Advertisement', *Punch*, 10 September 1859, p. 103.

47 'Rampant Idiots', *Punch*, 27 December 1856, p. 251.

48 'Extraordinary Flight of Geese', *Punch*, 14 February 1857, p. 70.

49 'Work for Weak Intellects', *Punch*, 23 April 1859, p. 169.

50 'Appropriate Airs', *Punch*, 24 March 1860, p. 119.

51 'Punch's Essence of Parliament', *Punch*, 12 April 1862, p. 143.

52 'Fashionable Entertainments for the Week', *Punch*, 23 June 1877.

53 Ronald Pearsall, *Collapse of Stout Party: Victorian Wit and Humour* (London, 1975), p. 149.

54 Gatrell, *City of Laughter*, p. 547.

55 Mark Ford, 'Introduction' to Charles Dickens, *Nicholas Nickleby* [1839] (London, 1986), p. xiii.

56 Dickens, *Nicholas Nickleby*, p. 156.

57 Ibid., p. 147.

58 Ibid., pp. 267, 423.

59 Ibid., p. 463.

60 Ibid.

61 Ibid., p. 746.

62 Ibid.

63 Charles Dickens, 'Idiots', *Household Words*, VII/167 (4 June 1853), p. 313.

64 Ibid.

65 Ibid.
66 Ibid.
67 Dickens, *Nicholas Nickleby*, p. 90.
68 Dickens, 'Idiots', p. 315.
69 Ibid., pp. 314–15.
70 McDonagh, *Idiocy*, p. 15.
71 Dickens, 'Idiots', p. 314.
72 Ibid., p. 315.
73 Charles Dickens, *Barnaby Rudge: A Tale of the Riots of 'Eighty* [1841] (Oxford, 2003), p. 52.
74 Ibid., p. 37.
75 Ibid., p. 202.
76 Tobias Smollett, *Roderick Random* [1748] (London, 1975), pp. 66–8.
77 Dickens, 'Idiots', p. 317.
78 George Eliot, *Brother Jacob* [1860] ebook (Gearhart, OR, 2013).
79 Elizabeth Gaskell, *Half a Lifetime Ago* [1855], ebook (Milton Keynes, 2013).
80 Mary Cowling, *The Artist as Anthropologist: The Representation of Type and Character in Victorian Art* (Cambridge, 1989), p. 125.
81 Ibid., p. 126.
82 Ibid.
83 L. P. Curtis, *Apes and Angels: The Irishman in Victorian Caricature* (Washington, DC, 1997), p. xiii.
84 M. Dorothy George, *Catalogue of Political and Personal Satires Preserved in the Department of Prints and Drawings in the British Museum*, vol. XI (London, 1954), www.britishmuseum.org/collection, BM satires 16163.
85 Thomas Webster, engraved W. Ridgway, *Going to School*, *Art Journal* (June 1862), p. 138.
86 Ibid.
87 Dickens, 'Idiots', pp. 315–16.
88 Ibid., p. 315.
89 Isaac Newton Kerlin, *The Mind Unveiled; or, A Brief History of Twenty-two Imbecile Children* (Philadelphia, PA, 1858).
90 Ibid., p. ix.
91 Ibid., p. 2.
92 Ibid., p. 16.
93 Ibid., p. 25.
94 Ibid.
95 Thackeray, 'Review', p. 6.
96 Gatrell, *City of Laughter*, p. 432.
97 Coleridge, *Biographia Literaria*, p. 167.
98 Karen Halttunen, 'Humanitarianism and the Pornography of Pain in Anglo-American Culture', *American Historical Review*, C/2 (1995), p. 304.
99 Pieter Verstraete, 'Savage Solitude: The Problematisation of Disability at the Turn of the Eighteenth Century', *Paedagogica Historica*, XLV/3 (2009), p. 279.

6 Colonies, Anthropologists and Asylums: Race and Intelligence

1 Joanna Bourke, *What It Means to Be Human: Reflections from 1791 to the Present* (London, 2013), p. 3.
2 Antony Wild, *The East India Company: Trade and Conquest from 1600* (London, 1999), p. 108.
3 Edward Bancroft, *An Essay on the Natural History of Guiana in South America* (London, 1769), p. 326.
4 Watkin Tench, *Sydney's First Four Years* [1793], ed. L. F. Fitzhardinge (Sydney, 1979), pp. 283–5.
5 James K. Tuckey, 'Narrative of an Expedition to Explore the River Zaire, Usually Called the Congo, in 1816', in *Travel Writing, 1700–1830: An Anthology*, ed. E. Bohls and I. Duncan (Oxford, 2005), p. 246.
6 Ibid.
7 John West, *The Substance of a Journal during a Residence at the Red River Colony in the Years 1820, 1821,1822, 1823* [1824] (New York, 1966), Preface, pp. v, 3.
8 Paul Du Chaillu, *Explorations and Adventures in Equatorial Guinea* (New York, 1861), p. 150.
9 Isaac Ray, *A Treatise on the Medical Jurisprudence of Insanity* (London, 1839), p. 68.
10 Ibid., p. 72.
11 Ibid., pp. 66–8.
12 Ibid., p. 69.
13 Maria Nugent, *A Journal of a Voyage to, and Residence in, the Island of Jamaica from 1801–1805*, vol. I (London, 1839), p. 145.
14 Harriet Beecher Stowe, *Uncle Tom's Cabin; or, Life among the Lowly* [1852] (London 1955), pp. 235–6.
15 F.-E. Fodéré, *Traité de medécine légale et d'hygiène publique, ou de police de santé: tome premier* [1792] (Paris, 1813), p. 186 (author's translation).
16 West, *Substance of a Journal*, p. 154.
17 Ibid.
18 John West, *The History of Tasmania* [1852], ed. A.G.L. Shaw (Sydney, 1971), p. 333.
19 Étienne-Jean Georget, *Discussion médico-légale sur la folie, ou aliénation mentale* (Paris, 1826), p. 140 (author's translation).
20 Ray, *Treatise*, pp. 75–6, 80, 95.
21 Ibid., p. 91.
22 Theodric Beck, *Elements of Medical Jurisprudence*, 5th edn (London, 1836), p. 402.
23 James Mill, *The History of British India*, vol. I [1817] (New Delhi, 1972), p. 32.
24 Ibid.
25 Ray, *Treatise*, p. 71.
26 Mill, *British India*, p. 288.
27 Ibid., pp. 459–60.
28 Ray, *Treatise*, p. 71.
29 Ibid.

30 Fodéré, *Traité de médecine légale*, p. 203 (author's translation).
31 Ibid., p. 71.
32 Ray, *Treatise*, p. 69.
33 Reginald Heber, *Narrative of a Journey through the Upper Provinces of India from Calcutta to Bombay, 1824–1825*, vol. I (London, 1828), pp. 49–50.
34 Mill, *British India*, p. 340.
35 Ibid.
36 E. W. Landor, *The Bushman; or, Life in a New Country* (London, 1847), pp. 186–7.
37 Anon., *Some Account of the Conduct of the Religious Society of Friends towards the Indian Tribes in the Settlement of the Colonies of East and West Jersey and Pennsylvania* (London, 1844), pp. 176, 143.
38 Georget, *Discussion médico-légale*, p. 140.
39 Ray, *Treatise*, pp. 71, 80.
40 Bedford Pim, *The Negro and Jamaica* (London, 1866), pp. 6–7.
41 John Langdon Down, 'On the Condition of the Mouth in Idiocy', *The Lancet*, I (1862), p. 65.
42 Ibid.
43 Samuel Tuke, *Description of the Retreat, an Institution near York for Insane Persons of the Society of Friends* (York, 1813), p. 23.
44 Ibid., pp. 23, 134.
45 Ibid., pp. 23, 135, 141.
46 Murray Simpson, 'The Moral Government of Idiots: Moral Treatment in the Work of Seguin', *History of Psychiatry*, x (1999), pp. 227–43.
47 Frances Trollope, *Domestic Manners of the Americans* [1832], ed. Elsie B. Mitchell (Oxford, 2014), p. 165 (author's italics).
48 Nugent, *Journal of a Voyage*, p. 30.
49 Ibid.
50 John Philip, *Researches in South Africa, Illustrating the Civil, Moral and Religious Condition of the Native Tribes*, vol. II (London, 1828), p. 9.
51 James M. Phillippo, *Jamaica: Its Past and Present State* [1843] (London, 1969), p. 191.
52 Ibid.
53 Ibid., pp. 211–12.
54 Du Chaillu, *Explorations and Adventures*, pp. 28–9.
55 Édouard Séguin, *Traitement moral, hygiène et éducation des idiots et des autres enfants arriérés* [1846] (Paris, 1906), p. 462 (author's translation).
56 Ibid.
57 Ibid.
58 Simpson, 'Moral Government of Idiots', p. 230.
59 Séguin, *Traitement moral*, p. 461 (author's translation).
60 Simpson, 'Moral Government of Idiots', p. 241.
61 Anon., *Some Account of the Conduct of the Religious Society of Friends*, pp. 176, 143.
62 Ibid., p. 143.
63 George Wilson Bridges, *The Annals of Jamaica*, vol. I (London, 1858), p. 479.
64 William Buyers, *Travels in India* (London, 1852), p. 418.

65 *The Times*, 10 December 1840, p. 6, cited in Andrew Scull, Charlotte Mackenzie and Nicholas Harvey, *Masters of Bedlam: The Transformation of the Mad-doctoring Trade* (Princeton, NJ, 1996), p. 66.
66 J. G. Millingen, *Aphorisms on the Treatment and Management of the Insane* (London, 1840), p. 106, cited ibid.
67 West, *Substance of a Journal*, p. 117.
68 West, *History of Tasmania*, p. 331.
69 Ibid.
70 Ibid.
71 Henry Reynolds, *Dispossession: Black Australians and White Invaders* (St Leonards, NSW, 1989), pp. 67–70.
72 Ibid., pp. 71–2.
73 Philip, *Researches in South Africa*, p. 277.
74 Julia V. Douthwaite, *The Wild Girl, Natural Man and the Monster: Dangerous Experiments in the Age of Enlightenment* (Chicago, IL, 2002), p. 53.
75 Ibid.
76 Ibid.
77 J.M.G. Itard, *An Historical Account of the Discovery and Education of a Savage Man* [1800] (London, 1802), p. 23.
78 Ibid., p. 11.
79 Ibid., pp. 17, 21.
80 Ibid., pp. 26, 30, 45, 57.
81 Ibid., p. 32.
82 Ibid., p. 33.
83 Douthwaite, *The Wild Girl*, pp. 61–2.
84 Ibid., p. 62.
85 James Cowles Prichard, *Researches into the Physical History of Man* [1813] (London, 1826), p. 548.
86 Ibid., p. 9.
87 James Cowles Prichard, *On the Different Forms of Insanity* (London, 1842), pp. 208, 215.
88 Robert Knox, *The Races of Men: A Fragment* (Philadelphia, PA, 1850), p. 149.
89 Ibid., pp. 156–7.
90 Ibid.
91 Ibid., p. 185.
92 Arthur de Gobineau, *The Inequality of Human Races*, trans. Adrian Collins [1853] (London, 1915), p. 140.
93 Ibid., pp. 205–6.
94 Charles Dickens, 'The Lost Arctic Voyagers', *Household Words*, 245 (2 December 1854), p. 362.
95 Charles Dickens, 'The Noble Savage', *Household Words*, 168 (11 June 1853), p. 337.
96 Ibid., pp. 337–9.
97 Charles Dickens, 'Idiots', *Household Words*, 167 (4 June 1858), p. 313.
98 George W. Stocking Jr, *Victorian Anthropology* (New York, 1987), pp. 244–5.

99 Ibid.

100 Ibid., pp. 245–6.

101 Benjamin Collins Brodie, *Address to the Ethnological Society of London* (London, 1854), p. 4.

102 See Royal Anthropological Institute, *Fellows Database*, 2015.

103 Robert Dunn, 'Some Observations on the Varying Forms of the Human Cranium', *Journal of the Ethnological Society*, IV (1856), p. 34.

104 James Clark, 'Obituary Notice of Dr Conolly', *Transactions of the Ethnological Society of London*, V (1867), pp. 325–40.

105 James Clark, *A Memoir of John Conolly, MD, DCL, Comprising a Sketch of the Treatment of the Insane in Europe and America* (London, 1869), p. 111.

106 Ibid.

107 Ibid., p. 112.

108 'Pedro Velasquez', *Memoirs of an Eventful Expedition in Central America* (New York, 1850).

109 John Conolly, *The Ethnological Exhibitions of London* (London, 1855), pp. 13–14.

110 Ibid., p. 12.

111 Ibid., p. 16.

112 John Conolly, *Address to the Ethnological Society of London Delivered at the Annual General Meeting on the 26 May 1855* (London, 1855), p. 5.

113 Ibid.

114 W. H. Brock, 'Hunt, James (1833–1869)', *Oxford Dictionary of National Biography* (Oxford, 2004)

115 James Hunt, 'On the Study of Anthropology', *Anthropological Review*, I (1863), pp. 2, 4, 8, 17.

116 Stocking, *Victorian Anthropology*, pp. 25–7, 245–8.

117 Respectively: 'Proceedings of the Anthropological Society of Paris', *Anthropological Review*, I/3 (1863), p. 377; N. T. Gore, 'Notice of a Case of Micro-cephaly', *Anthropological Review*, I/1 (1863), pp. 168–71; H. G. Atkinson, 'On the Idiotic Family of Downham, in Norfolk', *Journal of the Anthropological Society of London*, IV (1866), p. xxxii; 'Anthropological News', *Anthropological Review*, VI/22 (June 1868), pp. 323–8; 'Reports of the Meetings of the Anthropological Society', *Anthropological Review*, I/1 (1863), pp. 187–91.

118 David Wright, 'Mongols in Our Midst: John Langdon Down and the Ethnic Classification of Idiocy, 1858–1924', in *Mental Retardation in America: A Historical Reader*, ed. S. Noll and J. W. Trent Jnr (New York, 2004), pp. 92–119, p. 104.

119 Stocking, *Victorian Anthropology*, pp. 25–7, 248.

120 E. Dally, 'An Enquiry into Consanguineous Marriages and Pure Races', *Anthropological Review*, II/5 (1864).

121 Walter C. Dendy, 'The Anatomy of Intellect', *Journal of the Anthropological Society of London*, VI (1868), pp. xxvii–xxxix (read to the society on 3 December 1867).

122 John Langdon Down, 'An Account of a Second Case in Which the Corpus Callosum Was Defective', *Journal of Mental Science*, XIII (1867), p. 120.

123 Karl Vogt, *Lectures on Man*, ed. James Hunt (London, 1864), p. 170.

124 See Wright, 'Mongols in Our Midst', p. 104, and Stephen Jay Gould, *The Panda's Thumb* (London, 1990), p. 137.

125 Stocking, *Victorian Anthropology*, pp. 25–7, 252.

126 Dendy, 'Anatomy of Intellect', p. xxxviii.

127 James Hunt, 'On the Negro's Place in Nature', *Memoirs Read before the Anthropological Society of London*, I (1863–4), pp. 16–17, 51.

128 Gad Heuman, *'The Killing Time': The Morant Bay Rebellion in Jamaica* (Knoxville, TN, 1994), pp. xiii–xiv.

129 Royal Anthropological Institute Archive, London (hereafter RAI), A5, letter 273.

130 Bedford Pim, *The Negro and Jamaica (Read before the Anthropological Society of London, Feb 1, 1866)* (London 1866), p. 7.

131 Ibid., p. 20.

132 Ibid., pp. 69–71.

133 RAI, A/5/59, 2 February 1866; A/5/100, 23 February 1866; A/5/147 9 March 1866; A/5/67, 29 June 1866; A/5/168, 5 February 1866; A/5/169, 6 February 1866; A/5/170, 26 February 1866.

134 Earlswood Annual Report, 1859; Surrey History Centre, Woking, 392/1/1.

135 John Langdon Down, 'Observations on an Ethnic Classification of Idiots', *Journal of Mental Science*, XIII (1867), pp. 121–2.

136 Ibid.

137 Ibid., p. 122.

138 Ibid., p. 123.

139 Gould, *The Panda's Thumb*, pp. 135–6.

140 'Reports of the Meetings of the Anthropological Society', p. 191.

141 O. Conor Ward, *John Langdon Down, 1828–1896: A Caring Pioneer* (London, 1998), p. 182.

142 Down, 'Observations on an Ethnic Classification', p. 123.

143 Gould, *The Panda's Thumb*, pp. 138–9.

144 Daniel Kelves, *In the Name of Eugenics: Genetics and the Uses of Human Heredity* (Cambridge, MA, 1985), pp. 245–9.

145 Fanny Parks, *Wanderings of a Pilgrim in Search of the Picturesque during Four-and-twenty Years in the East* (London, 1850), pp. 361–2.

146 Phillippo, *Jamaica*, p. 200.

147 Earlswood Annual Report, 1862, Surrey History Centre, 392 1/1.

148 Earlswood Annual Report, 1881, Surrey History Centre, 392 1/2/3.

149 Earlswood Annual Report, 1859, Surrey History Centre, 392 1/1; Earlswood Annual Report, 1867, Surrey History Centre, 392 1/1.

150 Earlswood Annual Report, 1863, Surrey History Centre, 392 1/1.

151 Earlswood Annual Report, 1871, Surrey History Centre, 392 1/1.

7 Into the Idiot Asylum: The Great Incarceration

1 William Parry-Jones, *The Trade in Lunacy: A Study of Private Madhouses in England in the Eighteenth and Nineteenth Centuries* (London, 1972).

2 David Wright, *Mental Disability in Victorian England: The Earlswood Asylum, 1847–1901* (Oxford, 2001), p. 21.

3 Ibid., pp. 12–15.

4 Ibid., pp. 42–3.

5 Ibid., p. 41.

6 Edward Vallance, *A Radical History of Britain* (London, 2009), pp. 205–82, 363–432.

7 Roger Knight, *Britain against Napoleon: The Organisation of Victory, 1793–1815* (London, 2014), pp. 62–3.

8 Ibid., pp. 125–6.

9 Vic Gatrell, *City of Laughter: Sex and Satire in Eighteenth-century London* (London, 2006), pp. 283–4.

10 Ibid., p. 487.

11 Ibid., pp. 530–46.

12 Ibid., pp. 453–5.

13 Thomas Paine, *Rights of Man* [1790] (London, 1985), p. 59.

14 Ibid.

15 Ibid., p. 60.

16 Ibid., p. 172.

17 Ibid.

18 Ibid., pp. 173–4.

19 Ibid., p. 174.

20 Ibid., p. 68.

21 John Carson, *The Measure of Merit: Talents, Intelligence and Inequality in the French and American Republics, 1750–1940* (Princeton, NJ, 2007), p. xiii.

22 Ibid., pp. 22, 26.

23 Paine, *Rights of Man*, p. 70.

24 Ibid.

25 Ibid.

26 Ibid., p. 163.

27 William Godwin, *Enquiry concerning Political Justice and Its Influence on Morals and Happiness*, 3rd edn (London, 1798), p. 449.

28 Ibid., p. 93.

29 Ibid.

30 Ibid., pp. 94–5.

31 Ibid., p. 95.

32 Francis Grose, *A Classical Dictionary of the Vulgar Tongue*, 2nd edn (London, 1788).

33 Godwin, *Enquiry*, p. 528.

34 Ibid., p. 457.

35 Ibid., pp. xxvii, 457.

36 Ibid., p. 157.

37 Ibid., p. 93.

38 S. Jarrett and C. F. Goodey, 'Learning Difficulties: Intellectual Disability in the Long Eighteenth Century', in *A Cultural History of Disability in the Long Eighteenth Century*, ed. D. Christopher Gabbard and Susannah B. Mintz (London, 2020), pp. 133–4.

39 Edmund Burke, *Reflections on the Revolution in France and on the Proceedings in Certain Societies in London Relative to That Event* [1790] (London, 1986), p. 132.

40 Ibid., p. 133.

41 Ibid., p. 174.

42 Anne Stott, *Hannah More: The First Victorian* (Oxford, 2003), pp. 128–9.

43 Ibid., p. 82.

44 Ibid., pp. 169–76, 208.

45 Susan Pedersen, 'Hannah More Meets Simple Simon: Tracts, Chapbooks and Popular Culture in Late Eighteenth-century England', *Journal of British Studies*, XXV/1 (1986), p. 107.

46 Hannah More, 'The Shepherd of Salisbury Plain', in *Cheap Repository Tracts Published in the Year 1795* (London, 1795), pp. 28–9.

47 Hannah More, 'The Beggarly Boy: A Parable', in *Cheap Repository Tracts*, pp. 3–10.

48 Hannah More, *Thoughts on the Importance of the Manners of the Great to the General Society*, 8th edn (London, 1790), p. 34.

49 Hannah More, *The History of Hester Wilmot* [1795–8] (London, 1810), pp. 10–11.

50 Hannah More, *Parley the Porter; or, Robbers Without Cannot Ruin the Castle, Unless There Are Traitors Within* [1795–8] (Manchester, 1870), pp. 1–6.

51 Ibid., pp. 11–12.

52 Ibid., p. 1.

53 Hannah More, 'The Grand Assizes; or, General Gaol Delivery' [1795–8], in *Works of Hannah More*, vol. II (London, 1834), p. 148.

54 Jarrett and Goodey, 'Learning Difficulties', pp. 134–5.

55 Robert Dingley, 'Tupper, Martin Farquhar (1810–1889)', *Oxford Dictionary of National Biography*, www.oxforddnb.com.

56 Ibid.

57 Martin Tupper, 'In Anticipation', in *Proverbial Philosophy: A Book of Thoughts and Arguments* (London, 1853), p. 16.

58 Tupper, 'Of Memory', in *Proverbial Philosophy*, p. 39.

59 Tupper, 'Of Reading', in *Proverbial Philosophy*, p. 159.

60 Reverend A. W. Hare, *Sermons to a Country Congregation* (London, 1838), p. 35.

61 John Wallace, *Simple Simon: A Farce in Two Acts* (Madras, 1805), pp. 2–11.

62 J. S. Mill, 'Utilitarianism' [1861], in John Stuart Mill and Jeremy Bentham, *Utilitarianism and Other Essays*, ed. Alan Ryan (London, 2004), p. 280.

63 Ibid.

64 Ibid.

65 Ibid., p. 281.

66 Ibid., p. 285.

67 Ibid., pp. 285–6.

68 Ibid., p. 69.

69 J. S. Mill, *On Liberty* [1859] (London, 1974), p. 177.

70 Wright, *Mental Disability*, p. 13.
71 County Asylums Act, 1808, 48 George 3 c. 96.
72 Wright, *Mental Disability*, p. 13.
73 David Englander, *Poverty and Poor Law Reform in 19th Century Britain, 1834–1914* (London, 1998); Trevor May, *The Victorian Workhouse* (Oxford, 2011); Kathryn Morrison, *The Workhouse: A Study of Poor-law Buildings in England* (London, 1999).
74 Wright, *Mental Disability*, pp. 19–21.
75 County Asylums Act 1845, 8+9 Victoria c. 126.
76 Lunacy Act 1845, 8+9 Victoria c. 100.
77 Wright, *Mental Disability*, p. 19.
78 Ibid., pp. 19–20.
79 Ibid., p. 15.
80 Andrew Scull, Charlotte Mackenzie and Nicholas Harvey, *Masters of Bedlam: The Transformation of the Mad-doctoring Trade* (Princeton, NJ, 1996), pp. 66–8.
81 John Conolly, 'On the Management of Hanwell Lunatic Asylum', *Journal of Psychological Medicine and Mental Pathology*, II (1849), pp. 424–7.
82 Such as Samuel Gaskell, superintendent of the Lancaster Lunatic Asylum: Samuel Gaskell, 'Visit to the Bicêtre', *Chambers's Edinburgh Journal*, 158 (9 January 1847), pp. 20–22; 'Education of Idiots at the Bicêtre', *Chambers's Edinburgh Journal*, 161 (30 January 1847), pp. 71–5; 'Education of Idiots at the Bicêtre, Part 3', *Chambers's Edinburgh Journal*, 163 (13 February 1847), pp. 105–7.
83 Wright, *Mental Disability*, pp. 42–3.
84 Ibid., p. 157.
85 Ibid., p. 159.
86 John Langdon Down, 'Observations on an Ethnic Classification of Idiots', *Journal of Mental Science*, XIII (1867), pp. 121–2.
87 Wright, *Mental Disability*, p. 41.

8 After Darwin: Mental Deficiency, Eugenics and Psychology, 1870–1939

1 Idiots Act 1886, 49+50 Victoria c. 25.
2 Matthew Thomson, *The Problem of Mental Deficiency: Eugenics, Democracy and Social Policy in Britain, c. 1870–1959* (Oxford, 1998), pp. 12–13.
3 Ibid., p. 15.
4 Ibid., pp. 21, 51.
5 Roger Smith, *Between Mind and Nature: A History of Psychology* (London, 2013), p. 106.
6 Cited in Daniel J. Kelves, *In the Name of Eugenics: Genetics and the Use of Human Heredity* (Cambridge, MA, 1995), p. 3.
7 Smith, *Between Mind and Nature*, p. 107.
8 Richard L. Dugdale, *The Jukes: A Study in Crime, Pauperism, Disease and Heredity* (New York, 1877).
9 Ibid., p. 32.

10 Oscar McCulloch, *The Tribe of Ishmael: A Study in Social Degradation* (Indianapolis, IN, 1891).

11 José Harris, 'Between Civic Virtue and Social Darwinism: The Concept of the Residuum', in *Retrieved Riches: Social Investigation in Britain, 1840–1914*, ed. David Englander and Rosemary O'Day (Aldershot, 1995), p. 68.

12 Peter Quennell, ed., *Mayhew's London Underworld* (London, 1987), p. 176.

13 H. G. Wells, *The Time Machine* [1895] (London, 2005), p. 46.

14 Ibid., p. 25.

15 Kelves, *In the Name of Eugenics*, p. 92.

16 Ibid.

17 Charles Darwin, *The Descent of Man and Selection in Relation to Sex* [1871] (London, 2004), p. 54.

18 Ibid.

19 Ibid.

20 Ibid., pp. 55, 109.

21 George Romanes, *Animal Intelligence*, 4th edn (London, 1886), pp. 4–8.

22 George Romanes, *Mental Evolution in Animals* (London, 1883), p. 181.

23 H. G. Wells, *The Island of Dr Moreau* (London, 1896).

24 Henry Maudsley, *Body and Will* (London, 1883), p. 246.

25 Stephen Jay Gould, *The Mismeasure of Man* (New York, 1996), p. 176.

26 Ibid., p. 178.

27 Ibid., pp. 178–80.

28 Ibid., pp. 225–9.

29 Thomson, *The Problem of Mental Deficiency*, pp. 23–4.

30 Ibid., pp. 26–33.

31 John Carson, *The Measure of Merit: Talents, Intelligence and Inequality in the French and American Republics, 1750–1940* (Princeton, NJ, 2007), pp. 177–82.

32 Gould, *Mismeasure of Man*, pp. 188–9.

33 Henry Herbert Goddard, *The Kallikak Family: A Study in the Heredity of Feeble-mindedness* (Norwood, MA, 1912) p. 33.

34 Gould, *Mismeasure of Man*, pp. 198–201.

35 Anon., 'The Feeble-minded Control Bill House of Commons Meeting Dec. 5th 1911', *Eugenics Review*, III (1912), pp. 355–8.

36 Ibid., p. 355.

37 Ibid., pp. 355–6.

38 Ibid., p. 357.

39 Thomson, *The Problem of Mental Deficiency*, p. 39.

40 C. V. Wedgwood, 'Wedgwood, Josiah Clement, first Baron Wedgwood (1872–1943)', revd Mark Pottle, *Oxford Dictionary of National Biography* (Oxford, 2004); Thomson, *The Problem of Mental Deficiency*, pp. 37–46.

41 The National Archives (hereafter TNA), NATS 1/727 (1917), *Central Association for the Care of the Mentally Defective: Request for Information regarding Rejection of Soldiers for Mental Deficiency, 1917–18*.

42 Jan Walmsley and Simon Jarrett, 'Intellectual Disability Policy and Practice in Twentieth-century United Kingdom', in *Intellectual*

Disability in the Twentieth Century: Transnational Perspectives on People, Policy and Practice, ed. Walmsley and Jarrett (Bristol, 2019), p. 180.

43 Jan Walmsley et al., 'Community Care and Mental Deficiency, 1913 to 1945', in *Outside the Walls of the Asylum: The History of Care in the Community, 1750–2000*, ed. P. Bartlett and D. Wright (London, 1999), pp. 184–5.

44 Ibid., p. 186.

45 Walmsley and Jarrett, 'Intellectual Disability', pp. 180–81.

46 Walter Hedley, *Report of the Departmental Committee on Colonies for Mental Defectives* [Hedley Report] (London, 1931).

47 Maggie Potts and Rebecca Fido, *'A Fit Person to Be Removed': Personal Accounts of Life in a Mental Deficiency Institution* (Plymouth, 1991); Walmsley and Jarrett, 'Intellectual Disability', p. 182.

48 Walmsley et al., 'Community Care', pp. 185–6.

49 Kelves, *In the Name of Eugenics*, p. 114.

50 Walmsley et al., 'Community Care', p. 186.

51 Kelves, *In the Name of Eugenics*, p. 113.

52 Richard Overy, *The Morbid Age: Britain and the Crisis of Civilisation, 1919–1939* (London, 2010), p. 93.

53 Aldous Huxley, *Brave New World* [1932] (London, 2014), p. 50.

54 Overy, *The Morbid Age*, pp. 93–135.

55 Walmsley and Jarrett, 'Intellectual Disability', p. 184.

56 Smith, *Between Mind and Nature* (London, 2013), p. 108.

57 Karl Pearson, 'On the Inheritance of Mental Disease', *Annals of Eugenics*, IV/3–4 (1930), p. 374.

9 Back to the Community? From 1939 to the Present

1 Stanley P. Davies, *Social Control of the feebleminded* (New York, 1923).

2 Albert Deutsch, *The Mentally Ill in America: A History of Their Care and Treatment from Colonial Times* (New York, 1937), p. 378.

3 Karl Binding and Alfred Hoche, *Allowing the Destruction of Life Unworthy of Life: Its Measure and Form* (Berlin, 1920).

4 Henry Frielander, 'The Exclusion and Murder of the Disabled', in *Social Outsiders in Nazi Germany*, ed. Robert Gellately and Nathan Stoltzfus (Princeton, NJ, 2001), p. 147.

5 Robert Gellately and Nathan Stoltzfus, 'Social Outsiders and the Construction of the Community of the People', in *Social Outsiders*, ed. Gallately and Stoltzfus, p. 11.

6 Suzanne E. Evans, *Forgotten Crimes: The Holocaust and People with Disabilities* (Chicago, IL, 2004), pp. 15–16.

7 Frielander, 'Exclusion and Murder of the Disabled', pp. 151–6.

8 Evans, *Forgotten Crimes*, pp. 17, 143–4.

9 Matthew Thomson, *The Problem of Mental Deficiency: Eugenics, Democracy and Social Policy in Britain, c. 1870–1959* (Oxford, 1998), p. 276.

10 Ibid., pp. 276–7.

11 Ibid., p. 277.

12 Thomson, *The Problem of Mental Deficiency*, p. 278.
13 Maggie Potts and Rebecca Fido, *'A Fit Person to be Removed': Personal Accounts of Life in a Mental Deficiency Institution* (Plymouth, 1991), p. 45.
14 Ibid., p. 52.
15 Ibid., pp. 60–61.
16 Ibid., pp. 86–9.
17 Sheena Rolph et al., *Witnesses to Change: Families, Learning Difficulties and History* (Kidderminster, 2005), p. 77.
18 Ibid., p. 49.
19 Ibid., p. 19.
20 Ibid., p. 48.
21 Ibid., p. 78.
22 Jan Walmsley and Simon Jarrett, 'Intellectual Disability Policy and Practice in Twentieth-century United Kingdom', in *Intellectual Disability in the Twentieth Century: Transnational Perspectives on People, Policy and Practice*, ed. J. Walmsley and S. Jarrett (Bristol, 2019), p. 186.
23 Kathleen W. Jones. 'Education for Children with Mental Retardation: Parent Activism, Public Policy and Family Ideology in the 1950s', in *Mental Retardation in America: A Historical Reader*, ed. Steven Noll and James W. Trent, Jr (New York, 2004), p. 325.
24 Ibid., p. 326.
25 Janice Brockley, 'Rearing the Child Who Never Grew: Ideologies of Parenting and Intellectual Disability in American History', in *Mental Retardation in America*, ed. Noll and Trent, p. 150.
26 Wolf Wolfensberger, *The Origin and Nature of Our Institutional Models* (New York, 1983), pp. 14–15.
27 Brockley, 'Rearing the Child', pp. 330–41.
28 George Thomson, *The Foreseeable Future* (London, 1957), pp. 123–5.
29 Michael Young, *The Rise of the Meritocracy* [1958] (Abingdon, 2017).
30 Ibid., p. xvi.
31 Thomson, *The Foreseeable Future*, p. 125.
32 Young, *Rise of the Meritocracy*, p. xvi.
33 Thomson, *The Problem of Mental Deficiency*, pp. 280–81.
34 'Report of the Royal Commission on the Law Relating to Mental Illness and Mental Deficiency' (1957), Her Majesty's Stationery Office (hereafter HMSO), 1957.
35 Mental Health Act 1959, 7+8 Elizabeth 2 c. 72.
36 Thomson, *The Problem of Mental Deficiency*, p. 293.
37 'Report on Ely Hospital: Report of the Committee of Enquiry into Allegations of Ill-treatment of Patients and Other Irregularities at the Ely Hospital, Cardiff' (1969), HMSO.
38 'Better Services for the Mentally Handicapped' (1971), HMSO cmd 4683.
39 Nigel Evans (dir.), *Silent Minority* (ATV, 1981).
40 'Report of the Committee of Enquiry into Mental Handicap Nursing Care (the Jay Report)' (1979), HMSO cmd 7468.
41 'Care in the Community: A Consultative Document on Moving Resources for Care in England' (1981), Department of Health and Social Security (DHSS) and House of Commons (HC) (81) 9.

42 'President's Committee on Mental Retardation' (Washington, DC, 1976), cited in Deborah S. Metzel, 'Historical Social Geography', in *Mental Retardation in America*, ed. Noll and Trent, p. 434.

43 Philip M. Ferguson, 'From Social Menace to Unfulfilled Promise: The Evolution of Policy and Practice towards People with Intellectual Disabilities in the United States', in *Intellectual Disability*, ed. Walmsley and Jarrett, pp. 199–200.

44 Metzel, 'Historical Social Geography', pp. 434–5.

45 Wolfensberger, *The Origin*, pp. 13–17.

46 Robert B. Edgerton, *The Cloak of Competence: Stigma in the Lives of the Mentally Retarded* (Berkeley, CA, 1967), p. 216.

47 Ibid., pp. 217–18.

48 Wolf Wolfensberger, 'A Call to Wake Up to the Beginning of a New Wave of "Euthanasia" of Severely Impaired People', *Education and Training of the Mentally Retarded*, 15 (1983) pp. 171–3.

49 Valerie Sinason, 'Foreword' in D. Niedecken, *Nameless: Understanding Learning Disability* (Hove, 2003), pp. xv–xviii, quoted in Jan Walmsley, 'Labels, Death-making and an Alternative to Social Valorisation: Valerie Sinason's Influence on My Work', in *Intellectual Disability and Psychotherapy: The Theories, Practice and Influence of Valerie Sinason*, ed. Alan Corbett (London, 2019), pp. 135–6.

50 Guoron Stefánsdóttir, 'People with Intellectual Disabilities in Iceland in the Twentieth Century: Sterilisation, Social Role Valorisation and "Normal Life"', in *Intellectual Disability*, ed. Walmsley and Jarrett, pp. 131–2; Wolf Wolfensberger, 'A Brief Overview of the Principle of Normalization', in *Normalization, Social Integration and Community Service*, ed. R. J. Flynn and K. E. Nitsch (Baltimore, MD, 1980).

51 Stefánsdóttir, 'People with Intellectual Disabilities in Iceland', pp. 129–41.

52 Simon Jarrett, 'The Meaning of "Community" in the Lives of People with Intellectual Disabilities: An Historical Perspective', *International Journal of Developmental Disabilities*, LXI/2 (2015), p. 107.

53 Martin W. Barr, *Mental Defectives: Their History, Treatment and Training* (Philadelphia, PA, 1904), p. 2.

Selected Secondary Reading

Andrews, Jonathan, 'Begging the Question of Idiocy: The Definition and Socio-cultural Meaning of Idiocy in Early Modern Britain, Part 1', *History of Psychiatry*, IX/33 (1998), pp. 65–95; and 'Part 2', IX/34 (1998), pp. 179–200

Atkinson, Dorothy, Mark Jackson and Jan Walmsley, *Forgotten Lives: Exploring the History of Learning Disability* (Kidderminster, 1997)

—, et al., *Good Times, Bad Times: Women with Learning Difficulties Tell Their Stories* (Kidderminster, 2000)

Carson, John, *The Measure of Merit: Talents, Intelligence and Inequality in the French and American Republics, 1750–1940* (Princeton, NJ, 2007)

Cowling, Mary, *The Artist as Anthropologist: The Representation of Type and Character in Victorian Art* (Cambridge, 1989)

Dickie, Simon, *Cruelty and Laughter: Forgotten Comic Literature and the Unsentimental Eighteenth Century* (Chicago, IL, 2011)

Digby, Anne, and David Wright, eds, *From Idiocy to Mental Deficiency: Historical Perspectives on People with Learning Disabilities* (London, 1996)

Douthwaite, Julia V., *The Wild Girl, Natural Man and the Monster: Dangerous Experiments in the Age of Enlightenment* (Chicago, IL, 2002)

Edgerton, Robert B., *The Cloak of Competence: Stigma in the Lives of the Mentally Retarded* (Berkeley, CA, 1967)

Eigen, John Peter, *Witnessing Insanity: Madness and Mad Doctors in the English Court* (New Haven, CT, 1995)

Evans, Suzanne E., *Forgotten Crimes: The Holocaust and People with Disabilities* (Chicago, IL, 2004)

Frielander, Henry, 'The Exclusion and Murder of the Disabled', in *Social Outsiders in Nazi Germany*, ed. Robert Gellately and Nathan Stoltzfus (Princeton, NJ, 2001)

Gatrell, Vic, *City of Laughter: Sex and Satire in Eighteenth-century London* (London, 2006)

Goldstein Jan, *Console and Classify: The French Psychiatric Profession in the Nineteenth Century* (Chicago, IL, 2001)

Goodey, C. F., *A History of Intelligence and Intellectual Disability: The Shaping of Psychology in Early Modern Europe* (Farnham, 2011)

—, 'What Is Developmental Disability? The Origin and Nature of Our
    Conceptual Models', *Journal on Developmental Disabilities*, VIII/2
    (2001), pp. 1–18
Gould, Stephen Jay, *The Mismeasure of Man* (New York, 1996)
—, *The Panda's Thumb: More Reflections in Natural History* (London, 1980)
Harris, José, 'Between Civic Virtue and Social Darwinism: The Concept
    of the Residuum', in *Retrieved Riches: Social Investigation in Britain,
    1840–1914*, ed. David Englander and Rosemary O'Day (Aldershot, 1995)
Jackson, Mark, *The Borderland of Imbecility: Medicine, Society and the
    Fabrication of the Feeble Mind in Late-Victorian and Edwardian England*
    (Manchester, 2000)
—, '"It Begins with the Goose and Ends with the Goose": Medical, Legal
    and Lay Understandings of Imbecility in *Ingram v. Wyatt*, 1824–1832',
    Social History of Medicine, XI/3 (1998), pp. 361–80
Jarrett, Simon, 'The Meaning of "Community" in the Lives of People with
    Intellectual Disabilities: An Historical Perspective', *International
    Journal of Developmental Disabilities*, LXI/2 (2015), pp. 107–12
Kelves, Daniel, *In the Name of Eugenics: Genetics and the Uses of Human
    Heredity* (Cambridge, MA, 1985)
Lund, Roger, 'Laughing at Cripples: Ridicule, Deformity, and the Argument
    from Design', *Eighteenth Century Studies*, XXXIX/1 (2005), pp. 91–114
McDonagh, Patrick, *Idiocy: A Cultural History* (Liverpool, 2008)
—, Tim Stainton and C. F. Goodey, *Intellectual Disability: A Conceptual
    History, 1200–1900* (Manchester, 2019)
McGlynn, Margaret, 'Idiots, Lunatics and the Royal Prerogative in Early
    Tudor England', *Journal of Legal History*, XXVI/1 (2005), pp. 1–24
Mezler, Irina, *Fools and Idiots? Intellectual Disability in the Middle Ages*
    (Manchester, 2016)
Nitsch, K. E., *Normalization, Social Integration and Community Service*
    (Baltimore, MD, 1980)
Noll, Steven, and James W. Trent, Jr, eds, *Mental Retardation in America:
    A Historical Reader* (New York, 2004)
Overy, Richard, *The Morbid Age: Britain and the Crisis of Civilisation,
    1919–1939* (London, 2010)
Pedersen, Susan, 'Hannah More Meets Simple Simon: Tracts, Chapbooks
    and Popular Culture in Late Eighteenth-century England', *Journal of
    British Studies*, XXV/1 (1986), pp. 84–113
Potts, Maggie, and Rebecca Fido, *'A Fit Person to Be Removed': Personal
    Accounts of Life in a Mental Deficiency Institution* (Plymouth, 1991)
Rolph, Sheena, et al., *Witnesses to Change: Families, Learning Difficulties
    and History* (Kidderminster, 2005)
Scull, Andrew, Charlotte Mackenzie and Nicholas Harvey, *Masters of
    Bedlam: The Transformation of the Mad-doctoring Trade* (Princeton,
    NJ, 1996)
Simpson, Murray, 'The Moral Government of Idiots: Moral Treatment
    in the Work of Seguin', *History of Psychiatry*, X (1999), pp. 227–43
Smith, Roger, *Between Mind and Nature: A History of Psychology*
    (London, 2013)

Stocking, George W., Jr, *Victorian Anthropology* (New York, 1991)

Tave, Stuart M., *The Amiable Humorist: A Study in the Comic Theory and Criticism of the Eighteenth and Early Nineteenth Centuries* (Chicago, IL, 1960)

Thomson, Matthew, *The Problem of Mental Deficiency: Eugenics, Democracy and Social Policy in Britain, c. 1870–1959* (Oxford, 1998)

Trent, James W., Jr, *Inventing the Feeble Mind: A History of Mental Retardation in the United States* (Berkeley, CA, 1994)

Verstraete, Pieter, 'Savage Solitude: The Problematisation of Disability at the Turn of the Eighteenth Century', *Paedagogica Historica*, XLV/3 (2009), pp. 269–89

Walmsley, Jan, Dorothy Atkinson and Sheena Rolph, 'Community Care and Mental Deficiency, 1913–1945', in *Outside the Walls of the Asylum: The History of Care in the Community, 1750–2000*, ed. Peter Bartlett and David Wright (London, 1999), pp. 181–203

—, and Simon Jarrett, eds, *Intellectual Disability in the Twentieth Century: Transnational Perspectives on People, Policy and Practice* (Bristol, 2019)

Wolfensberger, Wolf, 'A Brief Overview of the Principle of Normalization', in *Normalization, Social Integration and Community Services*, ed. R. J. Flynn and K. E. Nitsch (Baltimore, MD, 1980), pp. 7–30

—, 'A Call to Wake Up to the Beginning of a New Wave of "Euthanasia" of Severely Impaired People', *Education and Training of the Mentally Retarded*, XV (1983), pp. 171–3

—, *The Origin and Nature of our Institutional Models* (New York, 1983)

Wright, David, *Mental Disability in Victorian England: The Earlswood Asylum, 1847–1901* (Oxford, 2001)

—, *Downs: The History of a Disability* (Oxford, 2011)

Young, Michael, *The Rise of the Meritocracy* [1958] (Abingdon, 2017)

Acknowledgements

Many people and organizations have been instrumental in enabling me to complete this book. My overwhelming gratitude and thanks are due to Professor Joanna Bourke, who was my research supervisor at Birkbeck, University of London when I first began this work. I can never thank her enough for her unwavering, inspirational and insightful support for my project from the beginning. The Wellcome Trust generously supported three years of my work for this project. My inspiration for this work has come from the many people with learning disabilities that I have worked with and alongside for many years. Quite simply, without them, this would not have been written, so I am truly thankful to them. I hope this work does them justice. My thanks are due to the courteous and helpful staff at the various archives and libraries where I carried out my research, in particular the National Archives at Kew, the Wellcome Trust Library, the British Library, the Heinz Archive and Library at the National Portrait Gallery and the library and archive of the Royal Anthropological Institute. Thanks are also due to Brigitte Lacoste, who helpfully checked and advised on my translations from French to English. The following have given up valuable time reading my work and offering invaluable feedback: Dr Chris Goodey of the University of Leicester, Professor Chris Mounsey of the University of Winchester, Dr Heather Tilley of Queen Mary University of London, and Dr Patrick McDonagh of Concordia University, Montreal. Professor Jan Walmsley and Dr Liz Tilley of the Open University, and the Social History of Learning Disability Research Group, have been invaluable allies and willing testing grounds for my research. My thanks to Amy Salter, Alex Ciobanu and Michael Leaman at Reaktion Books, for their excellent and knowledgeable support. I am most of all grateful to my wife, Dianne, for her patience, support and wise words, which are always true, even when I'd rather not hear them.

Parts of chapters One and Four are reproduced or adapted from my '"Belief", "Opinion" and "Knowledge": The Idiot in Law in the Long Eighteenth Century', in *Intellectual Disability: A Conceptual History, 1200–1900*, ed. P. McDonagh, C. F. Goodey and T. Stainton (Manchester, 2018). Thanks are due to Manchester University Press for permission to reproduce this material. Parts of Chapter Two are reproduced or adapted from my 'Laughing about and Talking about the Idiot in the Eighteenth Century', in *The Variable Body in History*, ed. C. Mounsey and S. Booth (Oxford, 2016). Thanks are due to Peter Lang Copyright AG for permission to reproduce this material.

Photo Acknowledgements

The author and publishers wish to express their thanks to the below sources of illustrative material and/or permission to reproduce it. Some locations of artworks are also given below, in the interest of brevity:

Artokoloro Quint Lox Limited/Alamy Stock Photo: p. 214; Beinecke Rare Book and Manuscript Library, Yale University, New Haven, CT: p. 227; Boston Public Library: pp. 82, 83, 222; British Museum, London: pp. 36, 174; from the Commission de Lunatico Inquirendo, *An Inquiry into the State of Mind of W. F. Windham, Esq. of Fellbrig Hall, Norfolk* (London, 1862), photos courtesy Wellcome Library, London: pp. 147, 148; from James Cook, *Voyage dans l'hémisphère austral, et autour du monde*, vol. IV (Paris, 1778), photo courtesy John Carter Brown Library, Providence, RI: p. 101; from Charles Darwin, *The Expression of the Emotions in Man and Animals* (London, 1872), photo courtesy Wellcome Library, London: p. 254; from Charles Dickens, *Barnaby Rudge* (Philadelphia, PA, 1841), photo courtesy University of California Libraries: p. 170; from Jean-Baptiste Du Tertre, *Histoire generale des Antilles habitées par les François*, vol. II (Paris, 1667): p. 111; from James Grant, *Sketches in London*, 2nd edn (London, 1840), photo courtesy Wellcome Library, London: p. 237; from Francis Grose, *Supplement to The Antiquities of England and Wales* (London, 1777), photo courtesy Philadelphia Museum of Art, Library and Archives: p. 57; courtesy of the Huntington Art Museum, San Marino, CA: p. 81; from *Illustrated London News* (11 March 1864): p. 219; from Carl Linnaeus, *Amoenitates academicae, seu, Dissertationes variae physicae, medicae, botanicae*, vol. VI, 2nd edn (Erlangen, 1785), photo courtesy the Digital Archive of the University of Maryland, Baltimore: p. 94; Los Angeles County Museum of Art: p. 99; The Metropolitan Museum of Art, New York: pp. 34, 41, 45; photo John Minihan/Evening Standard/Hulton Archive via Getty Images: p. 294; Minneapolis Institute of Art, MN: p. 80; from Alexander Morison, *Outlines of Lectures on Mental Diseases*, 2nd edn (London, 1826), photo courtesy Wellcome Library, London: p. 233; photos courtesy National Library of Medicine, Bethesda, MD: pp. 131, 260; National Maritime Museum, Greenwich, London: p. 91; National Portrait Gallery, London: p. 157; The New York Public Library: p. 165; from *Punch; or, the London Charivari* (23 June 1877): p. 163; from William

Index

Page numbers in *italics* refer to illustrations

Normansfield Training Institution
for Imbeciles 240, *294*
Nugent, Maria 186, 187, 192

O'Brien, John 303
Old Bailey 30, 31, 41–50, *49*, 60,
84–5, 137–9, *137*, 151
Onslow, Arthur 34
Ordinary Life, An 296–7

Paine, Thomas 219, 221–4
Park House, Highgate 171, 204,
239, 240, 241
Patagonians *see* Fuegians
Pearson, Karl 274
Percy Commission 292–4
Péron, François 97
'Peter the Wild Boy' 67, 200
physiognomy 72–5, *74*, 77, 96,
144, 164, 175, *209*
Philip, John 192–3, 198
Phillippo, James 192
Pim, Bedford 190, 209
Pinel, Phillippe 96, 125, 191, 200,
204
Pioneer Corps 280
Place, Francis 95
Poor Law 37, 236
Poor Law Amendment Act 1834
123, 218, 236, 250
Prerogativa Regis 24
Price, Richard 48
Prichard, James Cowles 201, 203
Pufendorf, Samuel von 106–7, 108
Punch magazine 160–62, 179
*Fashionable Entertainments
for the week 162*

Radford, Mary 48, 80, 84
Ray, Isaac 134–5, 186–90
Recapitulation Theory 211
Reed, Andrew 239–40
Report of the Committee of Enquiry
into Mental Handicap
Nursing Care 296
Roberts, Henry 35–7, 40
Rogers, Robin 287–8
Rogers, Roy 287–8

Romanes, George 255–6, 258
Rowlandson, Thomas 174
A Cake in Danger 45
Wonderfully Mended 30
Royal Albert Hospital for Idiots
and Imbeciles 240
Royal Commission on the Care and
Control of the Feeble-Minded
262–3, 265
Royal Commission on the law
relating to mental illness and
mental deficiency 287, 292–4

St Lawrence's Hospital, Surrey
295–6
see also Caterham Imbeciles
Asylum
Saint-Sauveur, Jacques Grasset de,
Hottentot 99
Salpêtrière Asylum, Paris 96, 124,
127, 191, 204
'savages' 98, 108, 112–18, 119, 183,
185–6, 194, 195, 197–8, 198–9,
202, 207, 212, 213, 253
Scharf, George, *'The Giraffes with
the Arabs who brought them
over to this Country' 143*
'science of man' 93, 103, 110, 118, 183,
185, 216
scientific racism 201–2
Séguin, Édouard 167, 191, 194–5,
204, 239, 277
sermons 85–7
servants 76, 79–81
Shelford, Leonard 133
Shriver, Eunice *née* Kennedy 300
Silent Minority 295–6, 297
'Simple Simon' 62–5, 231–2
Simon, Théodore 263–4
Sinason, Valerie 302–3
slang 30, 44, 55–62, 67, 70, 154–6
Smollett, Tobias 162–3
Roderick Random 29, 169–71
social valorization 303
South Sea Islanders 87, 101, 116, *117*,
207, 211
Special Olympics *299*, 300
stadial theory 114–15, 118, 205